MW00636644

Praise for
How To Become Self-Employed In Seattle

It helped me learn how to create a business in 3 days!

- Molly, Seaview Barber Company

Jenny MacLeod is like a wizard who takes a bunch of dry tax/regulation stuff and then presents it in a way that makes it feel exciting - like you and your new business are about to do something really special together and don't worry, you have totally done every legal thing that you have to do. :)

- Jessica, former Underwear Designer

Not only did I feel more confident in setting up my business, I also felt like I was getting the pep talk I needed about "trying out my dream job." When everything feels really hard, this book is a great reminder of how to tackle each problem and remind you about why you chose self-employment.

- Rachel, Spruce with Rachel

Even having owned a business for nearly 4 years now, I still learned from the book. Not only did I learn from content on things like bookkeeping and filing taxes, but I also learned from the reminders throughout the book about choosing your own style and how to start the work that you don't necessarily enjoy doing.

- Amy, Sassafras Boutique

I cannot recommend this book [enough], for it's practical, well organized and informative approach which has helped me take a more organized approach to starting my own practice.

- George, Strang Career Coaching

Owning this book is like having a business coach at your fingertips.

- Christina, Marketing Staircase

Super-comprehensive tips and answers to kick start you into making the jump in entrepreneur-land. I even bought one for a friend who's starting her own business.

- L. Burke, Make a Scene

I firmly believe this book could change the way you think about your business.

- SyKin, Amazon Reviewer

I like that it focuses on the technical aspects of business (legal, taxes, etc.), while also encouraging you to carve out your own path. It is very practical in that it gives you a step-by-step process into setting up your business, and then excellent advice for how to build it as you go.

- Jon, Pontrello Acupuncture

A couple of times I tried to start side businesses that sputtered out, and now, having read this book, I feel actually ready and armed with practical guidance for how to proceed, step-by-step.

- Jennifer, Amazon Reviewer

She simplifies and clarifies and I felt totally inspired to keep doing what I'm doing.

-- Daniel, Musician

It's a business development book with heart.

- Ann, Consultant

I wouldn't be where I am without this book.

- Robyn, Kale Love

How To Become Self-Employed in Seattle

How to Become Self-Employed in Seattle

A Guidebook, Companion, and Reference

Jenny MacLeod, Girl Friday :)

2018 Edition

CRAFT PUBLISHING
SEATTLE

Disclaimer

This book was written to explain the basics of starting and doing business. It is not comprehensive. These are recommendations.

This book provides general information only. *This is not legal advice! Please verify what is required for your own business.* **If you have specific questions, contact an attorney.**

I'm not a lawyer or accountant. I am somebody who figured out how to jump through the hoops and created a business in order to be self-employed. I'm sharing what I figured out the hard way in the hope of making it easier for you.

I am not liable for damages of any kind (including, without limitation, lost profits or any special, incidental, or consequential damages) arising out of or in connection with any information provided in this book. This guide has worked for my clients and myself, but every business is unique.

ISBN 978-1-945827-02-0 (paperback)
978-1-945827-04-4 (ebook)

Font Information: TW Cent MT, headings; Cambria, body text;
Wingding, manicules; Desyrel, handwriting

Published by Craft Publishing
Seattle, Washington

First Edition, First Printing 2016
2018 Edition, First Printing 2018

"[I'm] copywritten, so don't copy me." —Missy Elliott

To order multiple copies, please contact the author at jennygirlfriday.com

To my clients,

who taught me so much + make work a true pleasure

To Birch and Finlay,

who make me laugh + feel proud everyday

To Alex,

who is always doing something new + is the best companion

This is for all the people who have
the courage to be themselves

Table of Contents

Where do you want to start?

I'm ready to get my business licenses!

Go to page 61.

I want to know what to expect for the journey.

Go to page 33.

I would like an overview of business topics.

Read the introduction sections on pages:
130, 160, 206, 263, 302.

I want to meet the author and learn more about the method in this book.

Go to page 9.

I'm really concerned about taxes!

Go to page 129.

•

This book is designed for you to either flip around or to read cover to cover.

Hello (Or—You Can Do It)

Congratulations! By picking up this book, you're one step closer to your dream of being self-employed. It is an exciting process and lovely way of life. If we were meeting over a cup of coffee, I would ask you about all of your ideas and say, "It sounds wonderful. You can totally do it."

Becoming self-employed is a lot easier than people think—once you know what's involved and give yourself some time for the journey.

What's hard is finding the right guidance. Sure, there are lots of books, classes, and web guides for new businesses, but the problem is that they include lots of things you don't need to know—things related to having employees, getting investors, and creating huge business plans. If you're new to the field of business, it's hard to weed out all the extraneous stuff.

It helps to know right away that being self-employed is different from being a small business owner. Often, the two terms get lumped together, which causes confusion. When people choose self-employment, it's because they want a job that they really like for whatever reason: a flexible schedule, unique work, time to travel, more money, or creative control. Self-employment is about earning the living you need for a lifestyle that makes you happy.

Usually people in this camp don't advertise right away that they own a business. If you ask a self-employed person what they do, they might answer, "I'm a therapist."
"Oh, where do you work?"
"I work for myself."

Their interest is in the job, not the business.
When people build a business, they take pride in the entity they create —whether it's a shop, service agency or some other organization. Interactions with these folks sound more like this.

"What do you do?"
"I own a business."
"Oh, what kind?"
"Residential painting."
"Cool, so you paint houses?"
"Yeah. You might have seen our vans around town."

The pride and investment comes in the owning of the business more than the actual services that the business provides.

So, why are self-employment and small business ownership confused? Because, there is no legal category for just being a person who works. Only a business can provide a job. So, in order to work for yourself, you have to create and maintain a legal business. And since you're in charge, you are the owner (and not the employee) whether you like it or not. At that point, you're lumped in with other business owners, and what follows is that you are required to meet all the same obligations that larger businesses face.

You might be thinking: *That doesn't seem fair!* And, *I don't care about business...I hate numbers; that sounds too hard. I just want to do my work; I don't want to run a business.*

Don't worry. Here's the good news: it's all doable and learnable. You don't need a background in business. Most of the things you have to do are based on common sense and not that hard once you know what they are. They are things that people have been doing for a long time like setting goals and working towards them, making trades or barters, making agreements, and figuring out income requirements. Even paying taxes. Best of all, since you're the boss, you have a lot of control over how to run the business side.

Yes, in the beginning it will take some time to learn what's involved and to create your own systems, but after a while, the business side will take much less time. And, if you consider all the time you're saving by not being someone else's employee—from staff meetings and commuting to dealing with politics—it is probably a trade up.

My Point of View

The methods in this book are based on some ideas and values that I've developed over the last four years while working for self-employed folks. I want to be up-front with you about my point of view.

- Most people do not need a business plan.
- I suggest a build-as-you-go technique.
- Once you learn the requirements of doing business, you can meet them however you want.
- It's better not to take out any loans.
- Doing things your way is best for business.
- Start as soon as possible, and then give yourself one to two years to develop the business side.
- Learn all the parts of business, and then outsource the jobs you don't like.

It really is a privilege to make your own work. Even though there are challenging times, it is a luxury not everyone can afford. It's good to take moments to enjoy yourself and revel in the process.

This Book Is About Trying Your Dream

Every self-employed person I've met says something like, "I don't think I could ever work for a boss again." The sense of satisfaction, empowerment, and engagement that comes from working for yourself is hard to describe. There is a feeling of aliveness that seems to balance out all of the challenges.

This book is about trying out your dream job. Whether or not this venture works out as you hope, I'm pretty certain that you'll be glad that you tried.

You will be part of a group of people who gets in the arena.

> The credit belongs to the man who is actually in the arena, whose face is marred by dust and sweat and blood; who strives valiantly...who spends himself in a worthy cause; who at the best knows in the end the triumph of high achievement, and who at the worst, if he fails, at least fails while daring greatly. (Theodore Roosevelt)

You're a participant, not just a bystander.

It's also likely that you'll inspire others around you. You'll have new knowledge, more experience, and likely more confidence, no matter where your career takes you.

It is my joy and pleasure to help you make this transition to self-employment. I believe that the best way to be happy is to love your work and to be yourself throughout the day. Furthermore, I believe you're helping to make the world a better place—because happy people make for a better society.

I'm thrilled to present to you a guide for becoming self-employed in Seattle. It is the result of my working with dozens of clients to set up their businesses, as well as my own. My goal is that 80 to 100% of these words apply to you, making your journey as smooth as possible and setting you up for success. My hope is that this information will save you lots of time, money and stress—giving you more time and energy for the work that you want to do.

How to Use This Book

The pathway to self-employment is unique for each person. The basic approach presented in this book is to get going, learn by doing, and create a custom business set up that matches you.

Make it Yours & Go in Any Order

I invite you to make this book yours—to mark it up, use the checklists, and write in the workspaces. There's something magical about putting pen to paper. You will get more out of this the more you engage with it.

If something is not applicable to your situation, I invite you to put a line through that page, or even to tear it out.

This book is designed for you to go in any order. You may skip around as needed. Or, work through the book from front to back.

Required and Recommended— For the Quickest Read

This is the 1, 2, Go section in the middle of the book. All the pages are marked with a grey bar down the side.

Keep Going: The Five Areas of Business

These pages are marked with gray tabs. Please think of this section as a menu (not a mandate).

Some Points on Language

This book is for both service providers and product makers. This creates a challenge with choosing words. I will use these terms interchangeably: *client* and *customer*, *service* and *product*, *rate* and *price.*

Bank means any financial institution, including credit unions.

Self-employment, working for yourself, and *freelancing* all mean that you have created a job for yourself.

The word *business* has so many different meanings and connotations. I will use it to mean:

- the flow of work (including income)
- structure that you work for
- field of ideas, concepts and practices related to conducting business.

You Do NOT Need to Do Everything in this Book

Only a fraction of this book covers things you must do—the legal requirements of business. The rest of the topics are presented in case they are relevant and helpful to you. Pick and choose what fits your needs and style. Come back to the book as needed.

This book is about getting started. It is not comprehensive; it is not designed to be. My goal is to make every word, or nearly every word applicable to you. Instead of presenting a myriad of options, I've been selective—curating information, steps, and important thoughts to help you get going on your self-employment journey.

Are there things you might have to do that are not covered here? It's possible. Each person and field varies too much to be covered all in one book. The idea here is that if you work through the essentials of business (with the help of this guide), you can check those basic steps off your list. Then, armed with more knowledge and experience, you can find the additional information that you need.

1, 2...Go!

Really, there are just two things to do to get started:

1 Get licensed.

2 Get your first customer.

Then it's Go Time!

This Book on One Page

Here's the master plan of this book, presented on one page. 1, 2...Go! with some details.

1—Get Licensed

- Understand the requirements of small business
- Make some decisions
- Form an LLC (optional)
- Get a state license
- Get a city license
- Fulfill requirements for your field (if applicable)

2—Get Your First Customer

- Define your service/product
- Choose a rate/price
- Figure out how to find clients/customers

Go!—Do Your Work and Build Over Time

- Do business
- Set up shop
- Learn as you go
- Keep Going: Build the business side over time

Notes:
The first two steps can happen in as little as a week. "Go!" generally takes six months to two years.

Think of this journey like you're going to graduate school. You'll be working a lot, you might incur some debt, you'll be learning new things, and you'll have more options and earning power when you're finished.

My Business Story

My Business Almost Didn't Start

When I decided to work for myself, I figured that the first step was a business plan. I went to Half Price Books in the U. District and picked out a handful of books—since I love to skim and compare.

I sat in my attic office and started with *Business Plan for Dummies*. I was excited; I figured it would provide a nice, straightforward path. (I mean, this is for *dummies*, right?) Immediately, my heart sank. It felt like a huge textbook, and the pages looked dense, with lots of steps and filled with loud fonts, lots of graphics, icons, charts, pullout boxes and lists. I turned to the next book—a million steps and bulleted lists. The next was no better. I was overwhelmed. Why does my business plan have to be the equivalent of a master's thesis here?

The smell of coffee drew me down to the kitchen. I must've looked dejected, because my husband asked, "How's it goin'?" instead of heading back to his work outside.

"Writing a business plan is going to take forever. But, I guess I have to do it...."

"Have you read *The Art of the Start* yet?" (By Guy Kawasaki) He had grabbed one or two of the books earlier, as he had a few business ideas of his own.

"No, why?" I asked, hopeless and irritated. I was in a lousy mood and didn't want to be 'fixed' at the moment. Also, I hated the idea that he might know something that I didn't—since this was *my* project.

"You should really take a look at it. He describes a different way of getting started. Basically, you make a prototype and start talking to everyone about it. And you think about a personal mantra."

I was skeptical and resistant. It sounded a little too easy, too risky and too different. I'd only heard of businesses developed in secret over years of time—based on lots of research, testing, and re-testing. I ignored his suggestion for a few days...and then decided to pick the book up.

A Different Way

Guy Kawasaki presented a *totally* different way to get started. The first chapter was a much needed motivator to get moving, and then later in the book, he presented a format for a shorter, sleeker business plan. His methods seemed to match the current business climate. And, they felt exciting!

One of the beginning steps was to *get going*. Kawasaki explained:

> This means building a prototype, writing software, launching your website, or offering your services. The hardest thing about getting started is getting started...Remember: No one ever achieved success by *planning* for gold. (Chapter One)

I took his words to heart and decided to build a prototype of my services. I decided that at the most basic level, I needed to define my services somehow, and then find some people to try it out with. I spent time imagining working with my first client and soon realized that I would need a few tools—such as an invoice and receipt—and that some nice looking business cards would give me more credibility. It took me a few days to remember that I would also need a business license!

I almost hit another roadblock with that one...because I wanted the business name to be perfect and I couldn't decide on one. Thank goodness my sister explained that I could change it easily with DBAs. (See page 61.) So, I registered an LLC, changed my email signature, and, voila, I was in business.

It worked! I started getting clients, and I built things as I went—receipts, business cards, and policies—all in response to upcoming meetings or questions. For example, when a new client asked to pay me using PayPal,

I got it all set up just in time for our first session. When people started asking if I had a website, I figured I had better make one, so I set up a very basic site in WordPress. (Later, I changed to Squarespace.) I got in the habit of saying, "Sure, let me get back to you on that."

The process only took a few months. In another life, I would still have been reading books about business plans.

This Should Be Easier!

Since I was doing work for other self-employed folks, I was able to learn about business along with them. It was a happy synergy...although I had to discover some things the hard way. For example, I had gotten a state business license, but didn't know that I needed a city license as well. Sheepishly, I called the city to register. At the end of the call, I asked, "Is there anything else that I need to do?"

She assured me there wasn't. But guess what? A few months later, I discovered that all businesses are required to register with the county. I wondered what else I had missed, so I started checking online resources for new businesses.

It was strangely hard to find what I needed to do as a self-employed person. It all seemed so confusing. There were so many steps, terms and things that didn't apply to me; I wasn't sure what was required of me, and what wasn't.

This should be easier! I just wanted to do my consulting work, and this was taking so much time. If it was difficult for me—someone who likes to research new things—then it must be difficult for others as well. It also didn't feel fair. Being great at teaching yoga, doing massage, building violins, or copywriting is totally different from working through the online maze of requirements for a new business.

I started asking: *How can I make this easier for people?*

Realizations About Self-Employment

After quite some time, I started to realize some things about self-employment in particular:

- Being self-employed is different from owning a small business.
- Creating a job for yourself is different from building a company.
- Many of the resources are designed to cover all circumstances, so they look very complicated.
- As a self-employed person with no employees, there are only a few requirements.
- You have to know a lot of the jargon in order to know what applies to you and what doesn't.
- As long as you understand how to meet the requirements of having a business, you can do things however you want.
- Small business advice may or may not apply to you as a self-employed person.

Since there was no place to send clients for clear advice and help, I decided to build some materials myself. In addition to creating lists for tax reporting and license renewals, I made checklists for getting licensed. With extreme satisfaction, I watched client after client finish in one hour what had taken me a few years to complete. It was magic.

Of course, getting licensed is just the start. Building and maintaining the business is another matter. I started observing patterns, and again noticing that the trajectory for growth of self-employed people is different than what is typically covered in the books about business.

And thus, the method in this book was born.

The Method

1—Get licensed
2—Get your first customer
Go!—Do your work and build over time

Important Ideas

This method is based on some foundational ideas.

1) If you understand the requirements of business, then you can do things however you want.

This means that first you will learn what is required when you own a business. These topics are explored in the *Prepare for Licensing* section as well as the *Legal and Taxes* section. We'll cover how you get licensed and what is required of you each year.

One of the best habits to start immediately is to get all deadlines on your calendar. That way, you won't be surprised when it's time to make a report or send in taxes. This is covered in the *Go!* section.

Sadly, and ironically, most people ignore this aspect of business and sometimes feel irritated that they have to get licensed and pay taxes at all. It's understandable, but it will only cause stress—now and later. If you can have the courage to face this challenge in the beginning, you'll have nothing to fear moving forward. And you can plan your time more effectively and charge enough to cover your taxes and licensing costs.

2) Do things your way.

Do things your way—when it comes to setting up your business, doing business, and doing your work. If you do things your way, it will feel easier and go more smoothly. You'll be happier. You can sustain your efforts, keeping you in the game longer, increasing your chances of meeting your goals.

Take the *should* out of your business vocabulary as soon as you can. Once you decide to do something because you *should*, you're setting up a need for willpower, and there's only so much of that to go around. In addition, it means that you're doing something that you don't want to do. These things weigh on our minds, take energy, and are hard to stick to. It's far better to figure out how you want to do something and then do it that way.

For example, if you find yourself exclaiming, "I wish I could just hire a bookkeeper!" then listen to that. If instead, you get QuickBooks because people say that you should, then it's quite likely not to work out. Most people in this situation will let all the paperwork pile up, making it increasingly hard to face the task...and they'll avoid doing that work as much as possible. If you choose the *shoulds*, not only will you get behind, but this little voice will be in your head all the time, saying things like, "You need to work on those receipts!" or, "Why haven't you finished those invoices yet?" These thoughts are distracting and unhelpful.

On the flipside, if you hire the bookkeeper, you'll likely be able to pay their fee with a few more hours of the work you love to do. You'll feel so happy and relieved that the task is done and that you didn't have to do it.

When you pick a system you like, you'll stick with it and you'll do it with pleasure. It won't take willpower. You'll have more of that for your core work and your personal life. You'll be able to put more effort into your skill or craft. Not to mention, you'll feel better, smile more and stand taller. This is a great way to live and it gives you an attractive and radiant energy which is noticeable to friends, family, and potential clients.

3) Becoming self-employed usually takes time and perseverance. Set yourself up to last through the journey.

You are essentially crafting a custom job—one that is centered around your talents and passions with a schedule that fits your life and systems to suit your preferences. Crafting always takes time. You've got to build in the basics, then adjust, refine, and tailor. This takes time and effort—and your heart and soul. In the beginning, you'll likely be working a lot, and you may not be earning what you need.

Set yourself up to last through the journey. This is a marathon, not a sprint. Be ready to persevere, and get the support that you need—mental, physical, spiritual, emotional, and financial. Make a plan to have extra money coming in another way, and find ways to cut your spending.

It takes time for a seed to turn into a plant offering fruit, for whiskey to mellow in the casket, or for a leather chair to soften. Give yourself enough time to see the fruits of your labor.

4) Understand the terms and basics of doing business with a fresh (positive) attitude.

In order to know the requirements of being self-employed, and to do things your own way, you'll need to be familiar with some business basics: some terms, requirements, and a few strategies. Happily, most of us already know how to conduct business and we engage in aspects of it all the time. For example, we are doing business when we buy or sell things on Craigslist, hire a neighbor to cat sit, or announce a party or event. What might be new are some of the terms and the specific tasks that you're required to do.

To learn the business side of being self-employed, it helps to have a positive attitude. However, many of us have feelings and associations with words like accounting, marketing, bookkeeping, taxes, operations, and the word business itself. Often, people think of these as boring, dry, or perhaps associated with greed. Take a moment to imagine a whiteboard with the word BUSINESS written across the top, and all of these associations written or drawn down below. Now, erase it all clean. Write the word BUSINESS again, and add words like: relationships, joy, satisfaction, value, freedom, fairness, service, accomplishments, mutual benefit. These words are also a part of business!

Now, let's add a few more things: meeting requirements, knowing a few numbers, finding and keeping clients, details, self-management. We'll cover these things in the section Keep Going: The 5 Areas of Business. (I chose five categories so that you can look at one hand and think about them all.)

It can take a little time to learn the basics of business, but you don't need to understand it all to get started. Plan to learn as you go. The more you interact with the terms and processes of business, the more comfortable you'll feel.

Knowing some of the business basics and terminology will also help you as you interact with friends and family. Out of concern, interest, and helpfulness, it's likely they will ask questions or offer advice. Once you're informed, you'll know which advice to avoid, and how to answer their questions. People often ask questions in *business-ese*, such as "What are your operating costs?" "What's your marketing plan?" If you know these terms, it'll be easier to answer them. "It costs me about $350 a month for business expenses." "For now, I'm using word of mouth and flyers." Your confidence will reassure people and keep them from worrying about you.

5) If possible, avoid loans…or keep them small.

Loans are expensive. First, you pay interest. Second, when you have a chunk of money in the bank, it is easy to buy things you don't actually need...which means spending extra money on things. It is common to think buying a lot of stuff is the way to set up a successful business. This is unhelpful thinking. The heart of a business is an excellent product or service and happy customers—the kind who want to do repeat business with you and spread the word about you. It is not a slick logo, website, or fancy desk chair. (Additionally, if you've spent a lot of money on something like a logo or tool, it can be hard to change it if you need to. You'll feel tied to your investment. In this way, loans can hamper your refinement process.)

You will also have pressure on yourself to repay the loan. If it was from family, there is additional pressure to meet the expectations of whoever gave it to you. Your spouse might have expectations. *Her business had better work because we took out that loan!* It's another little voice in your head that can be a distraction. If at all possible, find a way to earn the money you need to invest back into your business. Perhaps you can get a part-time job or just wait a little longer for bigger purchases. It may take more time, but you'll feel more freedom and autonomy as you go. You might have to scrimp on things like going out or buying clothes, but it'll be worth it.

If you really must borrow money, first see if you can borrow from yourself—your own savings or retirement funds. If not, then a family member or low-interest loan can be helpful. If it's from family, agree on a low-cost monthly repayment plan, or ask for a one or two-year grace period. Just set it up in a way that you can fulfill your commitment. Then, if you're paying the loan on time, as agreed, you will avoid any negative feelings or pressures. If you do borrow money from a family member, be sure to talk through their role in your business, if any at all, and whether or not you'll accept any advise.

By earning what you need as you go, you'll be nimble and lean. You can adjust and change. This offers freedom and autonomy now, which is the point of self-employment! You're building for a great future, while enjoying the present.

6) Prepare your mind for the journey.

Planning to *build-as-you-go* does require a certain mindset, that is, a set of strategies and attitudes. Understanding what the journey is actually like will help you to prepare sufficiently, so you can make it to the end! We'll explore these topics in a section called *About the Journey*. One of the most important attitudes is to think of this like going to school. It helps to put spending time and money into context for yourself and your family.

When you know what to expect, and how to handle things, you'll experience less stress and be able to keep going.

Are you sure I don't need a business plan?

You probably don't need a business plan...but it really depends on your situation. In some cases, a business plan is necessary. In my view, there are three main reasons to write a business plan:

- to think through all the elements of doing your business
- if you're applying for funding from a bank or investors
- if doing things in a traditional way will calm you.

If you want to do a business plan, then go for it. Just be sure to pick a deadline and make appointments with yourself on your calendar. If you get stalled, get help from a class, a friend in business, or a coach. Using books for guidance is okay, although beware, they can vary greatly on approaches and sometimes make the process overly complicated.

My favorite guidebook is *The Art of the Start* by Guy Kawasaki. You can also find his template for business plans online.

If the business plan sounds like a drag and is holding you back, then consider other pathways. You can get the same results different ways. Working through this book, setting up a website, or going through a crowdfunding process will get you there, too.

At its core, a business plan looks at:

- What you are selling

- Who is going to buy it from you
- What compels people to buy from you
- How you will run the business

These are important things to know. However, you don't need to have the complete answers before starting. You can learn a lot of this as you go, using your experience to refine the answers.

Just get going, and build a cycle of doing, then reflecting and adjusting.

Lastly, you're not forming a start-up or trying to develop a business to sell to someone else, so those strategies don't fit here. You're setting up the business structure in order to be self-employed and to have a job that you love.

Why Build-As-You-Go Works

It's way more fun to build tools and ideas for a real audience than a hypothetical one. It saves you time and money and focuses your efforts. You'll revise things in response to customer input. All the while, you'll be building a reputation, the base of your brand.

Most people who've started a business will tell you that the reality veered from the business plan projections immediately. It's unsettling to always differ from the plan. Instead, with a build-as-you-go approach, you make goals, do the work, and adjust as needed. It feels better; it's more nimble. There's actually a name for this very approach in the tech world; it's called *iterative design.*

How long will this take?

How long it will take depends on so many factors. In general, preparing and applying for business licenses can take as little as two to four hours. It can also take months if you like a lot of time to process, or prepare mentally before starting something. Due diligence (more on page 75) varies according to your field.

Finding your first customer can take a day or a year, depending on how ready you feel and how you get the word out.

For almost everyone, it takes a full year to get the basics of your business foundation built, and another year to really revise and streamline your systems and services.

Some more factors are: the amount of time you plan to devote to this work, what your support system is like, and how skilled you are at managing yourself.

Emotions are another aspect. For many people, becoming self-employed has a way of bringing up deep-seated feelings—family expectations about earnings and success, questions about identity, courage, risk-taking, and knowing what you truly want.

These emotions are important and will affect your timing as well. They show up randomly. If you have someone to talk to—a loved one, partner, therapist or trusted friend—it will really help you to keep going. Consider getting more self-knowledge a part of your on-the-job training!

Different Results Require Different Methods

To engage in this journey is to be a pioneer. Doing work in a rapidly changing world, in your own unique way, is a lost art. You'll be reinventing a wheel, but at least it's one that you love. It can feel lonely sometimes. It's natural to doubt yourself.

Trust your instincts. Ask the questions: *What's best for me? What's best for my clients?* If you find that your answers are different or novel, then congratulations! You're an innovator. Seth Godin, thought leader and business author, writes about being a "purple cow." If you were driving along and saw a purple cow, you would notice it—it stands out. It makes you stop and look at it and wonder why it's purple...and then it might make you want one. Novelty is good! It's beneficial to stand out—when it's based on real and authentic reasons.

It sounds so easy, but in reality it feels risky to stick your neck out. Once you've figured out some cool new thing to do, it can be tempting to look around and notice that no one else is doing that same thing...and then to doubt yourself. *Maybe I should change it....*

Here's an example: Currently, I have no fees for cancellations, late arrivals, or no-shows. I do not suggest this for everybody. Here's why it works for me. My clients are busy and can feel that they are under a lot of pressure. My goal is to make their lives easier. If they're stuck in traffic and worried about being late, they might associate this feeling with me. Instead, I want all of our interactions to feel calm and good.

Lots of people have suggested I change this. I've thought about it...maybe I should charge. But then, when I heard the word should, I went back to the core questions about what's best for me and my clients. I might change it one day, if a different policy is better for me. But it works for now.

All of this is to say that if you want results that look different, they will require different methods. If you want to be self-employed, it's likely because you want something different than the typical American work experience. This is where you get to make up your own way. It's the only way to craft a job that you love, that fits your personal style, values, skills, and practical needs. So embrace it!

Welcome to the club...although it is a strange club, full of empowered, satisfied people who have no need for a club.

Best to you in your journey. This book was made just for you.

Warming Up

A Couple of Business Concepts for Self-Employed Folks

•

About the Journey

A Couple of Business Concepts for Self-Employed Folks

Introduction

Let's take a fresh look at what it means to do business—especially as a self-employed person.

At its core, business is the act of exchanging things of value. In these terms, doing business is a very normal, helpful, and sometimes friendly activity. It feels good to offer your service or products, and it feels good to get paid!

Sometimes in our modern world, we forget this. The word *business* has so many different connotations and meanings, and often has a bad reputation. It helps to claim this word for yourself, to be at peace with it, and to understand what *doing business* means for you and your work.

Creating a business and keeping it going requires you to wear many hats. We'll look at a handful of these—five areas of business that need development and tending. We'll also review how businesses grow and change over time—the demands, the mix of tasks, and the payoffs.

Anyone Can Do Business

The simple truth is that anyone can do business. There are a number of requirements and once you know these, you can meet them however you choose.

Consider this: people have been doing business since the beginning of time. It is just this: the act of exchanging goods and services. In prehistoric times, cavemen may have traded meat for some berries. In the middle ages, perhaps it was a loaf of bread for some ale. Eventually, currency was introduced, so bits of copper were used to buy a soda.

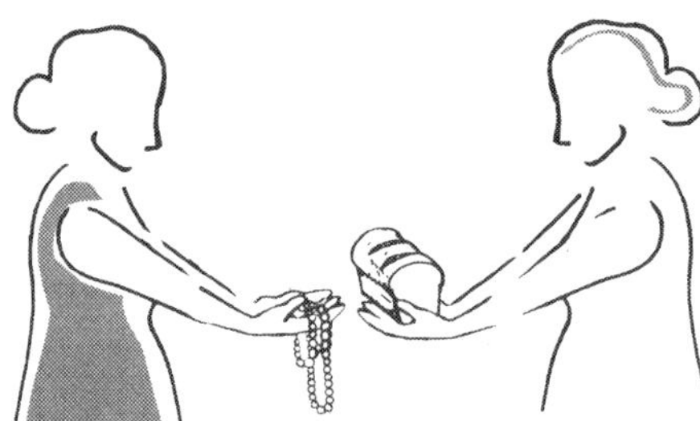

At some point, "business" became a field, something to study, a category of work—complete with practices, terminology, and textbooks. That's when it turned into something that only a few people do. That's when it became intimidating.

You don't need an MBA to be self-employed or to do business. You don't even need to take a business class. All you need is the willingness to learn the basic requirements, a little terminology and a few strategies.

Whatever you do—

Start simple. Choose your own methods. Learn and grow as you need to.

ProTip: Sometimes people who've been in business for years will help you the least because they will tell you all the things you *"have to do"* and forget that business is possible without all the complicated systems that they've come to rely on. To get better help, ask very explicit questions: *Did flyers work for you? Do you have a late payment fee?*

Business on One Hand

To create your work and keep it going, there are a handful of business areas to attend to. These are terms you likely know—let's look at them in everyday language, as they apply to being self-employed.

We'll explore each of these five areas in the *Keep Going* section.

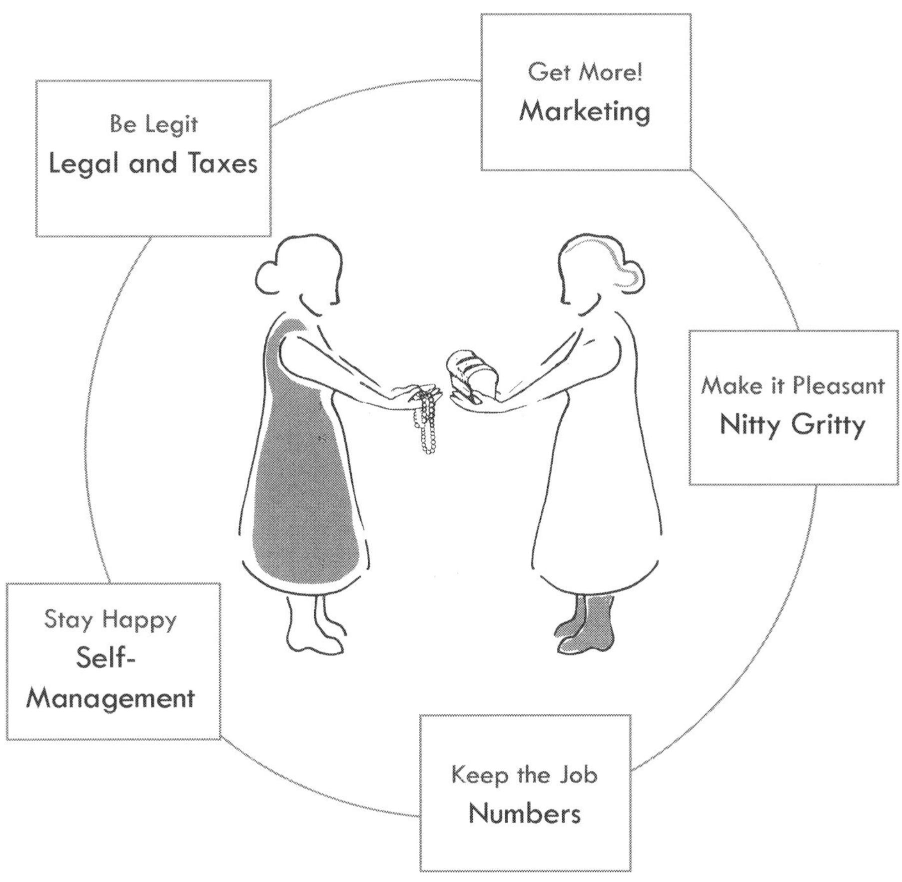

First, you must be allowed to conduct business. This is the **legal** aspect, where you meet requirements—namely getting licenses, following rules and regulations, and paying **taxes**.

To get repeat business, you need to find clients. This includes getting the word out there and letting the world know you exist. This is **marketing**.

To make the transactions go well is to pay attention to the *operations*, or **nitty gritty**.

You need to make enough money if you want to keep this job. This requires handling a few **numbers**.

To stay happy, and keep your quality up, you need to **manage yourself**.

•

Look at your left hand. Start with the thumb.

Legal and Taxes
Numbers
Marketing
Nitty Gritty
Self-Management

Marketing
Numbers
Nitty Gritty
Self-Management
Legal and Taxes

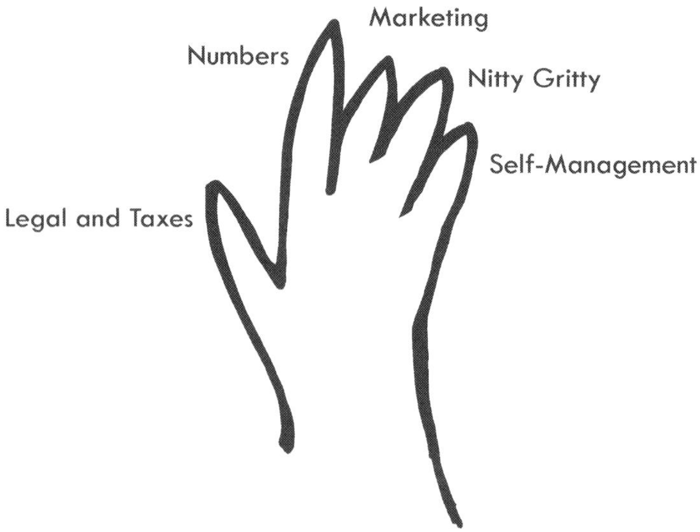

Requirements—The Have-Tos

Here's what you have to do:

- Get all licenses and permits required
- Make reports to various government agencies
- Pay taxes
- Act lawfully (follow any rules and regulations)

You can choose any methods you want to meet these requirements. How you track receipts, manage time, use technology, choose clients, and create your job description are all up to you. If you want to clean houses dressed in a cat outfit, ask for payment only in rolls of quarters, and throw all your receipts in a laundry hamper, that's fine as long as you are licensed, make your reports, and pay taxes.

Getting familiar with these requirements will help you to create systems that fit your needs and personality. All too often, people treat the laws like a monster in the closet. They look the other way and get stressed whenever they think about them. If you turn and face the monster, the fear goes away, and you end up saving time, stress, and money. You realize it's not really a monster after all, just a set of rules that you'll come to know and might even appreciate.

Learning some of the practices and terminology will also help you to be more comfortable. Even if you outsource certain tasks, like taxes and bookkeeping, you'll better understand conversations with other professionals and make better choices.

The Four Modes

My sister Liza used to do the chalkboards for the Starbucks store where she worked. As time went on, she got better and better and was soon doing boards for other local shops. She decided to hang up her barista apron and become an artist for pay. She imagined spending all her days in her studio, drawing and painting with her favorite music playing.

Like many new self-employed folks, she was shocked to discover that she spent only a small amount of time doing the work she wanted to do. Instead, she was meeting with shop owners, writing up proposals, making business cards, and sending a million emails.

Many people new to self-employment are surprised to find themselves in a similar spot. Sometimes they think: *I've jumped from the pan to the fire, maybe I should go back.* Do not despair! This phase doesn't last forever. It is normal in the beginning, but the business tasks diminish over time, leaving more time for craft doing and development

Below is a model to illustrate the four modes of self-employment. The definitions are on the next page.

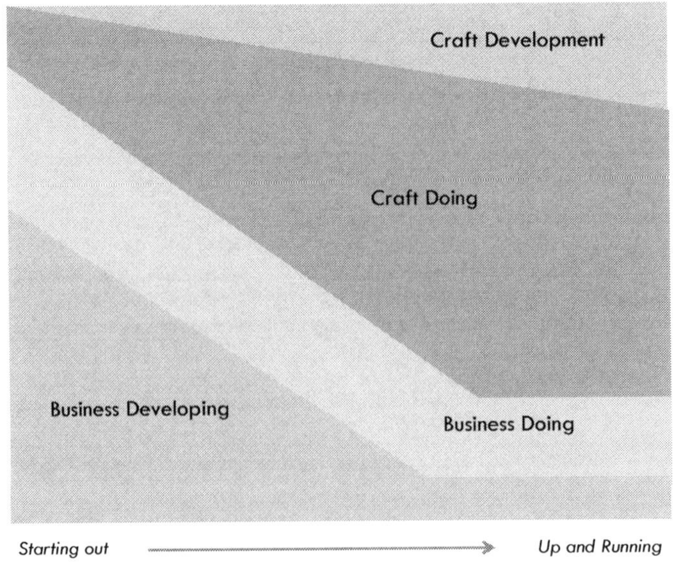

Starting from the base and moving up:

Business Development: This is the building the business side of self-employment. It includes things like creating a website, designing business cards, creating your systems, doing research or education related to marketing, creating your accounting system, and learning about taxes.

Business Doing: These are the regular tasks of maintaining a business. These never go away, although they can get more efficient. Some examples are setting up appointments, making invoices, putting up flyers, and tweaking your website.

Craft Doing: This is the reason you're doing all of this—when you're delivering your service or making your product.

Craft Development: This is improving your service offering or product. It involves additional training, coaching, reading, and developing new skills. This is one of the fun parts! It's also a great investment which increases the value of your offering, leads to price increases, and creates more job satisfaction.

You will always have to do all four, but over time, if you continue to build and revise, *Business Development* and *Business Doing* will take less time.

Phases of Business Development

The nature of your work will grow and change over time. What you're learning and working on the first year will be different than your third or seventh year. Think of it as a four-year growth pattern—just like going to high school or college—after which you graduate. This thinking honors the learning curve and offers hope in the challenging times.

Let's compare business growth to the typical 4-year student experience.

Freshman Year—Everything is exciting and new!

Student Experience: Lots of questions. It's taking a lot of work to figure out the lay of the land. Who are the best teachers? Will I make friends? Can I handle this?

Typical business activities include: getting licensed, finding customers, creating marketing materials, making a website, learning billing and book-keeping, adjusting services and prices. (There is a lot going on!)

Sophomore Year—You know what you're doing

Student Experience: We know how to pace ourselves; we've got some better study habits and favorite tools. We know where we fit in. We're still pretty excited.

Typical business activities: learning how to do tax reporting, renewing licenses, refining the website and marketing materials, adjusting prices, adding some policies, perhaps finding some referral partners.

Junior Year—Nose to the grindstone

Student Experience: We've got some serious classes and we're starting to think about college. We're in a group or comfortable without one.

Typical business activities: getting systems streamlined for bookkeeping, billing, and tax reporting, marketing efforts. Charging more and enforcing policies. Dialing in on best-fit clients, learning to say no to bad-fit ones. Exploring outsourcing for some of the business tasks. Developing weekly routines. Seeking out more support or colleagues, whether informally or through a formal networking group.

Senior Year—A full workload, and possibly some new dreams

Student Experience: We've got our systems in place, we have friends in our classes, and we have some favorite teachers. We feel lighter because graduation is on the corner, and we're looking forward to more freedom.

Typical business activities: getting better at time and financial planning for getting time off, and making enough money. Perhaps a re-brand—finding a new look and new language to find our A+ clients. Adjusting services to fit our preferences, whether it's adding or refining. Adding special touches. Regularly connecting with others.

•

Of course this pathway is different for each person. These are examples offered to illustrate the changes over time. The idea of graduation is not that leave your work, but instead, that you'll be finished with most or all of the business development—that you'll have a sense of freedom, accomplishment, and more earning power. Your brain can be released to think about other things.

In Summary—A Couple of Business Concepts for Self-Employed Folks

Business is that act of two people exchanging goods or services. Everyone can do it.

Most or all of your business activities will fall into five categories, which you can count on one hand:

- Legal and Taxes
- Numbers
- Marketing
- Nitty Gritty
- Self-Management

Learn the requirements of doing business as soon as possible!

As you're building and running a business, you'll be in different work modes. Craft Doing and Craft Development are the fun parts—when you're doing the work you love. In addition, it will take time for Business Development and Business Doing. The mix of these four modes changes over time.

Each year of the business will be different, and feel different—just like high school. Your freshman, sophomore, junior, and senior years will have unique joys, tasks, and challenges.

About the Journey

Introduction

Now that we've reviewed a few business concepts, let's look at the human-nature side of building your self-employment work.

This is not like getting a new job. It really is a journey. It takes time and lots of learning by doing. It takes courage to keep going. In addition to the fun parts, you will sometimes be challenged, feel hopeless, and get lonely. You will need to change and grow.

In addition, people will react to you in all kinds of ways. Sometimes they will be helpful; often times, they will not.

This chapter presents some mental shifts and strategies to help you manage your own expectations as well as how to communicate with others... so you can stay engaged with building your business and enjoy yourself more along the way.

It Helps to Behave As If You're Going to School

It's funny. Everyone seems to understand that when you go to school—whether for a certificate, a degree, or advanced degree—life will be hard for a bit, you'll go into debt, and you'll be busy. The idea is that in the end, you'll have more job opportunities, and your life will be better.

Becoming self-employed and building a business is exactly like going to school—you learn, grow over time, get busy, and often take a decrease in pay. Maybe you have debt, but maybe not. Then, if you can stick with it for two to three years, you'll have a better job, probably earn more money, and have more knowledge, choices, and happiness.

The difference is you don't have a piece of paper at the end...and people tend to forget that you're in a learning process. This causes some problems on a couple of levels. When you're working through challenging times, you might doubt your choice, lose hope and give up prematurely. Loved ones observing you might notice how hard you're working and get worried. They might think you're making a mistake and you're working too hard for a modest wage. This can lead them to subtly pressuring you to get a job again or bringing up concerns in unhelpful ways.

Help yourself by acting as if you're going to school. Communicate the following with others, so they can be supportive.

You might be extra busy and living on a tighter budget, and you might get tapped out at times and not be as available as you've been before. It's a temporary period. It's totally worth it.

A Transition Plan

We all know that "Rome wasn't built in a day." And, yet, our culture seems obsessed with stories of overnight success. It is common for business authors to highlight the ventures that took off quickly. Sure, some people get lucky and take off right away, but for most people, success takes longer.

It takes time to find customers, to keep customers, to build a referral base, and to shape a reputation. It's more like planting a grapevine than a sunflower. Grapevines grow quickly enough but take up to seven years before yielding fruit. In my experience, it takes most self-employed people anywhere from six months to two years or more to get fully up to speed. And another year or two for the business to thrive.

Growth works best when you have some time to build your business without the pressure to earn your full income. For this, you need a *Transition Plan*—a way to have enough income to support yourself for a set period of time. You can achieve this in a variety of ways. Here are some strategies I've observed with clients and friends.

- Have a full-time job in which you can transition to fewer hours, as needed
- Have a part-time job
- Have a partner who earns most of the household needs
- Get a roommate
- Be a long-term house sitter
- Draw from an inheritance or trust fund
- Cash out some of your 401K. (This often advised against, or done as a last resort. There are penalties too. I encourage clients to meet with an accountant or financial advisor if exploring this option.)
- Get a loan from a family member—to be paid back way in the future
- Use crowdsourcing, such as kickstarter.com or indiegogo.com
- Reduce weekly spending (See page 336)

Combine your strategy with a fixed period of time—perhaps nine, twelve, or twenty four months. Just like being in school, this provides a deadline to work toward. It also helps you to remember that the transition isn't forever.

Two Versions of You

Self-employment requires you to fill two roles—the business manager and the talent. Each one serves a different purpose and requires different skills and ways of thinking. It's important to separate these out from each other, so you know which version to call on at various times.

Talent You is the one that brings the value. It's you performing your service or making your product. It's the heart of your business. It's why you want to be self-employed.

Business You is required to keep your job. It's what you're developing by reading this book. For some of you, this will be totally new, and perhaps uncomfortable. For others, this side might be more familiar. Developing *Business You* is essential in order to make money, keep your job and stay happy in this work.

Business You needs to manage *Talent You*, making sure that your schedule isn't overloaded and that you get rest, support, opportunities to learn, and some rewards.

Knowing that you're playing a role can help you to make decisions and do things that might seem hard. For example, let's say you meet a potential client, and they're excited to hire you...but, you can tell they're going to take a lot of extra work. Maybe they're tricky to deal with; maybe they challenge you on lots of decisions or email you constantly. And perhaps on top of all that, they're asking a lot of questions about price in a way that suggests they might only pay you begrudgingly.

It's easy for *Talent You* to think: *Well, at least it's some money, and really, I just want to do my work, so what does it matter?*

That's where *Business You* can step in and explain: *Wait a minute. Dealing with this client will take a lot of time and create extra stress. This takes away valuable energy that could be spent elsewhere, such as marketing for the clients I want, or getting my workshop cleaned up. Taking this job is too big of an opportunity cost. I need to find a way to say "No, thank you".*

Business You channels other sides of yourself or other people to do things that are new and unfamiliar, such as talking about your services to potential clients, learning a piece of tax code, or sending out your bills.

Sometimes people think: *I'm a writer, how can I do this tax stuff?* Or, *I'm an artist, I can't do marketing.* That's fine. That's your *Talent You* talking. *Business You* can learn to do what's needed.

Knowing All the Requirements Brings Empowerment and Freedom

Here's my pitch to you: learn these as soon as possible.

Once you know that basic requirements for starting and maintaining a business, you can meet them however you want. That is the only true responsibility you have as a business owner. The rest of it—marketing, tools, policies, client interactions—all of it, can be done however you like. This knowledge brings an incredible freedom.

In addition, learning about licensing and taxes takes the fear away. It can be very tempting to put this off—it's hard to know where the process starts and if it will ever end. Add to this a natural fear of taxes taking a lot of your money away! The problem is that fear and dread have a way of growing—like a monster in a closet. They gnaw at you, keep you up at night, take up valuable brain space, and, if ignored too long, can cause some real problems. If you face this knowledge up front, you will sleep better and feel better from the beginning. With the fear gone, you'll have more of your brain and heart freed up to do your work and build your business.

Participating in the process of licensing and working on taxes will help you determine who needs to be doing this work for your business. You might discover that you don't mind the work so much. Or, if you find that you really dislike it, you can decide to hire a bookkeeper or accountant. You can feel good about this decision because you tried it first.

Lastly, once you know the language and processes, it'll be easier to understand things when you meet with other professionals. You can make more informed choices, and understand and utilize advice.

Think Sequentially

Imagine building a house from the ground up. You can't pour the concrete foundation, put in light switches, and paint all at the same time. Similarly, when you go to college, you don't take twenty-five classes all at once...you do a few each term. Partly this is because the order of things matter; also, you will spread yourself too thin if you're switching between too many tasks.

The same idea applies here. Building a business is a big, multi-pronged project with a lot of little steps. It is common to feel pressured to work on everything at once. *I have to get the website up, meet with an accountant, make those new invoices and—oh, yeah, figure out how to get a logo!* This is frazzling to the brain and generally gets in the way of progress.

There's a saying:

> You can have everything you want, just not all at once.

Eventually, you will get all your projects done if you can pace yourself and put them in order. Learn to think sequentially about your goals. That is, focus on one thing, and then, when it's done, all the way done, then start the next project.

For example, you might say to yourself: *First the website. Then the logo. Right now, I'm going to focus all efforts on the website. I need it for a variety of reasons. It'll be fine without the logo. Afterward, I'll start meeting designers or looking online for logo stuff.*

Sometimes it's helpful to attach time periods to projects. For example: *This month I'm working on the website, next month is the logo, and after that the invoice.* Other times, it's better to give each project as much time as it needs. It just depends on your personal style.

Index Card Exercise

If you're not sure how to prioritize your projects, here's an exercise to help. Get some index cards or scraps of paper. Write each project on a separate card. First, observe how many you have! When I do this with clients it's common to have eight to fifteen cards. Just this activity can be quite sobering and also quite validating. No wonder they've been feeling crazy and overwhelmed!

Sort them into priority order. You might instinctively know, or you might have to think through each task. Consider various factors: how important it is, how much effort, time, and money it might take, and if any are a prerequisite for other projects. If you're still not sure, put them in any arbitrary order.

Now, take the top goal, set it somewhere so that you'll see it regularly—on your desk or fridge perhaps. Put the others away. When you finish the top goal, then go get the next one.

Doing this exercise with actual index cards can really clarify thinking since you can look at all the projects at the same time. It can also work conceptually. When I'm driving or walking to work, I often think about projects I need to do, and then imagine writing them on cards...and picking the top card.

Do Things Your Way

One of the great things about working for yourself is that you get to do things your way. This is not only a perk, it is also a strategy. You're more likely to stick with systems that you like.

There's a common perception that there's one right way to do business. In reality, as long as you meet the legal requirements for your business, and report your numbers to various tax agencies, you can do things however you want.

Take bookkeeping, for example. I'm often asked, *Do you use QuickBooks? Do you teach your clients how to use QuickBooks?* People are obsessed with QuickBooks! No. My approach is to teach clients to read the tax form first, and then to decide on how to meet the requirements in a way that fits their style. For some, it's a box with no lid for receipts, and for others it's a notebook. Some use an Excel spreadsheet. And, yes, for just a few of them, QuickBooks is the ticket.

Another example is social media. Everyone says you *have to* do social media; it's the new way and it's the future. Here's my reaction: if you want to, then do it. If you don't like it, don't. Find a different way to network or advertise. Be yourself; work the channels that you like. When you're happy, you're motivated, and people will want to work with you. The idea for self-employment is freedom, not new burdens.

In addition, sometimes your unique way of doing something helps you stand out from the crowd.

Do the Business Tasks You Like and Get Help for the Rest

For some reason, there's a pervading notion that being self-employed means you have to do everything yourself. There's a problem with this thinking. It would require learning too many things at once. You'd be switching roles constantly and doing tasks you don't like or that you're not good at. Being self-employed doesn't mean going it alone!

Outsourcing

After you learn the various aspects of business, figure out which ones you like and which ones you don't. Then, find ways to outsource the things you don'e like! It might sound expensive, but consider the following. You're likely to get higher quality results on those tasks. You'll experience less stress. You can focus better on doing your primary work. Often, you can earn the money to pay that other person in less time than it would take to figure out how to do that task yourself.

Trading/Bartering

Sometimes you can trade or barter—maybe with another self-employed person, a knowledgeable friend, or a family member. This can be a great, low-cost way to get things done, to learn, and to add energy to projects. In addition, it's nice to have some company and a sense of teamwork.

Bartering can also be a little tricky. Here are some strategies to keep in mind. Make sure that the tasks you've bartered for are actually helpful. For example, if someone creates a website for you that you can't make changes on, or don't like, then it wasn't actually helpful. Treat anyone who wants to trade as someone you would hire. Look at the work they've done for others, find out what they normally charge, and create an agreement, including a timeline for the project.

One important note: bartered income must be reported and is taxed. (More on page 282.)

Information

When you need information, find friends or family who can explain things well. It's amazing what people will do in exchange for lunch or a bottle of wine! If you like to learn from books, get recommendations. Going into the bookstore or library can be daunting. In addition, there are lots of unhelpful or outdated books that look good on the cover. Finding the right book can be incredibly empowering, allowing you to learn and move at your own pace.

Support

Get support for yourself. It's a bit of a lonely journey. Find a *co-traveler* (someone who's also self-employed) or someone to lean on or just talk to, such as a coach or therapist.

It's best to spend the majority of your time doing what you're good at. You'll be happier, and you'll develop your expertise. Get help for the rest.

Other People Don't Always Understand

Many, many people will not understand what you're doing. There are lots of reasons for this. It's hard to picture how being self-employed works. People are really attached to the mainstream model of work. Doing something different challenges people. They might be jealous. And, for some people, independence can look like irresponsibility.

Even if people are happy for you, they'll often be worried. This is likely because they haven't taken the same time you've had to think, research, and engage in your venture. Unfortunately, these concerns can come out as unnecessary advice or questions that are a guise for fears. Also, almost everybody knows someone who has opened a business that failed. They will want to tell you these stories.

So, be careful who you talk to. For people who don't get what you're doing and are likely to give you grief about it, be concise and then change the subject. Give them the simplest version of where you're at, make it sound safe, and be confident. Say: *Yes, I've decided to work for myself.* Or: *Business is great. I've got some new clients this month.* The more confident you are, the better.

If possible, try not to engage with these people in a conversation. Don't go into details. Answer questions with just one sentence that sounds like a conclusion, not an invite. For example, you might say, *I've got a plan. I'm working on it.*

Pro Tip: If you find yourself feeling defensive or stuck in a conversation, excuse yourself to go use the restroom.

It is very normal for friends and loved ones to doubt in the beginning. Keep in mind, this is usually not about you! It's most often a reflection on themselves, and our society in general.

A lot of times, folks will come around later, once they see that you're doing fine.

Plan to Build as You Go

You do not need to create the whole business at once. Also, things don't need to be perfect the first time you use them. Building parts of the business in response to real world clients provides motivation to get things done, saves you time in the long run, and often creates the best results.

For example, imagine that you've gotten your licenses and you've found your first customer. You can make the invoice and menu of services in preparation for working with that person. Imagining a real meeting means you'll think through more details and you'll be energized to finish prepping on time. The deadline is meaningful. And then, after working with them, you can make revisions for the next client.

Imagine that for the first year, everything is an evolving prototype.

To build as you go:

- Try it out: provide your service, or sell your product
- Reflect and revise
- Get information as you need it
- Rinse and repeat!

Building as you go in response to the customers in front of you also helps you build the right number of tools—not too many, and not too few. I grew up in a time when business owners had letterhead. I planned to make some right away, thinking it was an important beginning step. But then I got busy working on other tasks in response to my actual clients, such as invoices, a website, and a menu of services. A year went by, and then I realized to myself: *Wow, I guess I don't need letterhead because I'm not really sending letters out.* Making that letterhead would have been fun, but the time and money was spent better elsewhere.

Pick a Date

To make this journey real, pick a date—either to start the process, or to finish the 1,2…Go! section. Put it on the calendar.

Start talking about it. Say things like: *By September, I will have my business up and running.* Or: *Next month, I'm going to start offering my services.*

Hint: You can change it later.

•

Write your date and goal here:

Momentum Part One: Dealing with Roadblocks

It's hard to get a freight train moving. It takes enormous energy in the beginning, and yet the movement is so slow. It looks labored, and it is. But once it's moving, it's moving fast! And it takes less energy to keep it moving.

It's all about momentum.

In the beginning, roadblocks can slow you down or halt progress. Later, when you're really moving, you'll be able to blast right through most of them.

Roadblocks need to be named. Name roadblocks, whether they are big or small. This is very important! The little stuff might not seem worth worrying about, but if something's bothering you, it will continue to do so. Try to be neutral with your language, and don't blame yourself. Here's an example: *Wow, I keep putting off setting up my business banking accounts. For some reason, that just feels really hard.*

Here are two strategies for small and medium roadblocks.

Quick Strategy

Tell somebody about the roadblock, and ask for their help or even just company with trying to solve it. For example, if you feel blocked about opening a business account, ask someone to go with you. Or if you're starting a website, ask them to sit next to you while going through the set-up process.

Simply making an appointment gets something on your calendar, having a friend makes it feel more pleasant, and a second set of eyes and ears can help you catch details.

Problem / Solution Strategy

1 Identify your roadblock. Write it down or say it out loud. Then give it some time. The answer might come to you. If not, then...

2 Figure out when you need to deal with it. Write a due date on your calendar.

3 Identify what's holding you back. What makes this thing hard? Is it unpleasant? Are there things you don't know how to do? Does it fit it into your schedule?

4 Now, write down solutions for the above. Figure out how you'll get what you need.

5 Block out time in your calendar to do the work.

•

For some of the deeper roadblocks...well, there's no easy answer. Usually, they are related to fear. It helps to acknowledge what you fear, and at some point, to explore it. You might journal about it, talk to a therapist, or meet up with someone in the field to hear their story or get their advice. Maybe they have faced similar fears.

Sometimes doing your work in spite of your fear will help you overcome a roadblock. Experience will give you more confidence and will help you discover which fears are real or imagined. For what it's worth, almost everybody deals with these. Steven Pressfield writes a lot about the creative process. He poses that the deeper the fears, the more validation that you're on the right path. He talks about "Resistance" and all its forms in his three non-fiction books: *Do the Work!*, *The War of Art*, and *Turning Pro.*

For me, when all else fails, I try to remember: *Other people have figured this out. So can I.*

Momentum Part Two: Progress, Not Perfection

Progress is progress. And it is the only way to get to perfection…if perfection is even possible.

If you're a hard-core perfectionist (meaning you have very high standards for yourself), you will have to trick your brain. It's hard to shake the habit of wanting things to be the way you imagine them in your head.

Try this: Tell yourself you want to be perfect at the process. And process includes making imperfect things, so you can reflect, get feedback, and then revise them to make them better. This process creates stronger products in the end.

If it's hard for you to put things out into the world that don't seem perfect yet, that's okay! You can label things with words like *DRAFT*, *PROTOTYPE*, or *BETA*.

Eventually, you'll be in the habit of making things that are good enough. When you allow things to be good enough, they exist. That is way better than perfect in your mind.

Inspirational Stories

Claire, Apparel Artist in Ballard

Claire was working full time as a barista while sewing curtains and bridesmaids' dresses on the side. She was feeling stuck—this wasn't the side work she wanted to be doing. Since childhood, Claire had always dreamt of being a designer and having her own shop. She had been sewing her whole life, trained as a fashion designer, and studied couture in London.

We worked together for about two years. We made a weekly schedule with protected time to design and sew what she wanted to create. Claire starting saying *no* to projects not in line with her dream. We created a website and systems for bookkeeping and taxes that fit her style. We also tried out different ways to market her clothes and accessories, and increased her prices. Now, she's designing and sewing four days a week, selling at a downtown boutique and local markets, and doing a ton of custom work. She has created a complete line of clothes and made a Look Book. She's on her way.

Jeff, Read-Aloud Stories and Marketing on Capitol Hill

Jeff told me he'd rather do any job than go back to a corporate life. He was a writer of poetry, children's books, and essays. There was no time leftover for that after a sixty-hour-a-week job. When times got tough, he started looking at corporate job postings. I reminded him of his earlier statement. We decided to build a part-time consulting job for him—copy and marketing strategies—in order to support his writing.

It's working! He's finding that the marketing is all about story too. He's enjoying both the work, as well as the fact that he can switch gears on a regular basis between strategic thinking, poetry, and creative writing.

Roxie, Radical Beauty and DIY Hair In Green Lake

Roxie had built up an amazing website in her spare time, all about hair, beauty, empowerment, natural products and feeling free. When we met, she had nearly 70,000 unique visitors to her site every month. Her goal was to start earning some regular income in order to leave her part-time job so she would have more time to spend with her daughters and pursue other work interests.

Roxie had some great ideas that we put into action. We added affiliate links everywhere, we reached out to like-minded businesses with organic advertising opportunities, and she launched a line of natural hair care products. Now, three years later, she's left her part-time job, and her earnings from the website are steady. With that base income, she's more free to explore some of her other interests, such as photography, teaching, and writing.

•

What do you want? What will your story be?

In Summary—About the Journey

You are stepping into a new way of working. You need some new mental frames and strategies to deal with the challenges.

Think of building your business as if you're going to graduate school. Make a *transition plan* that includes a way to earn enough money to pay all your bills—so you have time to develop your business.

Realize, there are now two versions of you: *Business You* and *Talent You.*

Learn the requirements of business. This empowers you and brings peace of mind. Give yourself time; it's a learning process.

Think sequentially. Work on projects in order, not all at once.

Do things your way! You'll enjoy your work more and it'll be more sustainable.

Don't go it alone. Do what you like, and get help for the rest.

Other people won't understand. Be ready for them, don't take it personally.

Plan to build as you go. It's called *iterative design*. You can make changes in response to customers and experiences.

Pick dates to get projects started. Put these on the calendar and talk about them.

Be inspired by people who've gone before you! Be an inspiration to others. What story will we tell about you?

1, 2...Go!

1. Prepare for Licensing
   Get Licensed

2. Get Your First Customer

Go! Do Your Work + Set Up Shop

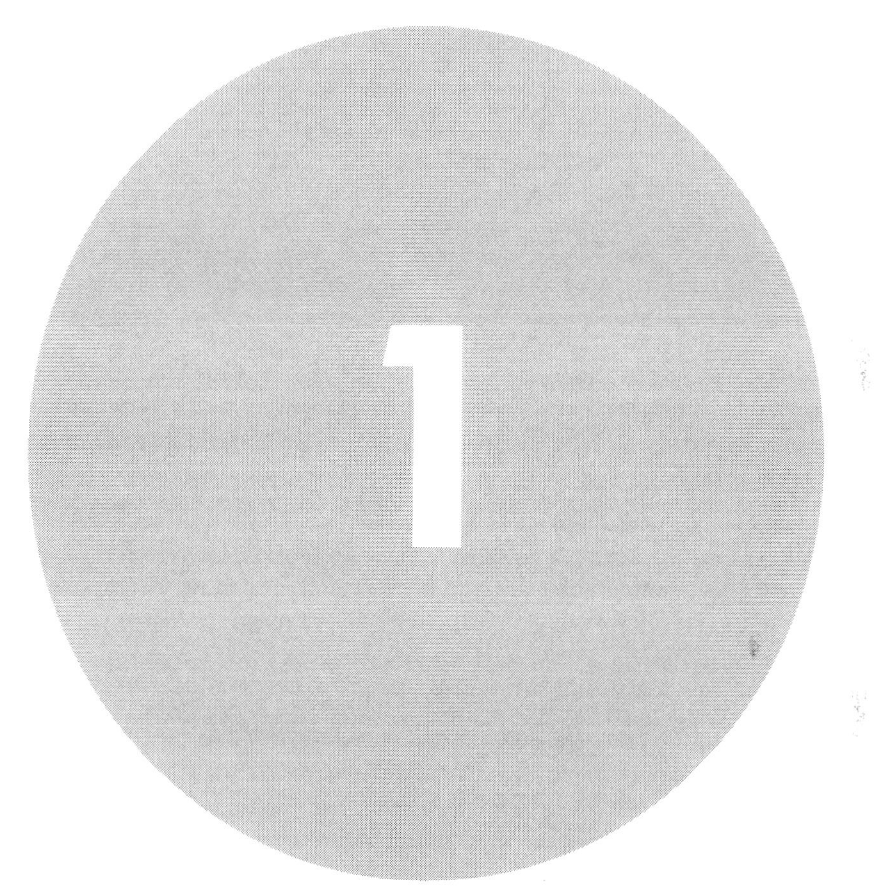
1

Prepare for Licensing

Recommended for everyone. Check when complete.

Decisions

- Business Entity—Sole Proprietor or LLC (Or PLLC)
- Determine Legal Name
- Create Primary Business Name
- DBAs
- Write Description of the Business
- The Start Date

Research and Review

- NAICS Code
- Categories of Business Activity
- Location
- Your Due Diligence
  - *Professional or special license(s) needed?*
  - *Permits required?*
  - *Rules or regulations to know?*
- Determine If You Need to Collect Sales Tax
- Example Starting Costs

Notes

Introduction to Prepare for Licensing

Getting licensed is actually pretty simple. You'll be asked for your address a million times, along with a few basic questions about your business, e.g., your expected income, location, if you're hiring employees, etc.

Having said that, a lot of people get tripped up filling out these applications if they haven't prepared ahead of time. That's what this chapter is for! We'll cover some terms you need to know and make some decisions, so you'll be ready to skip through the licensing process. Please be aware that websites change and move. If any of the links don't work, perhaps search for the terms or call the related government agency.

The checklist is provided to help you keep track of your progress. Feel free to add notes to the checklist and to record your choices as you go along, so you can refer to it when applying for your licenses.

Important notes:

- Some things apply to everyone, and some things vary by occupation. I'm providing the basics. It'll be up to you to find out what else you need; that is what due diligence is all about. (Covered on page 71.)
- If you plan to hire employees, you will have additional responsibilities that are not covered in this book. (See page 357.)

Some people like to get help from a small business expert or lawyer. This can be extremely valuable. I still encourage you to work through this chapter first to become familiar with the terms. Then, you can better understand their advice and utilize their expertise to fill in the gaps.

ProTip: people will try to give you additional advice. Help them help you by staying on task. At this step, you want to understand only what's needed to get set up as a legal business. Do this first before digesting other advice.

Lastly, have fun! You're creating something new. Make it your own!

Business Entity: Sole Proprietor or LLC (Or PLLC)

One of your first decisions is to choose what type of business entity you want to have. There are different types; each have their own requirements, obligations, and benefits. Most self-employed folks pick either *Sole Proprietor* or *Limited Liability Company, or LLC.* (Or if your work requires a professional license, then a special version of an LLC is required called a *PLLC*, or *Professional Limited Liability Company*.)

Some people choose to set up an S Corporation. That is beyond the scope of this book.

Sole Proprietor

The simplest option is the *Sole Proprietor*. In this case, you and the business are considered one and the same. There's no real structure to set up or maintain. You are simply required to have licenses and pay taxes. The structure is free; that is, there are no additional costs for being a sole proprietor besides licensing fees.

There are no special obligations or benefits. The main advantage is that the paperwork is the most streamlined. There is a risk, though. If for some reason, someone sues your business, they are suing you personally. If they win and you owe them damages, they will come out of your personal assets, such as your savings accounts, retirement, or properties.

One benefit to having a sole proprietorship is that checks can be made out to your name—so that makes banking easy. You can even use a personal banking account versus a business account. (Having said that, it's best to get separate accounts for your business. We'll look at those later.)

Note: It's fairly easy to change from a sole proprietor to an LLC, if you change your mind.

Limited Liability Company, or LLC (Or Professional Limited Liability Company, or PLLC)

The second option is an *LLC*, or *limited liability company*. (If you work in a field that requires a professional license—lawyers, massage therapists, counselors—then you must get a *PLLC*. They cost the same, function the same, and are grouped with LLCs. Generally, if you read about LLCs, here or in other places, the information applies to PLLCs as well.)

In this case, the business is a company that is separate from you. This offers a layer of protection. When someone sues a LLC, they can take the company's assets, but not the personal assets of the owner. If Jane Q. Carpenter builds a house that collapses, she can lose everything if she gets sued. Her home, her savings account, all of it. But if JQ Carpentry, LLC gets sued, a plaintiff can only take the assets that belong to the business. (In my case, my company assets only include a small business savings account, my computer, printer, and lots of great books.) The idea is that your home and personal monies are protected.

Having said that, it is possible to get around that protection—depending on the case and the lawyer. If you want to know more on the subject, I suggest meeting with a small business lawyer to share more about your specific situation.

You must apply with the Secretary of State of Washington to be granted the LLC entity. It costs about $200. You must renew each year on the anniversary month, for about $70.

Some people consider it an additional benefit that the LLC label looks and sounds super legit. Some find that it helps potential clients, friends and families all take your business seriously. This can be a boon for certain types of businesses, especially if you have a unique job or one that doesn't require any degrees or licenses, like a consultant or artist.

For an LLC, you will need to get a separate banking account, since it's a company separate from you. (More LLC stuff on page 81.)

Here's a cool thing about LLCs. If you're the only owner or member, you don't have to do anything different for the IRS! You use the same forms as a sole proprietor because the finances work in exactly the same way. In fact, the IRS refers to you as a *"disregarded entity."* Your entity is not regarded! You are ignored. ☺ This allows you to use the simplest reporting option. (If you want to be regarded as a corporation or partnership, you may do that instead if you meet those requirements. Regarded entities have their own special forms.)

•

Once you know which type of entity you'd like, enter it onto the checklist.

Legal Name and DBAs

When you register your business, you'll be asked for the legal name. This is like the root name. It'll be on all your licenses and tax forms. You can still do business under different names. These are called DBAs (doing business as) or trade names. Here are a couple rules to know:

☞ If you're a sole proprietor, your legal business name must be your own legal name.

☞ If you're an LLC, your legal name must include limited liability company, limited liability co., LLC, or L.L.C. in the name somewhere. The 'LLC' tells everyone this is a registered entity they can look up with the Washington Secretary of State.)

☞ Your legal name can be changed—for a $30 fee, using a form called: Amended Certificate of Formation/Registration

☞ DBAs for an LLC may NOT include any variation of the LLC label. (For example, my official business name is Girl Friday LLC. If I want a DBA for Jenny Girl Friday, that's fine. But it can NOT be Jenny Girl Friday LLC.)

Example with a Sole Proprietor—
Legal name: Alexander MacLeod
DBA/Trade Name: Old Time Entertainment

Example with an LLC—
Legal Name: Girl Friday LLC
DBA/Trade Names: Girl Friday, Jenny Girl Friday, and Jenny MacLeod

•

DBAs cost about $5 each with the state. (They are free with the city.) They can be added at any time. This is great to remember, since we're employing a build-as-you-go mentality.

Business Name

Your business name is the name you actually use—whether it's your legal name or a DBA. It's the one on your business cards, flyers, and invoices.

Pick one that you like! For whatever reason—it's fun, it's traditional, it's outrageous. Pick one that your target customers will like. (You can change it later.)

If you don't have one yet, brainstorm ideas. Perhaps ask some friends to help. Then, narrow down your list, using the ideas on page 64. Resist the temptation to hold out for the perfect name. If it comes to you, great. Otherwise, just pick a decent one and get going.

Here are some different types of name structures...to help with your brainstorming.

A Clear Description—e.g., Custom Cupcakes for Parties

Your Target Customer—e.g., First-Time Landlord

What You're Selling/Benefit—e.g., Peace of Mind Estate Planning

Something Clever/Eye-catching—e.g., Not a Number Cards & Gifts

Combine the one of the above with your name or initials—e.g., tk Consulting

Combine one of the above with your neighborhood—e.g., Green Lake Dog Walkers.

Narrow your list down to your top 5:

-
-
-
-
-

To narrow further:

- Review available domain names. Go to namecheap.com, and put in your desired name. If what you want is not available, see page 252 for ideas.
- Check to see if other businesses have this name already. Go to the Washington State Look Up tool at: http://apps.dor.wa.gov/BRD/
- Research any trademarks with this name. (See page 72.)
- Look at the usability of your name.

  Is it easy to spell?
  Is it easy to say?
  How does it look written out?
  How does it look as a URL?

Narrow your choices to your top three:

-
-
-

Description

You will be asked to provide a detailed description of your business activities on all license applications. This can be a phrase or a couple sentences.

This has several purposes. First, the state can check to see if you have the correct permits or licenses. Second, it's part of the public record for consumers. Third, it is used to assign your *NAICS* code. (See page 67.) If you care about the code, be sure to craft language to match the one you want.

It's okay to be concise, but be sure to include the main elements of your work.

Incomplete Example: Massage Therapy

Good Example: Massage Therapy: treatment-based, in clinic settings, spas, and private homes.

Practice your description here. Think about what you do, where, with whom, categories of service, and specialty offerings.

The Start Date—Some Considerations

When you apply for your licenses, you will be asked for a start date. You can make it the date of filing or pick a different one.

Sometimes the specific date of filing will be on the LLC certificate or city license. However, in the database, it will show a different date— usually the first of the month of filing.

Here are a few things to keep in mind:

- If you register an LLC, you will renew on the anniversary month, so it might be practical to choose a certain month over others. I suggest sometime between January and April—since you'll be busy with tax season work anyway.
- Pick a date that's memorable. You will be asked about it from time to time, and it's nice to have a solid memory of your start date.
- Lastly, you might have the opportunity to make it fun or meaningful. Mine was 4/9/13*. I love how the first two numbers add up to make the year. Whatever your records say, it's nice to remember your original filing day, and perhaps celebrate business anniversaries.

*Later, I changed my start date to 5/1/13, because May Day is my favorite day of the year. But my certificate still says 4/9/13,—which I still like to see too.

NAICS Code

This code is used for statistics only. Usually it is assigned to you by the state. From time to time, you'll be asked for it. (Opening a business banking account is one example.) So, it's good to know what it is, or where to find it!

NAICS stands for North American Industry Classification System. It collects statistics about business and industry. It was originally developed in the 1930s, and has evolved over time. Every business is given an NAICS code—which also puts your business into a specific category—and you cannot change it. It's kind of fascinating to see all of the business categories.

Typically, the state assigns this to you, using the business description that you provide. To find out what you've gotten, use the business lookup tool.

1 Go to the business lookup tool at: www.dor.wa.gov/content/doingbusiness/registermybusiness/BRD/
2 Put in your business name.
3 Look at the results, find your name and click on it.
4 It will show your business profile, and the NAICS code will be there.

(Note: If the above link has stopped working, try these terms in search: *DOR, business, look up*.)

If you're curious, or want to find one that fits your business, you can go to NAICS.com. It's possible that you could get a specific code assigned to you if you craft your business description to match, or, you call the state to about requesting a specific code. The BLS (The Washington State Business Licensing Services) phone number is 800.451.7985.

List your ideas here: ______________________________.

Types of Business Activity: Service, Retail, Wholesale, Manufacturing

It is important to understand the categories of business activity and to know which ones you'll be doing. Why?

☞ You'll be asked about them on your Washington State Business License application.

☞ Later, you'll be asked to report your business activities by category to both the state and the city.

☞ In order to make these reports, you'll need to figure out the total sales by category. You can track this as you go or add them up later.

Service—This is whenever you help others through words or actions... and you are NOT improving physical items. For example, if you're a consultant or workshop teacher, you're providing services.

Retail—Anytime that you sell a product, or, provide a service that improves a physical thing, you are involved in retail.

Product example: You sell a painting at a street fair.

Service example: You install and paint a bookshelf for someone.

Wholesale—Wholesale refers to anytime you provide products or services when someone else is collecting the payment and sales tax from the customer.

Product example: **Roxie** makes amazing ShamPhree kits. She sells them to hair salons at wholesale prices. The salons sell to the customers and collect sales tax.

Service example: **Anne** is a color consultant. She sometimes subcontracts with an architect. An architect gives a bid to a client. Part of that bid includes Anne's services. The architect collects payment and sales tax for the entire job, then pays Anne.

Manufacturing—Manufacturing is anytime you make something. Some examples are artwork, furniture, body lotions, jewelry, and publishing written works.

•

Often, the same work will be a part of multiple categories.

Some examples:

Nikki makes stunning jewelry and then sells it directly to consumers in Washington. This means she is both *manufacturing* and *retailing*.

Alan is a commercial photographer specializing in arts, culture and adventure. He primarily works for businesses—providing photos for websites or advertising. In addition, Alan sometimes provides photos for individuals for personal use. Usually these are clients he meets on the job who request a personal photography session. And/or, when Alan shoots events, such as business conferences and festivals, attendees will sometimes purchase photos afterward. He's both providing *services* (for the business use) and *retailing* (for the private individuals).

Alex writes captivating articles about adventures in the Pacific Northwest for his blog and sometimes for magazines. He also sells products he has made from time to time. He is *manufacturing*, *retailing*, and selling *services* (for the ads).

Which categories apply to your work? Circle or check:

Service	Wholesale
Retail	Manufacturing

Location(s) of Business

Licensing forms will ask for the location of your business. This refers to the city or cities where you're conducting your business activities—that is, where you are physically when you're offering services or selling products. If you're shipping products or providing services over the phone or Internet, then the location is where you are at when working on your computer and handling these products.

If you do business outside of Seattle, you'll need a license for each city. And, you'll need to pay taxes for each city—if they collect them. (Some cities collect tax; others do not.) Additionally, if you work in a different county, you'll need to check their requirements too.

For example, if you are a massage therapist with an office in Seattle, you just need a City of Seattle business license. If you decide to start doing in-home treatments in Shoreline, you'll need to get a license from the city of Shoreline.

To make it easier on yourself, consider starting just in Seattle. Then you can add other cities later.

For more information, you can:

- Call the BLS (The Washington State Business Licensing Services) at 800.451.7985.
- Make an appointment with Greater Seattle SCORE. They offer free advice to small business owners. Go to www.seattle.score.org
- Look on the website of each city. For a list of all cities and websites, go to: www.mrsc.org/Home/Research-Tools/Washington-City-and-Town-Profiles.aspx

Due Diligence

When you open a business, it's your responsibility to find out what is required and to make sure that you're following all of the laws that apply to you and your work. This is what doing your *due diligence* is all about. Examples of what you might need are special licenses, permits, regulatory endorsements and, inspections.

For some jobs, there are *no special requirements*. Examples: consultants, writers-for-hire, or artists.

For some, you need a *professional* or *special license* to practice in your field. Examples include massage therapists, counselors, and day care providers.

Certain products require *permits*. For example, if you make foods in your kitchen to sell at farmers markets, you need a Cottage Food Operation permit.

Some fields have *rules and regulations*. Massage therapists, for instance, are required to put their license numbers on all advertising.

There is help available! Here are some options.

If you want to do this yourself:

- Check the List of Licenses on the Washington Department of Licensing website: www.dol.wa.gov/listoflicenses.html
- Check the City Regulatory Endorsement page: www.seattle.gov/business-regulations/businesses-that-require-a-regulatory-endorsement
- Look for relevant permits on the Washington Business Hub site: http://business.wa.gov/start.html#LicensesPermits

- Use the State of Washington Business Licensing Wizard. Go to: http://bls.dor.wa.gov/licensing.aspx. Then find the "Business Licensing Wizard" button.

It's a nice tool where you put in your trade, where you will work, and the nature of your business (entity, employees), and it creates a customized guide. Be warned...there's a lot of language on there, and it takes careful reading.

If you want help with this:

- Call the Business Licensing Service (BLS), and ask them what you need at 1.800.451.7985
- Check with Greater Seattle SCORE. They offer free advice to small businesses at www.seattle.score.org.
- Talk to someone in your field.
- Meet with a lawyer.

Trademarks

In addition to the above, you will also need to check to make sure that your name and graphics do not infringe on any trademarks.

- Check with the United States Patent and Trademark Office.

Go to: www.uspto.gov/trademark and scroll down. Select *Search Trademark Database*

- Check Washington State trademarks. Call the Secretary of State at 360.725.0377.

If you plan to hire employees

If you plan to hire employees, you will have additional responsibilities that are not covered in this book. Please read page 357.

Do I Have to Collect Sales Tax?

It's important to figure this out from the get-go, so you will know if you need to charge customers for this.

Generally speaking, if you make any products or do services that improve physical things (such as painting a house or tuning a piano), you need to collect sales tax. There are exceptions and special cases.

To be sure, check with the Department of Revenue (DOR):

- Look up your industry online,
  - Go to: www.dor.wa.gov
  - Select Doing Business from the top Menu
  - Select Business Types
  - Select Industry Guides

  OR

- Call the DOR and ask at 800.647.7706.

Please note, laws change! **It's important to determine for yourself, if you need to collect sales tax or not.**

Some examples of service industries that—

DO collect sales tax: interior designers, artists, hair-stylists
DO NOT collect sales tax: consultants and massage therapists

Some Fuzzy areas—

Yoga Teachers and Martial Art Teachers. When teachers provide yoga or martial art services *as a spiritual practice*, they do NOT collect sales tax. When teachers provide these in a fitness capacity (e.g. a gym), this falls under a different category, and they DO collect sales tax.

Writers, designers, photographers. Artists who sell their work directly to consumers for personal use DO collect sales tax—whether in physical or digital form. Artists who sell their work to businesses for use in marketing DO NOT collect sales tax.

How Much Does it Cost to Get Started?

The costs vary depending on your choices. Here are some examples of very basic start-ups just to give you an idea. (These costs are approximate and based on 2018 prices.)

Sole proprietor— Basic Option: *About $79 total*	City business license, $55 State business license + 1 DBA, $24 Free website Free business cards
LLC— Basic Option: *About $279 total*	City business license, $55 State business license + 1 DBA, $24 LLC registration, $200 Free website Free business cards
Sole proprietor— Mid Level Option: *About $235*	City business license, $55 State business license + 1 DBA, $24 Website—a year at $8 a month, $96 Business cards—$60
LLC— Mid Level Option: *About $435 total*	City business license, $55 State business license + 1 DBA, $24 LLC registration, $200 Website—a year at $8 a month, $96 Business cards—$60

In Summary—Prepare for Licensing

Now that you have made some decisions and know more of the language, getting licensed should be a cinch.

You've chosen your entity type (LLC or sole proprietor), legal business name, and DBAs. You've got a short description ready and have picked a start date. You've also reviewed NAICS codes in case you want to try to get a particular one.

Very importantly, you have determined if you need to collect sales tax or not.

You've done your due diligence, so you've researched all the requirements, permits, and licenses for your business type, as well as checking out trademarks. This will help you sleep better at night.

You also understand that every city where you conduct business will require you to get a license.

You're ready!

Get Licensed

Required and recommended. Check when complete, or mark NA.

Getting Set Up

- Get a Special Notebook
- Set up Email Folder
- Set up Special Place for Storage
- Meet the UBI Number

If Getting an LLC

- Review Terms
- Apply for LLC *(Or PLLC)* w/Secretary of State
- Wait for LLC Certificate and UBI
- Write Down UBI for Other Applications

Licenses

- State Business License
- Get an EIN *(optional)*
- Get City Business License Tax Certificate
- File New Business Form with King County

Finishing Strong

- Put Everything in Place
- Business Lookup Tool
- Record in Special Notebook:
    - *UBI Number*
    - *Assigned NAICS Code*
    - *How Often to Report to DOR*
    - *SOS - Login and Password*
    - *My DOR / SAW - Login and Password*
    - *File Local - Login and Password*

Introduction

Now that you're prepared, getting licensed should go pretty fast*, and is not that expensive. If you have your notes ready from the last chapter, the whole process should take only thirty to ninety minutes.

To set up a new business, we'll do the following:

1 Create an LLC (optional)
2 Get an EIN from the IRS (optional)
3 Get a Washington State business license
4 Get a City of Seattle Business License Tax Certificate
5 Fill out a New Business Set-Up form with King County

It is important to go in this order, and to make friends with your UBI number. This is your tax ID for Washington state.

Pro Tip: If you feel yourself stalling or getting overwhelmed, consider asking a friend to sit with you while you go through the licensing process. Often, a second set of eyes helps things feel easier.

Let's get started!

*Two important notes, at the time of this writing: All levels of government are currently transitioning to new online portals, so some things in this chapter may not match your experience exactly! Also, some are experiencing some technically difficulties. When in doubt, call to get help.

Currently, wait times for getting an LLC have increased to several weeks. It used to just take a few days. One option to speed up your process is to drive down to the Secretary of State office in Olympia for faster service.

Set Yourself Up for Success

The steps below sound really simple...and you might be tempted to skip or do them later. Please, do not skip these steps! You will thank yourself in the future. Having all the necessary information in one place will come in handy so many times.

1 **Get a notebook** to record everything that's related to licensing and taxes—all of your passwords, logins, and numbers for your business, such as your *UBI (unified business identifier)*—and for taking notes in every time you do research or call one of the government agencies.

If you like things organized, consider a notebook with tabs. Mark them: City, County, BLS, SOS (if you get an LLC), DOR*, and Federal. Otherwise, just write notes as needed, and flip through to find things.

You might be tempted to make it an electronic file. I encourage you to use a paper notebook. It's tangible, you don't have to back it up, and no virus can ruin it.

2 **Set up a folder in your email inbox** to store all emails and receipts related to government agencies. Perhaps name it "Legal + Taxes".

3 **Set up a special place to put all your official documents** such as licenses, license renewal reminders, any printouts from the web. They can be in file folders, or you might use a small metal file box, a special basket, or decorated box. Pick something that feels good to you—either because it looks nice or feels safe. You need to feel comfortable interacting with it and these documents. Make it easy to get to. I have a neat box that closes with a magnet flap and has a "leather" cover. I store it under a chair, so it's easy to slide in and out.

*

BLS is the *Business Licensing Service of WA*
DOR is the *Department of Revenue of WA*
SOS is the *Secretary of State of WA*

Meet the UBI Number

UBI stands for *Unified Business Identifier* and is used for business and tax purposes within the State of Washington, as well as security.

It's used in a similar way as your social security number (SSN). Think about all the times you've been asked for your SSN, or the last 4 numbers as part of a security question. Even though it was created for paying taxes, it's also commonly used as an identifier.

That is exactly how the UBI number is used within Washington. You will use it on all of your licenses, bank accounts, and some correspondence. Also, as soon as you're assigned this number, it is automatically sent to the Department of Revenue, so they can start collecting state taxes from you. (More information to come on this.)

There are two ways you'll receive your UBI—

☞ If you apply for an LLC, the Secretary of State will assign it to your business entity.

☞ If you are a sole proprietor, you will receive it with your state business license.

Important for LLCs: you must apply for your LLC first, and then use that UBI number with your state license application.

LLC Pathway—For Getting Licensed

For Starting as a Sole Proprietor, go to page 87

If you're getting an LLC, you'll be dealing with three different agencies of Washington State. It's easy to get them all mixed up. (Read more in the *Legal and Taxes* section. See page 131.)

Here is the pathway for setting up your licenses. **The order is important**. First, go to the Secretary of State (SOS) to set up your LLC. Wait for confirmation that it has gone through and for the UBI assigned to your LLC. This may take 3-5 business days or more. Once you've got the UBI, your LLC is ready to get a state business license.

Take your UBI over to the Business Licensing Service (BLS). The BLS will issue your state business license and will also send your information over to the Department of Revenue (DOR). Then your part is done. The DOR will get in touch with you about how often you will file your excise tax form (for state taxes)—either monthly, quarterly, or annually.

Before Applying for Your LLC: Some Terms to Know

For Starting as a Sole Proprietor,
go to page 87

These are some terms you'll come across when working with banks, or filling out your LLC application.

Certificate of Formation: The piece of paper that grants the status of your LLC is the *Certificate of Formation*. It is issued by the Secretary of State. The current version has some flowers on the border and the seal of the state in gold.

Articles of Formation: The *Articles of Formation* are the papers you fill out to designate which members will get what percentage, and who the managers are, etc.

Sometimes people mix up these terms. So, if a bank asks you for the Articles, they might really need the Certificate. Having said that, they might want the Articles to see which names are on the account. To be safe, bring both.

•

When you're a single member LLC, you fill all the roles. Here are some definitions, in case you're curious about them.

Member: The owners of an LLC are called *members*. The term makes more sense if you imagine a club of people starting a company. Each member (of that club) shares in the responsibility and gets a designated percentage of the profit.

Single Member LLC: Describes an LLC with only one member / owner. Sometimes people say *single owner*. This is a good synonym, although it's not the official term.

Manager: The person or persons who run the business are called *managers*. Now, imagine a club that is composed of grandmas who make knit products and don't want to deal with the business side. They might hire someone to set up the structure, file paperwork, and write checks on their behalf. This would be the *manager*.

Member-managed versus **manager-managed**: This term describes who is running the business—e.g., handling legal documents, banking, overseeing operations)—whether it's the member/s (owners) or manager/s (hired). Typically, single-member LLCs are *member-managed*.

Registered Agent: The person authorized to make reports and changes to the LLC.

Governor: The person in charge of managing the business of the LLC.

Executor: The person creating the LLC, and signing the formation application.

Apply for Your LLC— With The Secretary of State

Takes about 10 – 15 minutes, Cost: $200

For Starting as a Sole Proprietor, go to page 87

To get an LLC, you must apply with the Secretary of State (SOS), since you are setting up a legal entity.

It costs about $200 to start.
It costs about $60 to renew each year.

The SOS assigns your *Unified Business Identifier (UBI)*. This is your business ID number with the state.

The application is fairly straightforward. Mostly, you'll need to input your address in a million places. This is because you fill all the roles when you are a single member LLC.

On the Secretary of State website, LLCs are handled under the category of Corporations.

You may file on paper or online. For both, go to www.sos.wa.gov/corps/ on the Secretary of State website.

For the Paper Form

The paper form is very straightforward—only two pages, with instructions attached. For Agent type, choose "Noncommercial Agent". See more Helpful Hints below.

1 Go to: www.sos.wa.gov/corps/

2 On the right hand navigation, choose "Limited Liability Companies".

3 Choose: Paper Form.

4 Print and fill out.

5 Your name and contact information goes in every section.

To File Online

Filing online is fairly easy, and it's pretty quick, when you know the pathway.

Note: If things have changed, or if you get stuck, call the SOS to get help at 360.725.0377.

1 Go to: Go to: www.sos.wa.gov/corps/

2 Click on the "Corporations and Charities Filing System". It's the big green button on the right hand side.

3 Select "Create a User Account".

4 Choose "User Account".

5 Select "Individual".

6 Fill in the remaining information.

7 Record your Account login and password somewhere safe.

8 Log in to your new account.

9 On the left side navigation, find "Create or Register a Business".

10 Move the application, putting your name and information in every box. See helpful details below.

11 Checkout and print receipt. Well done!!

12 Wait for the LLC formation papers to arrive, along with your UBI. (At the time of this writing, this is taking several weeks.)

Helpful Hints

Initial Report Box - Somewhere in the beginning, there's a box to check to include this in your application. **Select this box!** (It will save you filing a report in a few months.)

Filling out Initial Report - Confirm information and submit.

Beware - There's a box that's easy to accidentally check. It asks if you're part of an address protection program....

Submitting the Name for Review - Once you enter your desired LLC name, it will show a list with similar names and tell you if the one you want is available. If yours is taken, you will have to find a variation, or change it all together.

Your LLC legal name *must* include one of the following:

- Limited Liability Company
- LLC
- Limited Liability Co.
- L.L.C.

Tenure - This is how long you want your LLC to exist.

Perpetual or Specific - Perpetual means that it is open until you close it, and is the usual choice. Use Specific if you're forming the LLC for a set period of time.

Place of Business - the city or cities where you intend to work.

Managed by: members or managers? - Single-member LLCs typically select 'member'.

Sole Proprietor Pathway—For Getting Licensed

For LLC Pathway, see page 81.

If you're planning to be a sole proprietor, then you'll be dealing with two different agencies of Washington State. It's easy to get them mixed up. We'll look at this more in the *Taxes and Legal* section.

For now, here's what you need to know. You will register with the Business Licensing Service (BLS). They will issue a UBI and state business license. Then they send your information over to the Department of Revenue (DOR). Your part is done.

The DOR will get in touch with you about how often you will file your excise tax form (for state taxes)—either monthly, quarterly, or annually.

Get Your State Business License

Takes about 15 – 30 minutes

Cost: $19 +$5 per DBA

All LLCs and most Sole Proprietors **must** get a Washington State business license.

The only **exceptions** are businesses that meet ALL of the following:

- you are a service business and collect zero sales tax
- plan to do business in your name
- make less than $12K each year
- require no specialty licensing
- work in a city that handles its own city licensing (such as Seattle).

Even when meeting all the criteria, I tell my clients to get a license with the state anyway. It doesn't cost very much, and they may be more protected or prepared if laws change. Plus, it's the only way to get a UBI, which is often asked for.

It takes about fifteen to thirty minutes.
It costs $19 for your license and $5 for each DBA.

Note: Strictly speaking, you do not need to renew your state license. If you have other permits or licenses attached to it, then will you need to renew those.

Note: you **DO** have to renew your LLC. This is separate from your state license.

The state license basically sets you up to collect state taxes—sales, use, and B&O (business and occupation tax). Besides issuing licenses, the Business Licensing Service (BLS) does other important things. The department checks to make sure people have correct permits and certifications, offers licenses for smaller cities, and holds your contact information in case a consumer has an issue.

You can apply through the mail or online.

Paper Form through the Mail

If applying **through the mail**, you must print the application found at:

www.bls.dor.wa.gov/forms/700028.pdf.

If you have questions about the paper form, call the BLS at 800.451.7985, or look through the notes below. See Helpful Hints below.

Apply Online

This process matches the current system. It's likely to change soon. If you get stuck or need help, call the Business Licensing Service 800.451.7985.

1 go to: www.bls.dor.wa.gov
2 Select the "My DOR" button in the top right corner. (Or, select "Get a WA state business license" to read more about the process.)
3 Find the button for New User—Note: In order to access My DOR, you will have to set up an a SAW account, which stands for Secure Access Washington.
4 Record your login and password somewhere safe.
5 Once in My DOR, find the button to apply for new license.
6 Fill out the application, confirm and pay.
7 Print your receipt for confirmation and bookkeeping.

Helpful Hints

The state will ask if you have a spouse. If yes, provide their name, DOB (date of birth), and social security number.

- They will ask if you already have a UBI. If you set up an LLC, use the one you were given.
- Self-employed workers are NOT considered employees.
- Bank information is optional.
- For DBAs, add all names that you'd like to use when receiving checks. For example, if you have an LLC, you might want to add your personal name as a DBA in case checks are written to you.
- When a list of cities is presented, Seattle is not there because it handles its own business licenses. Just hit the Next button.

Bravo!

Get an EIN (Optional)

(Federal)

Getting an EIN is optional. Probably, the answer is Yes.

Bank applications and programs such as TurboTax, and PayPal will ask for your *EIN*. It stands for *Employer Identification Number*. It was created for employers, and has a reputation of being standard for all businesses. Because of this, many people mistakenly think that you need an EIN. This is not the case. If you are a sole proprietor or single-member LLC, with no employees, then technically, you **do not need an EIN**. The IRS instructions explicitly say to use your SSN because that's what they will use!

Having said that, there are some advantages to getting an EIN. First, many application forms are set up for EINs, and not for SSNs. That is because an EIN has a different format: 00-0000000. This means companies will need to do a work around for you if using your SSN, which may take more time. The EIN will be faster and easier for them. Secondly, there is a privacy advantage with using an EIN for your business—your SSN can be restricted to personal use, and not out in the world in so many places.

If you elect to use only your SSN, and do not want an EIN, you can politely educate your banker that you are allowed to use your SSN. They might have to find a tricky way to get your SSN in their system—that is their problem to solve. If they don't believe you, you might ask to meet with the head of their department, or you show them an IRS publication explaining this. Instruct them to go to www.irs.gov, to search for "Single Member LLC", follow the link to find the publication. Have them look for the section on Tax Payer Identification.

If you would like to get an EIN—it is very easy, and it's free.

1 Go to: www.irs.gov

2 Search for "apply for EIN"

3. Find the search result that says "Apply for Employee Identification Number (EIN) Online"
4. Follow the link and the steps
5. You will receive your EIN immediately
6. Write it in your Legal and Taxes notebook

One thing to note—you may only apply for your EIN during their hours of operation! Currently, these are Monday through Friday, 7 a.m. to 10 p.m., Eastern Time.

City of Seattle
Business License Tax Certificate

Takes about 15 – 30 minutes

Cost: $55 or $110

Or, city *business license* for short. Everyone doing business within the city of Seattle needs a city license. (This is different, and additional to, the state license.) The standard cost is $110. If you are planning to make less than under $20K a year, then it is $55.

You can apply in person, through the mail, or online.

Apply In Person

Go to the Seattle Municipal Tower.

Financial and Administrative Services
Seattle Municipal Tower
700 5th Ave. Suite 5200
Seattle, WA 98104
Phone: 206.684.2489

Take with you: All the numbers + documents—UBI, EIN, your state license, LLC paperwork—and a form of payment.

Apply Through the Mail

Print the application off the website and mail it in. Go to: www.seattle.gov/Documents/Departments/FAS/Licensing/Seattle-business-license-application.pdf

See Helpful Hints below.

Apply Online using FileLocal

Seattle uses a new portal called FileLocal for license applications. You'll use this same portal to renew your license and report your earnings for the B&O tax (business and occupation tax).

It takes about 15 - 30 minutes to both set up your profile and apply for the license. If you get stuck, or the website is not working, call the city at 206.684.8484.

1 Go to: www.filelocal-wa.gov

2 Select "Create Business Account".

3 Go through the Sign Up process, wait for email confirmation.

4 Record your Login and password in a secure place.

5 Hurray! Now, sign into your account.

6 On your Home page, find the button "Apply for General Business License".

7 Work through all the screens.

8 Confirm, pay.

9 Print receipt for your records.

10 Celebrate!

Helpful Hints

- The city application will ask you for Contractor, FEIN, and Vendor numbers. If you don't have these, leave them blank. (FEIN is the same as your EIN. It stands for Federal Employer Identification Number. See page 91.)
- You are NOT an employee.

- NAICS code was assigned to you by the state when you obtained your Washington State business license. See page 67.

- UBI is the number that the state assigned you. Use the lookup tool online if you're not sure. See page 80.

- 16 Digit UBI - Sometimes the 16 digit version is asked for. Simply add the following numbers to the end: 0010001

Well done!

File New Business Set-Up Form with King County

For many of you, this will be nothing more than a hoop to jump through. The county taxes us on property used for business—both real estate and personal property. *Personal property* includes movable tools and equipment, such as furniture and computers (that you use for business). You report the cost, the county assesses the value, and then sends you a tax bill if they see fit. Generally speaking, if the total value is over a certain amount, you will owe taxes. If it's under, then you will NOT owe any taxes. In 2018, this amount is $7500.

Note: If your business owns land or a building, please call the county to find out what to do at 206.296.5126.

You need to fill out a New Business Set-Up form. You have three ways to get this:

- Call 206.296.5126
- Email: www.Personal.Property@kingcounty.gov
- Go to: www.kingcounty.gov/depts/assessor/Forms.aspx.
  Scroll down to the Personal Property Section
  Find "New Business Set-Up

Currently, the form is a one-page interactive PDF. Fill it out, and email it, or print and send it through snail mail. The address is on the form.

The form will ask for:

- Your business name, address, and UBI
- A list of all the property you use for business—e.g., computer, furniture, books, and tools (before sales tax)
- The monthly cost of supplies

It is free to set up your business account with the county.

Put Everything in Its Place

Let's finish strong! If you haven't already done so, please—

1. Record some of your important information in your notebook:
    - UBI
    - NAICS code
    - EIN (if you have one)
    - State taxes—How often do you report?
    - Secretary of State (If you have an LLC)—login, password
    - Business Licensing Service of WA—Login, password
    - Department of Revenue of WA—login, password
    - City of Seattle (File Local)—Login, password

2. Put all emails into a designated email folder.
3. Put all paperwork and your notebook into your special place for legal documents.

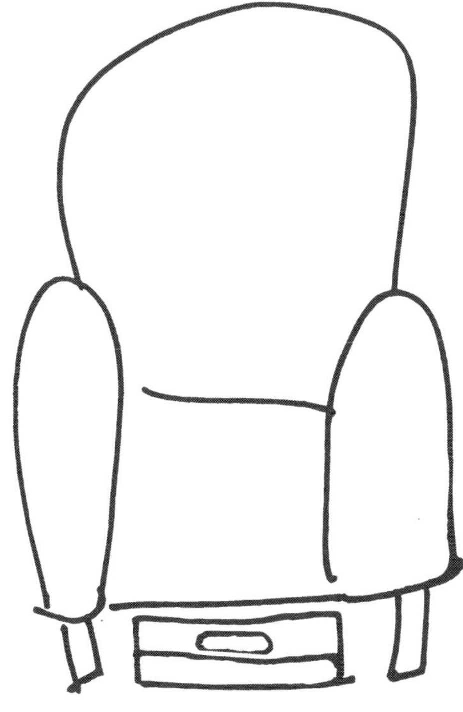

Business Lookup Tool

If you ever need to look up your business information, or someone else's, you can do so online through the DOR (Department of Revenue) or the SOS (Secretary of State).

For the DOR—

1 Go to: http://apps.dor.wa.gov/BRD/

Or, search for "DOR", "business", "lookup".

2 You can search by name of the owner, name of the business, or UBI number. Once you put in one of those, the search will list any of the businesses that match that information.

3 Select the one that you're looking for, and it'll give you their *database detail*, which includes the UBI, NAICS code, date when the account was opened with the DOR, active status, and the address.

For the SOS—

1 Go to: https://ccfs.sos.wa.gov/#/

Or, search for "Secretary of state wa", "business", "lookup". Scroll to the bottom of the page.

2 You can search by using a variety of words, including names, dates, UBI. Once you put in one of those, the search will list any of the businesses that match that information.

3 Select the one that you're looking for, and it'll give you their *database detail,* as described above, plus, a list of documents associated with the LLC, and the name of agents and/or managers.

Congratulations!

You have a business now. A lot of people talk about doing this and never do it. You have done it.

Find a way to celebrate or commemorate what you've achieved. This is a stepping stone, and it's good to pause and appreciate this moment.

Here are some ideas: buy a frame for your new licenses or a bottle of champagne. Go out to dinner. Purchase a fun tool for your business or for your work attire—a piece of furniture, some artwork, a fancy pen, maybe some cool shoes, or a new work bag.

Whatever you do, please, pause, enjoy yourself...and rest up for the next part of the journey.

How do you want to celebrate?

Summary—Get Licensed

We talked a little about the three business arms of Washington State:

- The Secretary of State (SOS) grants status to LLCs.
- The Business Licensing Service (BLS) gives licenses to both sole proprietors and LLCs.
- The Department of Revenue (DOR) collects our state taxes; your account with them is automatically set up when you apply for your business license.

You've learned a few new terms now. In addition, we talked about your Unified Business Identifier (UBI), which is used as an ID for your business within the state. And the EIN, a tax ID number with the Internal Revenue Service. Optional, and recommended for privacy and ease with banking.

The NAICS code is for statistical purposes only.

You jumped through all the hoops to get your licenses with the state and city, and then set up an account with the county.

You recorded all your important information.

And celebrated!

2

Get Your First Customer

Recommended for most. Check when complete, or mark NA.

Preparing	○ You're Prototyping
	○ Create a Price Sheet / Menu of Services
	○ Offer Discounts or Not?
	○ Create Transaction Tools
Get the Word Out	○ Define the Customer You Want
	○ Define What You Are Offering
	○ Create a Sentence Combining the Above
	○ Ideas for Getting the Word Out
	○ Pick 1 - 3 Ways to Advertise
Stay Motivated	○ Set a Goal for Getting First Customer
	○ Set a Second Goal
	○ "Act, reflect. Act, reflect."

Introduction

You're licensed! This means you're ready to do business. Before too much time goes by, figure out a way to get your first customer. Any customer! Do this as soon as possible—even if it's your neighbor or your mom.

Getting started will break the seal. Doing your work will teach you what you need and what you don't need, and it will give you confidence.

You're Prototyping

In lieu of sitting around thinking or writing business plans, you're going to learn by doing. You're going to prototype. This means your job is to get started and that things do not have to be perfect.

If it helps you to feel better, you can charge less during this period, and you can even tell people that you're prototyping your services or trying some things out.

Big companies have Research and Development departments or usability studies. That's what you're doing too. It's called *iterative design*.

So let's get you ready to prototype.

Make a Price Sheet / Menu of Services

Make a Price Sheet or Menu of Services. Type this up, and print some copies. Have them on hand so you're ready when someone asks you what you charge. It is more comfortable and easier to show them a list, than to say your prices out loud.

ProTip: Do not just do this in your head! It's important to see this on paper.

For Service Providers: make a list of services and rates. If you have one hourly rate, that's fine. Just be sure to list all of the types of services that you're offering.

Product Makers: list your products with their prices. Include wholesale and retail prices, if applicable, and any add on fees.

Write the season and the year on top of your list —such as *Spring 2018*.

If you're not sure what to charge, then just make up some prices that feel right. (You will likely change them later anyway.) Or read pages 174-178.

Please note—it's very tempting to change prices down for a friend or family. That's why you need them printed. Show them your regular prices, then feel free to offer a discount if you want. Be sure to include both the original and discounted prices on your invoice. This way, they will know they are getting a deal; they can feel the gift. And they won't expect these same prices forever.

Transaction Tools

Think through your first sales transaction. What tools will you need that day?

Each business is different, so I won't be able to direct you exactly. Imagine the entire transaction, and make notes about what details would make it go smoothly.

Ideas include:

- invoice and receipt
- knowing what kinds of payment you accept
- any policies (returns, rescheduling, late fees)
- packaging
- tags
- handout or info sheet of some kind.

When people make a purchase, it feels good and reassuring to have a token, or something tangible to mark what has taken place. For service providers, it helps if you can give clients something in writing—perhaps a handout describing your process or an info sheet related to your work.

For product makers, this isn't as necessary, although it is still an opportunity to add value. You might leave instructions for care of an item or some information on how it was made.

What else? You might flip through the chapter called *Nitty Gritty,* for inspiration.

You can write ideas here:

Getting the Word Out

You've got a service or product that you're excited about, prices, and transaction tools. Now's the time to find your first customer. It's time to get the word out!

Be creative. Be talkative. Tell everyone!

Before we talk about how to do this, I would like to pause and acknowledge that sometimes talking to people can feel difficult. Clients say to me, "I don't like having to sell myself." This feeling makes sense, and I have some good news. You don't have to sell yourself. Instead, think of it this way. You're simply informing people about the activities in your life; you're just sharing life news. If you were moving, or getting a new pet, you'd let people know.

In the same way, you can simply share about your work developments and be honest about your own feelings too. You can say things like, "Guess what? I'm almost ready to launch my website! I'm not sure if it looks right, but it's still pretty exciting." Or, "I've got a couple dozen products made, I think I'm ready to start approaching some boutiques." You'd be amazed at how making little comments here and there can lead to opportunities. Practice will make this easier too.

•

To help you get ready, define the customer you hope to work with and what you can do for them. If you make products, then think about where you want to sell them. Write these down, then create a sentence to use when talking to friends and family.

Some examples are:

"I'm offering in-home haircuts—especially for busy moms of young children."

"I make videos that tell a story. I want to work with local businesses that need a video for their website, or for nonprofits for fundraising events."

What sentence will you say? Try one here:

Here are some ideas for getting the word out:

- ☞ Start talking about it **all the time** with friends, family, neighbors, and people at work if you have another job. Tell them that you're excited to get started and that you're looking for customers or places to sell your work. This is a real and authentic, and will often lead to work or sales opportunities.
- ☞ Put the word out on Facebook or other social media. If you have an Etsy page or website, always include the link.
- ☞ Try some low-cost advertising: flyers, brochures, ads in school plays or directories. Offer your service or products at auctions.
- ☞ Create some incentives: say you're prototyping and charging a "Percentage of your future price," or offer a discounts such as New-to-the-neighborhood or Early-bird specials.
- ☞ Ask family, friends, or professionals to give you feedback. This will give you some ideas...and will often lead to connections or word of mouth marketing.
- ☞ Look for street fairs, expos, and trunk shows where you can have a table—whether you sell products or services.
- ☞ Tell baristas and bartenders.
- ☞ Just keep trying and keep thinking. Ask for ideas from friends or family.

Set Some Goals

Choosing some concrete goals with dates attached will make this venture feel more real. It will also help you when trying to get the word out. When chatting with people, you can say things like, "I'm hoping to find my first client this month." Or, "I have a goal to make at least one sale before Christmas."

When do you want to have your first customer by?

Write it here:

And write on your calendar. ___ (Check here, after putting on calendar.)

Will you do this work for free or for a discount?

Thinking ahead...after your first customer, set another goal for a set of clients or sales. Choose a number between three and ten. Select a due date for completing this set. Decide if they will get a discount.

Example: I want to have three more clients by September 24th, and I will give them a 50% discount.

Write out your goal here:

And write it on your calendar. ___ (Check here, after putting on calendar.)

ProTip: Do three things every workday toward your current goal.

"Act, Reflect. Act, Reflect." *

Whatever you do, keep moving! You're prototyping, which means the idea is to learn by doing and then reflecting...later. Not at the same time.

Take your critic hat off. Take action, do your work, try stuff. The more data you get, the better. Full disclosure, it might mean making mistakes. That's okay. That's how you'll learn.

Then, later, reflect on those actions. What worked? What didn't work? What tools or print materials do you need next time? You might keep a journal, or consider getting a business coach or therapist to help you with this.

Just think of what you'll know after six to twelve months! You'll be fine-tuning your service or product and your business practices, and you'll be making money all the while.

This way of building your business includes risk and takes courage. It will also be highly satisfying.

*Quote from Steven Pressfield's amazing book, *Do the Work! Overcome Resistance and Get Out of Your Own Way*

In Summary—Get Your First Customer!

It's official. The moment you've got your first customer, you're in business.

You're prototyping. You're taking action, and then later, you're reflecting and revising. This leads to a richer experience and refined service or product.

Get ready for your first customer by making a Price Sheet/Menu of Services—on paper. Create any tools for your first transactions such as handouts, tags, invoices, receipts, and contracts.

Get the word out! Do it anyway that you can. Talk about your business all the time. Set some goals to keep you moving.

And remember: "Act, reflect. Act, reflect."

Go!

Do Your Work + Set Up Shop

Recommended for everyone. Check when complete, or mark NA.

Marketing	○ Create an Email Signature
	○ Be Amazing and Collect Testimonials
Numbers	○ Number Goggles
	○ Set Up Bank Accounts for Business
	○ Important Banking Habits
	○ *Use business accounts for all transactions*
	○ *Transfer 30%* of deposits to business savings*
	○ *Print bank statements monthly*
	○ *Transfer "paycheck" to personal checking*
	○ How to Be a Rockstar at Taxes
	○ Set Up One Box with No Lid
	○ Know What to Collect
	○ Mileage Tracking Method
	○ Put Important Dates on Calendar

**40% if you collect sales tax*

Introduction

Start your business off right, with a few key habits.

These steps will be free or cheap and offer big bang for the buck. They provide an elegant structure for you to build the rest of the business on.

We'll lay the ground work for marketing by creating an email signature (making you look like a pro) and collecting testimonials.

Most importantly, we'll talk about how to be ready for the tax man!

If you follow the steps in this chapter—set up business banking, always save 30% for taxes (40% if you collect sales tax), collect everything in a big box, and put important dates on the calendar—you'll be set for taxes next year.

Email Signature

Adding an email signature does so many good things, it's fairly easy, and it's free.

First, it helps you to figure some things out—you can play around with job titles, company name, and taglines in a nimble, fun way. There's something about seeing it all on a screen that makes everything feel more real. Try out several ideas to see what works for you. You might even change them every few days.

Second, it serves many marketing purposes. It's a gentle way to announce what you're doing. It makes your venture look official, it makes you look professional, and it gets people's attention. By simply adding the signature, you'll likely have friends and family ask questions about what you're doing...which leads to moral support and perhaps some clients. Later, it can drive traffic to your website and express the mood of your business.

To start, add:	Your name Your business name/new role Phone number
Later, add:	Website with a link
Optional elements:	Tagline Social media links A quote Announcements

In most mail viewers, you can control the signature through the settings or preferences section.

I got one new client just through the email signature! An acquaintance saw it, checked out my website, and then sent her friend my way. That cost me zero advertising dollars and only 10 minutes of easy work.

Be Amazing and Collect Testimonials

In the beginning, people can get obsessed with marketing. This is often true for the newly self-employed person *and* their friends and family. "How are you going to find customers?" I was asked repeatedly, and you might be too. This can sometimes create a pressure to have a Marketing Plan with a capital M.

While this is a good question, it's not the right time to overly focus on it, or to worry about it. Right now, ask yourself, "How can I be amazing at my job?" This is actaully the foundation for all marketing. Hustle for clients however you can for now, and keep this in mind:

The way to find new clients is to know what you're trying to do and to do an amazing job, every time.

More official marketing efforts come after that. So, for right now, focus on taking care of your customer. If you're meeting a need or making a phenomenal product, your clients will talk about you. (They will also talk about you if you're doing a bad job!)

Word of mouth is powerful.

As much as you can, collect testimonials—for your website (present or future), Yelp reviews, brochures, etc. Put them all in one file for future use. (See page 234 for more on how to collect testimonials.)

Number Goggles—
Seeing Payments in a New Way

"Cool, I deposited $810 this week."

Doing work we like and getting paid feels amazing. It can also seem like we're making more money than we are. This is due to an old habit of being an employee. When you got a paycheck, the money was all yours—since the taxes had been taken out for you. But now, you're receiving payments to your business, which is different than receiving a paycheck.

When you make deposits for your business, only part of it comes to you personally. Some of it needs to be used for expenses, and some needs to be saved for taxes. It's important to start seeing checks in this way.

Here are some *very* ballpark estimates of what your take home pay will look like. Of course, these percentages will vary.

In general—

Service providers can expect to take about 60% home as a paycheck. Product makers, take about 40% home as a paycheck.

Let's walk through this together: after you collect payments from your customers, about 30% will need to be saved for federal taxes. Additionally, you'll need to set aside money for business expenses and supples for products (COGS), if applicable. (See page 179 for more info on COGS.) This varies according to each business. A beginning estimate for expenses and supplies is 10% for service providers and 40% for product makers. What's leftover is your paycheck.

We'll look at this in detail in the *Numbers* chapter. Once you've tracked your numbers for a while, you can fine-tune what percentage to set aside for expenses and supplies for products (or COGS).

If you're a service provider, this means your deposits will be divided as such:

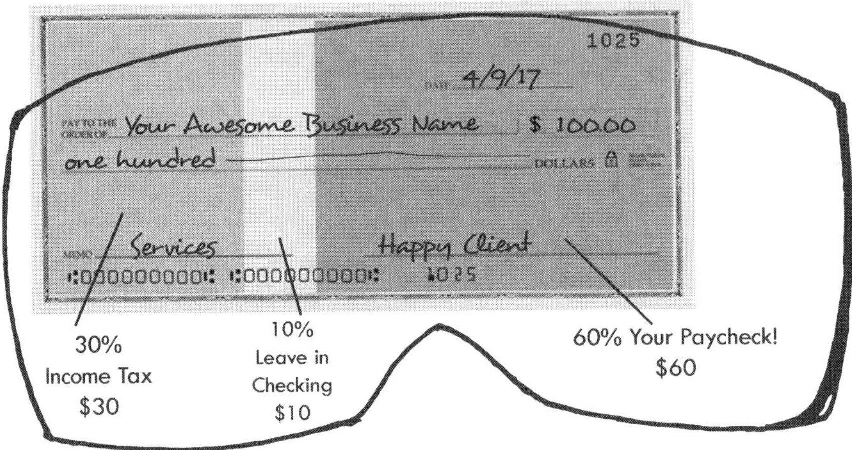

For a product maker, you have to collect state sales tax. This is currently 9.6%—and it is added on top of your whole bill. For sake of easy math, we'll round up to 10% when using Number Goggles. This means the percentages will add up to 110%. Your deposits might be split up as below:

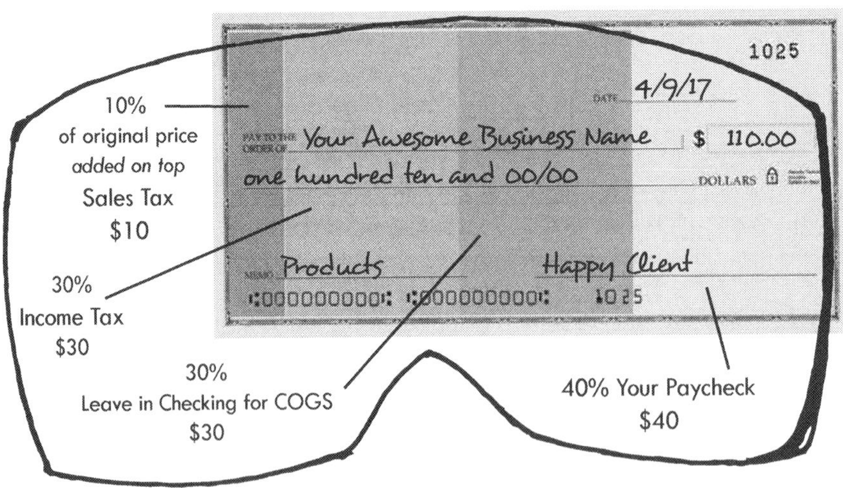

Using number goggles with our original example of $810, we can see our paycheck (as a service provider) would be about $480. Our paycheck would be about $320 if we made products.

Bank Accounts for Business

After you have your licenses, it's a good idea to set up official business accounts—checking and savings—as soon as possible. It takes a little work to do, but it's rewarding to see your business name on the debit card and checks, and it serves so many helpful purposes. Also, it is a great reminder that those deposits are not the same as your paycheck.

You will need to bring your business licenses. If you have an LLC, you'll also need the Certificate of Formation. Business accounts can cost a little more than personal-style accounts, depending on your bank. They also have different requirements, and these vary by institution.

For example, some banks require a minimum number of debit card transactions. Others require a minimum balance. Sometimes fees will be waived if you meet these requirements.

You can call your bank or look online to find out how the business accounts work and what you need to set them up. You might even shop around with different banks to find prices and rules that you like, as well as convenient locations. I like Umpqua Bank—the monthly fee is $7 for business checking. It's waived if you keep a minimum balance of $1000.

ProTip: It's most convenient if you can transfer money from your business checking to your personal checking. If all accounts are at the same institution, it's easy. If you prefer to use different banks for business and personal, check to see if they do bank-to-bank electronic transfers.

ProTip: If all accounts are at the same bank, ask about something called Bank Setoffs. This is where the institution can move money between your accounts to cover checks or withdrawals, without asking you. Many of us are familiar with banks moving money from savings to checking automatically—usually after we've set this up. Check to see if their practice is to do the same thing between your personal and business accounts...and if you have any choices in the matter.

Important Banking Habits to Start Now

Think about your business accounts in this way:

Checking Account: Run everything through here—deposits, paying for expenses and supplies for products (or COGS), and issuing your paycheck.

Savings Account: Use this primarily for saving for taxes. You might also use this for saving up for big purchases—although I'd recommend doing this separately by getting an additional savings account, or leaving it in checking.

Habits:

☞ With every deposit, transfer money over to savings immediately.

- If you DO NOT collect sales tax—transfer 30%.
- If you DO collect sales tax—transfer 40%.

☞ Print out your bank statements monthly.

☞ Transfer your "paycheck" into personal checking, or withdraw as cash.

Following these habits will make your life easier, now and later. It creates some nice records for accounting and in case you get audited. Everything is clear; you know what you actually have to spend. Your tax money is ready and waiting. It reminds you that only a portion of business income is yours.

How to Be a ROCKSTAR at Taxes

(Even if You "Hate Numbers")

Here's how to do the least amount of work possible, and still be ready for tax season. *Truly, this is the biggest favor you can do for yourself.* Your future self will thank you.

It only works if you do ALL four of these things:

1. With every deposit, always transfer 30% into business savings. If you collect Washington sales tax, then make it 40%.
2. Use the One Box Method on the following page. This includes reading about what you need to collect. (Covered on page 123.)
3. Mark your calendar with Important Dates. (Covered on page 124.)
4. Plan some work time in January*. You'll need to total up some numbers for tax reporting. You can get some help from a professional or friend, or can use the *Numbers* section of this book to do it yourself.

•

Tax time gets stressful when people don't have enough money, don't know how to file, or when they're surprised by a huge tax bill. This set of strategies is the antidote. If you've collected all the stuff, you'll be able to file all your taxes. If you've got the money set aside, you'll be able to pay them no problem. It will be a lot easier to learn to do taxes if you're not stressed.

* If Washington State requires you to file quarterly, set aside time each January, April, July, and October. If monthly, then mark work time on your calendar during the first week of each month.

One Box Method, Two Variations

The One Box Method is a totally legitimate way to prepare for taxes:

1 Find a box with no lid.

2 Throw everything in there.

3 In January*, get a bottle of wine and a calculator and do all of your accounting at once.

OR

1 Find a box with no lid.

2 Throw everything in there.

3 In January, hand it to your accountant.

If this appeals to you, then use this system. If you want to do more now, then please proceed to the second half of the *Numbers* chapter, starting on page 188.

* If Washington State requires you to file quarterly, set aside time each January, April, July, and October. (VERIFY) If monthly, then mark work time on your calendar during the first week of each month.

Most of the Job is Just Collecting Stuff

Even if you get a bookkeeper or accountant, it's still up to you to collect all of the stuff they need to figure out your taxes. Use this list below, or, when in doubt, throw everything and anything into your One Box.

Here's what you need to collect:

- Receipts for anything that you spend on the business
- Receipts for any supplies you use to make products (COGS)
- Parking receipts
- Bank statements
- Letters from the IRS, state, county, or city
- Some record of income—maybe deposit slips, copies of the invoices you give to clients, or receipts
- Mileage record (See page 199.)

Collecting stuff is the prerequisite to the entire accounting process. This is why I love the One Box Method because it's easy, very efficient, and it gets most of the work done.

Consider the accounting process:

1. Collect necessary stuff.
2. Sort and add up categories.
3. Put the right numbers into the right forms.
4. Pay any necessary taxes.

The last three steps only work if you've done step 1. Other bookkeeping methods are all variations on this theme; complexities are added to gain certain benefits. If you don't want to do all the work at the end, then you will basically need to sort and add as you go. (Covered in *Numbers*.) Software programs do just that, calculating automatically as you go, as long as you make entries correctly. The complexity, rhythm and tools are all up to you—what your style is, and which numbers you need to know.

Put Important Dates on the Calendar

Once you start a business, certain things are set in motion. It's helpful to understand your new requirements, and how they ramp up. It's so quiet the first year that sometimes people new to self-employment get surprised by all the things they are required to do later. It can feel like everybody wants a piece of you (and they do!).

The good news is that when your business is still small, you are not required to pay some taxes. You still need to file with everybody, so they know this is the case. Later, if you're making more money...and have to pay more taxes, it can be a nice confirmation of your success.

We'll go into detail about this later, for now, just get the dates on your calendar so you have a heads-up and will be ready. For all of these dates, please read them as "on or before" this date.

For Year 1—Year of Formation

April 15—First Quarter Estimated Tax payment due ~ IRS
June 15—Second Quarter Estimated Tax payment due ~ IRS
September 15—Third Quarter Estimated Tax payment due ~ IRS
December 31—Renew City Business License ~ Seattle

For Year 2 and Beyond
January 15—Fourth Quarter Estimated Tax payment due ~ IRS
January 31—Annual Report of Gross Sales (B&O) ~ Seattle
January 31—State Excise Tax* form due ~ WA Dept. of Revenue
January 31—1099-MISC forms due ~ Independent Contractors, if required
January 31—1099-MISC forms due ~ IRS, if required
April 15—Federal Taxes due ~ IRS
April 15—First Quarter Estimated Tax payment due ~ IRS
April 30—Personal Property Annual Report due ~ King County
June 15—Second Quarter Estimated Tax payment due ~ IRS
September 15th—Third Quarter Estimated Tax payment due ~ IRS
December 31—Renew City Business License ~ Seattle

You May Have to Add Some Custom Dates

1 If Washington State has you reporting quarterly or monthly, you will have additional due dates. (For more on quarterly reporting see page 123.) If quarterly, add these dates:

April 30th
July 31st
October 31st

2 If you have an LLC, add renewal on the anniversary month.

3 If you have special licenses or permits, add the due dates for these renewals to your calendar as well.

☞ Think about all the due dates this way: spring is really busy. Then you have one thing to do in summer, fall, and winter.

In Summary—
Do Your Work + Set Up Shop

Now that you're doing business, it's important to put a few systems in place. We reviewed some simple steps to take now that will lay a nice solid foundation for you to build on as you grow.

First, you want to announce you're here by adding an email signature.

As a foundation for marketing, you want to be amazing and start collecting testimonials.

With regard to handling money, there are some key steps and habits to establish now. First, set up business banking accounts, and commit to always transferring 30% (40% if you collect sales tax) into business savings. Start to see your payments in a new way; only a portion becomes your paycheck.

We also reviewed the BIGGEST FAVOR you can do for yourself—to set up a box with no lid to collect all receipts, bank statements and paper trails that you'll need for taxes. Lastly, we reviewed all the important dates. If you put them on your calendar, then you'll be prepared for re-licensing and tax season.

Keep Going: The 5 Areas of Business

☞ Topics to Read as Needed

Legal and Taxes
Numbers
Marketing
Nitty Gritty
Self-Management

About This Section

Building the business side takes time. For most people, this process takes six months to two years. This book walks you through creation of the basic foundation for each of the five areas: legal and taxes, numbers, marketing, nitty gritty, and self-management.

You don't need to do everything in each section. Use the checklists to track what you want to work on and any progress that you make.

You can structure building the business in different ways:

☞ As you need to—in response to a client or your next goal. For example, start your website because someone asked you about it. Or learn to make an invoice just before you meet your first client.

☞ On a schedule—assign tasks for certain time periods. For example, this month is Marketing; next month is Numbers.

Whatever you do, keep going.

Pro Tip: Whenever you're stuck, pick the easiest task first. Choose one goal at a time. Write it on your calendar.

Legal and Taxes

Things to review, choose, and do. Check when complete, or mark NA.

Overview

- Learn by Doing
- Understand Your Agencies
- List of Requirements

Topics

- Self-Employment Tax *(Federal)*
- Estimated Quarterly Tax Payments *(Federal)*
- 1099-MISC forms *(Federal)*
- W-9 forms *(Federal)*
- State Taxes - Three Kinds
- If You Want a Reseller Permit *(State)*
- Online Sales *(State)*
- King County Assessor *(County)*
- City Taxes - Two Kinds

Context

- List of Agencies
- Where All the Taxes Go
- Attitudes that Help

Introduction to Legal and Taxes

This chapter holds the keys to freedom, peace of mind, and sleeping all night long. We will review all of the requirements of owning a business. Remember, once you know what these are, you can do the rest however you want.

None of this is very complicated, but it can seem overwhelming at times because there is a lot of new vocabulary, and different agencies want different things. I promise, each time you interact with this information, a little more will sink in, and it will get easier over time! It's a lot like getting a freight train moving—at first, it takes so much energy to just inch it along... but then, once it's rolling, it takes very little to keep it moving.

Every government agency that you're a part of will want something from you. In our case, this includes Seattle, King County, Washington State, and the federal government.

In general, there are three ways you'll be interacting with these governing bodies:

- Getting licenses and meeting specific requirements of your field
- Making financial reports
- Paying taxes

Below is a chart to summarize what you will eventually need to know. It includes some terms that might be new to you. We'll cover them in detail later. You don't need to memorize or even understand everything just now. I just want to give you the whole picture, so that you can get a good overview, and to see that it is a finite list.

Important note: This covers the standard requirements for basic businesses. You may have additional ones, depending on your field.

All Types of Business Tax and Basic Licensing Requirements

If You Live in Seattle

	What you're taxed on	Type of Tax	License Required?	Renewal
City	Gross Sales, Retail Sales	B&O tax and Sales Tax	Yes	Yearly
County	Value of Personal Property*	Property tax	No	na
State	Gross Sales, Retail Sales	B&O tax, Sales tax, Use tax	Yes	No
Federal	Business Profit	Income tax, Self-Employment tax	No	na

** Equipment and supplies used to do business*

I want to mention a common challenge for learning this stuff. If you have nervous feelings attached to this topic, it can make this information hard to digest. For example, if hearing the words *IRS* or *taxes* makes you tense up with worry, your mind and body will sort of shut down and not let the information in. If this is your situation, remember that you have a plan in place for taxes! (See page 121.)

Plan to read and reread many of these pages. I'll introduce you to important terms and give you a context by talking about the various government agencies and taxes. The more that you can see the human side of all these hoops, the easier it will be to jump through them.

Understanding this content brings an amazing feeling of empowerment. It puts you in the driver's seat.

 Bottom line: You can do yourself a big favor by learning about all the taxes and licenses for your business as soon as possible. It will save you time, money and stress.

Learn by Doing and Repeated Exposure

For many people, legal and tax terms all sound like a foreign language. And actually, they are, sort of—they are a new set of workplace jargon for you to learn.

Have you ever had a new job that included a whole bunch of terms or in-house shorthand? You might have had a trainer to introduce you to things and show you around, "These are the TPS reports, and this is the thingamabob." You would try your best, and you'd remember some things, and others you'd forget. You'd have to ask questions, you would observe others and absorb what you could. That is how language is learned: over time, through use and repeated exposure.

Your challenge here is that you're not surrounded by others using this terminology. So it'll be up to you to re-read this information or find people to talk it through with. You might not understand it all right away, but as you go through the tax season and license renewal, it'll make much more sense.

For now, read through the information, and get as much as you can. Mark your calendar for due dates, and plan to really learn it next January to April. See Important Dates in "Appendix 5: Tools and Worksheets".

Whenever in doubt, or if you feel stuck, get help! Some targeted advice, even if you have to pay for it, can save you so much time and stress.

The more you interact with these terms, the easier it all gets. Before you know it, you'll be talking about things like *gross sales, 1099s*, and *W-9s* with ease.

Pro Tip: For this chapter, leave this book in the bathroom, so you can read it in small snippets.

Understanding Your Agencies—Part One: Overview

To keep track of all your reporting duties, think of it this way:

Every governing body that you're a part of requires something.

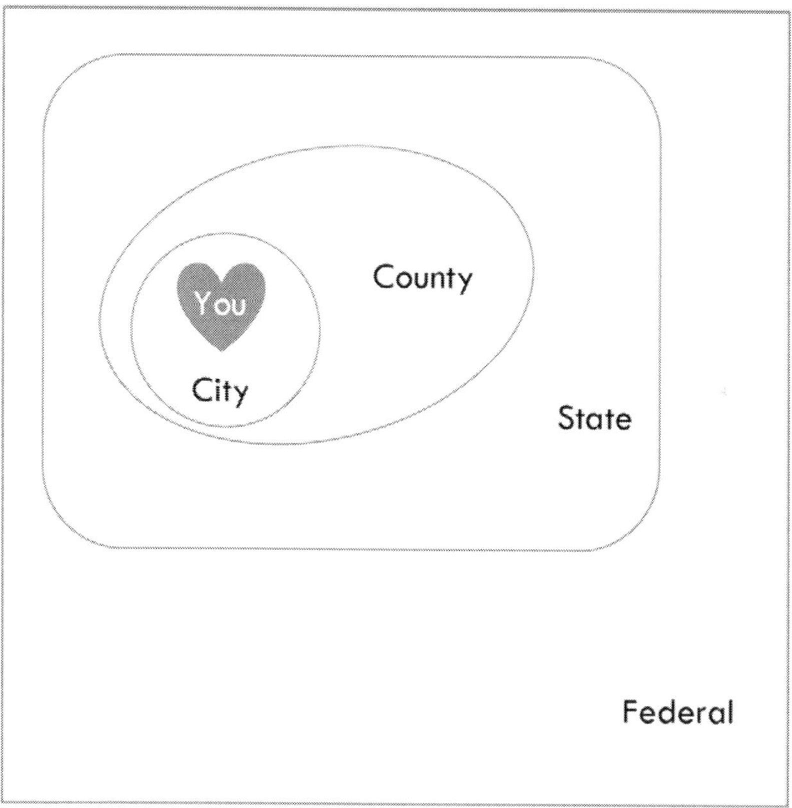

Getting to know your agencies will make life easier. Remember that they're not "out to get you." All these levels of government need taxes to pay for things. (See page 151.)

You'll be working with Seattle, King County, Washington State and the IRS. I often refer to these as city, county, state, and federal.

Quick List of Requirements

This is the standard set of requirements for basic businesses operating in Seattle at the time of this writing. *(Please note, it's possible that your business requires something not listed. See Due Diligence on page 75.)*

City

- Business License
- Annual License Renewal
- Annual Report of Income
- Annual B&O tax—if you make over $100,000
- Permits—if needed

County

- New Business Set-Up Form
- Annual report—called Personal Property Tax Affidavit
- Annual taxes—if your business property is worth more than $7500

State

- Business License—no renewal needed for actual license
- State Taxes —filed monthly, quarterly, or annually (frequency assigned by the DOR)
- Sales, Use, and B&O taxes—pay when you file
- If applicable—Annual LLC renewal, special licenses, small city business licenses (some are handled by the state)

Federal

- Federal Taxes—filed annually—Schedule C
- Taxes on your profit, sent in quarterly
- 1099-MISCs—if needed

Next, we'll look at specific topics related to license renewal and tax reporting.

What is Self-Employment Tax?

(Federal)

Whenever you earn money, whether it's through your business or as miscellaneous income, you have to pay both the standard income taxes AND self-employment tax.

The self-employment tax is a separate and additional tax that is used to fund your Social Security and Medicare accounts. When you are an employee, your employer pays half of this for you. When you're self-employed, you have to pay it yourself. It is around 15%. You will get a small tax credit, so it can end up being a little bit less.

Keep this in mind when you create your rates or pick your prices.

A good rule of thumb is to imagine that your combined taxes (income and self-employment tax) will be 30% of your income. For example, if someone offers you $45 an hour, you would need to save $15 of that for federal taxes. That means your net pay is about $30 an hour.

When negotiating with companies, it can be helpful to remind them of this tax burden and how much more they'd be paying if they hired an employee instead of a contractor.

Do I Have to Pay Quarterly Taxes?

(Federal)

Quarterly taxes, sometimes referred to as *quarterlies*, are shorthand for the *Estimated Quarterly Taxes* paid to the IRS. The idea is to spread your tax burden into four payments throughout the year, so that you don't have one huge, painful bill in April. This helps you, and it helps the IRS. It's possible to incur penalties if you don't send these in.

After you file with the IRS for the first time, the amount of these payments will be calculated for you—either by your online preparer, accountant, or using an IRS worksheet. Usually, it's your total tax bill for the year, divided by four, with a little bit added. It's nice that they assume your income will grow!

This leaves people in a funny place the first calendar year—because this amount hasn't been calculated yet, and may be hard to estimate while still in the building phase. In my experience, many self-employed folks I know didn't send any payments in during that first year, and none of them had any penalties *because their income was low enough.*

If you would like to start sending in payments the first calendar year, you can get a worksheet from the IRS website, call the IRS, or talk to an accountant. To find the worksheet, go to www.irs.gov and search for "self-employed". Follow the link to the "Self-Employed Individuals Tax Center". Find the section on "Quarterly Payments".

Here's something to keep in mind. It's quite common for these estimated quarterlies to be too low in the beginning. This is because they're based off of your income, which usually starts out low that first year, due to: starting mid-way through the year, spending a lot on starting the business, and/or because business is slow in the beginning.

Pro Tip: Be sure to save 30% of your gross sales, no matter what the estimated quarterlies work out to be. (Save 40% if you collect retail sales tax.)

The rhythm of payment is kind of funny; due dates are not evenly spaced. They are two, three, or four months apart. They are generally due around these dates—the actual date may change, if the 15th falls on a weekend or holiday.

- April 15th
- June 15th
- September 15th
- January 15th

The fourth payment can be skipped if it gets paid off with your annual filing.

It's a good idea to pay these taxes on time. It keeps you from getting behind, and it helps you to avoid penalties. Plus, it just feels great to get that money out of your savings account and where it belongs!

Check with an accountant if you would like more detailed information.

1099-MISCs and W-9s—
Like Peanut Butter and Jelly

(Federal)

Just like peanut butter and jelly, 1099-MISCs and W-9s go together.

As a self-employed person, it's quite likely you'll be both giving and receiving these forms, so let's take a look at a few situations calling for them and how they work together. More details about each are in the following sections.

The Basics

1099-MISCs are forms that must be filed with the IRS, whenever an independent contractor has provided services totaling more than the minimum defined amount. (In 2017, this was $600.)

A *W-9 form* is used to get a tax ID number and contact information from an individual or business. This information is required for filling out a 1099-MISC.

When to Give 1099-MISC Forms (and to Ask for W-9 Forms)

If you hire someone to do any work for you, whether they are a private individual or self-employed person, and the total is more than the annual minimum, you must fill out a 1099-MISC form for them. (You are required to do so, and there are penalties if you don't.) If you hire a corporation, you do not.

> *Example A*: My photographer cost $400 to do pictures for my website. I DO NOT have to fill out a 1099-MISC for her.

> *Example B*: My freelance designer charged me $700 for a logo and letterhead. I DO have to fill out a 1099-MISC for him.

Example C: Let's say I consult with a lawyer about getting a trademark and we meet a few times. For one calendar year, my bill comes to $1200. Since this lawyer works for a corporation, I DO NOT send him a 1099-MISC.

In order to provide the 1099-MISC form, you must ask for a W-9 from the person you are paying, so that you have their tax ID and contact information. Technically speaking, you are required to have a completed W-9 on file before issuing full payment to the independent contractor. Practically speaking, this is also a very helpful practice so that you don't have to worry about it during tax season!

ProTip: Avoid the January scramble! Make it a habit to ask for a W-9 on the same day you hire any individual...whether or not you plan to pay them over $600.

Receiving 1099-MISC Forms (and Providing W-9 Forms)

Whenever a self-employed person or business pays you more than $600 (or current minimum) within a calendar year, they will need to provide a 1099-MISC for you.

In order to do that, they will request a W-9 from you. They will need your tax ID number and contact information.

ProTip: Whenever someone hires you, offer a W-9 upfront...to save both of you one less detail during tax time.

More About 1099 / 1099-MISCs

(Federal)

1099 forms are essentially paper trails related to income. They are created by the IRS and completed once a year. You've probably gotten them before. For example, you might have gotten a 1099-INT from your bank. The INT refers to interest. Suffixes vary according to type of income.

A 1099-MISC is used to track miscellaneous income, hence the "MISC". If you've worked as an independent contractor or received a stipend, you've probably seen one before. Sometimes people call them 1099 for short, or use the term as a verb, as in—*Did you have to 1099 him?*

Independent contractors (IC) are people who work as individuals on a contract or freelance basis, rather than as an employee for a company. Sole proprietors and single-member LLCs are both considered ICs.

Some things to know—

- You can order the 1099-MISC forms from the IRS for free, or you can purchase at office supply stores
- Order or purchase these early! They can run out. Add to your November or early December calendar
- If you fill out by hand, they will be carbon forms
- These are currently due on January 31st—both to the independent contractors and to the IRS
- 1099s are usually accompanied by a 1096 form. The IRS will send this automatically to you if you order from them. Do not be alarmed! It is very simple, and acts like a cover letter. You DO need to send it in, along with the 1099s.

To see an example, go to www.irs.gov and search for "1099-MISC form". Follow the link.

More About the W-9 Forms

(Federal)

In order to fill out a *1099-MISC*, one needs the *Tax Identification Number*, or *TIN* of the payee. The W-9 form is used to collect this information. It's likely that you'll be both providing and receiving these forms.

Businesses have the option of using paper forms or interactive PDFs. In addition, the IRS instructions booklet explains that if you have another system for getting and storing TINs, then you can use your own method instead.

The TIN will usually be one of the following:

> *Social Security Number (SSN)*—if a sole proprietor, single-member LLC, or individual not in business
>
> Or
>
> *Employer Identification Number (EIN)*—a tax ID number given to businesses that have employees. Sometimes independent contractors will use an EIN.
>
> Or sometimes,
>
> *Individual Tax Identification Number (ITIN)*—a tax ID number given to those not eligible for an SSN. These are usually folks from other countries who may or may not have resident status.

To find the form, go to www.irs.gov, and search for "W-9". You may use print and use this form.

Remember, whenever you hire any individual contractor, ask for the W-9 right away, as soon as you shake hands.

Understanding State Taxes—Three Kinds

(State)

Sales tax: If you sell a product or do a service that improves a physical thing, you have to collect sales tax. Currently, the rate for Washington state is 6.5%. (If you live in Seattle, there is an extra city tax put on top of that, which gets to the 9.6% that you're familiar with.) The Department of Revenue (DOR) collects both the state *and* local (city) portion of this tax.

The state sales tax is 6.5%
The local (Seattle's) sales tax is 3.1%

Use tax: If you buy something out of state for your business, you are asked to pay *Use tax* to Washington State. (This also applies to purchases made online that didn't include sales tax.)

Basically, you're paying sales tax here for something you bought out of state. For example, if you buy a printer for $200 in Portland, you need to report this, and pay $19.20 in *Use tax*.

B&O: Last is the Business and Occupation tax. It is a percentage of gross sales of each type of business activity that you do (Service, Retail, Wholesaling, Manufacturing). These percentages differ by activity and industry.

You have to report this directly to the state on the state excise tax form. (This is separate from the B&O tax that the city collects.)

With the state, there is a *small business tax credit*. This helps a lot! You won't owe any taxes if you make less than a certain amount, depending on the industry. To give you an idea...if you're a service provider making $45,000 a year, the credit would cover it all, and you would owe nothing.

Important Note: You have to report your earnings even if you don't owe any tax!

Reseller Permit

(State)

If you buy supplies to make products or purchase goods on behalf of your clients, you might be interested in getting a reseller permit. This allows you to buy the above mentioned materials and items without paying sales tax at the time of purchase. You may only use the permit for this purpose. It is NOT for personal use.

Contrary to popular belief, a reseller permit doesn't actually save you money. It simply affects when the tax is paid. Technically speaking, you're not the one paying sales tax—your buyers are. If you pay sales tax when you buy supplies for products, you're simply paying upfront what the buyer will eventually reimburse you for.

For an example, let's look at Emily and her lovely essential oil rollers. (You can roll them right on your wrist!) To make these, she purchases glass bottles with the roller balls, the oil base, and essential oils. Suppose that combined supply cost is $4. Her labor includes buying supplies, selecting and mixing the oils with skill and love. To cover labor, Emily charges $8, making the total price $12 per bottle. For that amount, Emily must collect $1.52 in sales tax.

When a consumers pays the $1.52 in sales tax, they are paying tax on both the supplies used ($4) + labor applied ($8) to transform those supplies into a useful and beautiful product. Tax on the supply part ($4) is 38 cents + the labor part ($8) is $1.14.

Without a reseller permit, when Emily purchased the bottles she would have already paid that 38 cents per bottle. She beat the customer to the tax punch! She would still collect tax on the whole amount ($1.52), and send the labor part of the tax ($1.14) to the state. But she would report that she had already paid the 38 cents in tax for the supplies. She wouldn't pay that amount a second time.

On the other hand, if Emily gets a Reseller Permit, she would pay only $4 per bottle for her supplies (no sales tax paid by Emily for her supplies!). She would still collect the $1.52 in sales tax from the customer, but in this case she would send that entire amount to the state.

In both cases Emily keeps $12 for herself from each sale, and the state collects $1.52 in sales tax. Without the Reseller Permit, Emily pays a portion of the sales tax in advance, when she purchases her supplies. She gets reimbursed later from the customer. With a Reseller Permit, Emily doesn't pay any sales tax for her supplies, which allows her to conserve her own cash and even buy more supplies up front.

Sometimes the state will automatically send you a reseller permit. If one doesn't arrive, you may apply for one.

1 Go to www.dor.wa.gov.
2 Log in to your account.
3 Look for *Manage Account*. Select the arrow next to it.
4 Select *Apply/View Status of Reseller Permit*.
5 Follow the instructions.

If you don't want to use the reseller permit, there are two ways to handle sales tax. The most common is to take a deduction on your state tax form. It is called *Tax Paid at the Source* (see page 197). The other is to send in documentation to the state and receive a refund. Either way, you will need to keep all of your receipts to find these totals and to have as evidence.

Please know that not all stores accept a Reseller Permit. You may have to pay sales tax on your purchases even if you have a Reseller Permit if the store cannot accept it.

To learn more, talk to an accountant, call the Department of Revenue at 800.647.7706, or look online at www.dor.wa.gov. (Search for reseller permit.)

What about Online Sales?

(State)

Selling things online adds a layer of complexity. This is because sales are going across state lines, and they each have different rules and enforcement policies.

Currently, sellers must collect sales tax if the buyer lives in Washington. Sellers are NOT required to collect sales tax for buyers *outside* of Washington state. Additionally, it's important to know that we have a destination-based sales tax system—this means that if you're sending goods across the state, you have to charge sales tax rates based on the location of the customer.

Therefore, you must have a system for keeping track of all of these different totals.

- In-State Total Sales (aka Gross Sales) for *each location* in Washington with a different tax rate.
  (You will owe sales tax on these amounts.)

- Out-of-State Total Sales (aka Gross Sales)
  (You will NOT owe sales tax on this amount.)

Happily, you can usually set up your online store to collect sales tax for you for sales within the state (including the various locations), and it will also keep a record for you. This works on selling platforms, such as eBay, Amazon, and Etsy, as well as commerce sites you manage like Shopify, Squarespace, and Wordpress.

Usually, you can run reports that will show you all the totals that you need.

This is true at the time of this writing. I suggest looking into the current rules to check for your particular industry. You can read about it on the Department of Revenue's website.

1 Go to: www.dor.wa.gov

2 Search: *Online Sales of Goods*

Or, call the DOR at: 800.647.7706.

King County Assessor

(County)

The county collects taxes on property. We usually think of this related to real estate. It also collects taxes on property used for business, whether this is land or equipment.

The good news is if the value of your equipment used for business totals less than $7500, you will not have to pay any county taxes. However, you still need to set up an account and make an annual report.

Here's what to know and do:

- Know the term *Personal Property*: it refers to the physical things you use to do business (as opposed to land)—like computers, paper, tools, etc.

- Submit your New Business Set-Up Form (See page 97.)

- Once a year, you'll need to file a report with King County. It is called the King County Personal Property Tax Affidavit, and it's due every year on or before April 30th.

- You can do this annual report online, with their eListing.

- If you have no changes...you may email your report. Use the subject line "NO CHANGES"; include your name, business name, and UBI.

Note: If your business owns real estate, has an expensive lease, or pays for improvements on those structures, please consult with King County directly.

Understanding City Taxes—Two Kinds

(City)

Sales tax: If you sell a product or do a service that improves a physical thing, you have to collect sales tax. Currently, it's 3.1% in Seattle. (This gets added to the state sales tax of 6.5%—giving us a total of 9.6%.) The Department of Revenue (DOR) collects both the city *and* state portions of this tax.

The state sales tax is 6.5%
The local (Seattle's) sales tax is 3.1%

B&O: The city also collects Business and Occupation tax, *if your business activities total over $100,000.*

It is a percentage of gross sales of each type of business activity that you do (Service, Retail, Wholesaling, Manufacturing). These percentages differ by activity and industry.

Important Note: You have to report your earnings even if you don't owe any tax!

Understanding Your Agencies—Part Two: Review and Contact Information

City of Seattle

The city requires you to have a business license, shorthand for business license tax certificate. It collects city B&O tax, also known as business tax. Seattle uses an online tool called File Local.

www.seattle.gov/business-in-seattle
206.684.2489 (CITY)
File Local: www.filelocal-wa.gov

King County Assessor

The county collects property taxes. Usually, we think of these as related to real estate. With businesses, there are two types. All of you will have *personal property* for your business, the equipment and tools used for your business. If your business owns land or buildings, or leases property, you may have to pay those taxes as well.

www.kingcounty.gov/depts/assessor
206.296.0100

State of Washington

There are two departments that you will work with as a sole proprietor, and three if you have an LLC.

• **Business Licensing Service (BLS)**—The BLS issues the state business license. They give your info to other agencies that need to know about you, including the DOR, and make sure you have any additional permits, licenses and requirements that are related to your field or industry.

www.bls.dor.wa.gov
800. 451.7985

• **Department of Revenue (DOR)**—The DOR collects state taxes. We have three kinds of state taxes: sales, use, and B&O. The DOR collects all three of these taxes and sales tax for the city of Seattle. (However, the city collects its own B&O tax.)

They have a great customer service line. They will walk you through the reporting process.

www.dor.wa.gov
800.647.7706

• **Secretary of State (SOS)**—The SOS is where you file for an LLC or other structure such as a non-profit or corporation. If you want a business structure other than sole proprietor, you need to contact this department. This is where you file for an LLC (or other structures such as a non-profit, corporation, etc.)

www.sos.wa.gov/corps/
360.725.0377

Federal—Internal Revenue Service (IRS)

The IRS taxes your profit—with income tax and self-employment tax. There are two basic forms to file: *Schedule C*, which shows your profit or loss, and *Schedule SE* which calculates the self-employment tax. (If you depreciate vehicles or equipment, you'll have to use additional forms.) These get added right to your 1040. If you use TurboTax, it does all that for you.

www.irs.gov.
800.829.4933
For the Small Business & Self-Employment Center:
www.irs.gov/Businesses/Small businesses-&-Self-Employed

Where All Your Taxes Go

City of Seattle

Taxes on: *Gross sales*—according to business activity

Goes to: police, fire departments, parks & libraries, human services, neighborhood and economic development, and transportation

County

Taxes on: *property*—both real estate and *personal property* (equipment used to do business)

Goes to: courts, jail, public defense, sheriff, public health, emergency services, hazardous waste management, and parks

State

Taxes on: *gross sales*—according to business activity, including *retail sales*

Goes to: schools, colleges, police and fire departments, street lights, public transportation, hospitals, and social services

Federal

Taxes on: *income*, including any *business profit*

Goes to: education, defense, health care, and transportation—airports, waterways, and roadways

Everyone Wants a Piece of Me!

It can feel a little crazy sometimes. There are so many agencies to report to, and so many taxes. All you want to do is some good work for good people. Why do you have all this other stuff?!

It's true it feels like an undue burden. Big companies have specialists and whole departments to deal with this, and you only have yourself. It doesn't feel proportionate. It feels unfair. (It's one of the main reasons that I wanted to work for self-employed people.)

Hopefully, someday it will be easier for one-person businesses—one location, one department, streamlined reporting, and easier language. Until it has changed, the reality is that there are a lot of hoops to jump through and things to understand. Lots of agencies want a little bit of your money.

That's the bad news. The good news is that it's all doable, it gets easier over time, and when your income is low, sometimes you get credits or exemptions to reduce your tax burden.

There's also a lot of help out there for you.

Is it Fair?

When it comes to taxes, it's easy to fall into this woe-is-me trap when we're not prepared. I would like to offer a different point of view.

Point 1: All businesses are taxed because they rely on roads, electricity, etc. to do business. It's impossible to do business without using services provided by the government. It's a privilege that each business pays for. Some big companies pay all the taxes they are supposed to; some probably cheat. It's up to each of us to answer to our own standards and ethics. I usually make choices on what's fair, not what cheating companies do. It gives me a sense of integrity and peace of mind.

Point 2: Part of your self-employment taxes are being saved for you—your social security money and disability.

Point 3: People get mad about taxes when they are surprised, and don't have the funds. If you know they're coming, and understand how they work, you can charge enough from your customers and save the money properly. In general, I'm not a good money saver. But with taxes, it's different. It's not actually savings. Here's why: the money isn't actually ours. We're just collecting part of the government's money. Every time I deposit a check, I put 20%* into business savings for taxes. Every time.

Point 4: Life isn't fair. Once you face that, you can ask, *so what are my choices?* Our choice is to charge enough. And, if it's more than larger company competitors, so what! Don't compete with big businesses on price. Compete on an amazing products and customer service that delights customers.

**I've learned over time that 20% is enough to save for my taxes. I recommend that everyone starts by saving 30% to be safe, then adjusting after going through the tax season once or twice.*

Attitudes that Help—With All the Hoops

Here are some stories that I tell myself to make jumping through the hoops feel easier. They are probably true or mostly true. Anyhow, they help me stay calm as I work through the tangle of tax reporting.

☞ It helps to know upfront that the system is burdensome, and feels unfair. This way, you won't be surprised. You can prepare to be patient, take time, and get help.

☞ The system was created for businesses bigger than yours. Being self-employed is its own funny little category. My guess is that there are not enough of us, or money in us, to create a special system. So, we're lumped in with the bigger guys, and just have to make do.

☞ We need taxes to pay for roads, fire fighters, and libraries and more.

☞ The spirit of the system is that tools, regulations, and reports were all created to keep things fair. The idea of tracking business costs, is so that you don't pay too many taxes! It might feel like the system is clunky, but it didn't start that way. Each rule is in response to a real life situation. It grew over time as the needs grew. True, sometimes bigger businesses find loopholes and pay less money than they should, but that is an example of a private party taking advantage of the system. It doesn't mean the system is unfair in itself.

☞ It's worth it in the end. I love my job. I love my schedule. I love the people I work with. I don't have to commute. I don't sit in boring meetings. I spend way less time doing taxes and licensing stuff... than I spent at work in my old jobs doing unpleasant tasks.

- ☞ There's a lot of friendly help. Every time I've called the city, the state, the DOR, and the IRS, I've had a great experience. Each time, the person answered all my questions and explained the rules I needed with a lot of patience.

- ☞ Tasks will take time, and that's okay. Sometimes, you have to be on hold for twenty minutes. Sometimes paperwork takes a while. Sometimes, it takes months to get taxes done. Just take a deep breath, slow down, try to enjoy the pockets of stillness within the process.

- ☞ Learning also takes time. Eventually, all of these details, hoops, and words make sense. It just takes use and repetition. You'll get it.

Internalizing these stories—that the system was designed to be fair, that we need what taxes pay for, that we're in a weird category, and that things take time—will help you to slow down, take a deep breath, and keep moving through.

If you still feel anxious or confused, just try to remember that other "regular people" have figured it out. You can do it too.

In Summary—Legal and Taxes

You can do yourself a big favor by learning about all the taxes and licenses for your business upfront. It will save you so much time, money and stress to face it now. Almost everything you need to know is in this chapter. It is the most important chapter of this book.

If you know what taxes you'll have to pay, you can charge enough to cover them.

For the city, county, and state, you have to make a report even if you don't owe any taxes. Sending estimated quarterly tax payments to the IRS is helpful to you.

The system was designed to be fair. Jumping through these hoops gets easier over time...and feels totally worth it if you love your job.

Numbers

Things to review, choose, and do. Check when complete, or mark NA.

Context	Know Your Numbers
	Profit, COGS, and other Terms
Earn Enough	How to Earn Enough Money
	Define What You Need to Earn
	Income, Profit, and Your Paycheck
	Earning Hours vs. Admin Hours
	Calculate Earning Hours per Week + Year
	Choose Your Rates / Prices
	The A, B, Cs of Taxes and Number Tracking
Easy As A, B, C	Print Schedule C and Review
	The Numbers You'll Need to Track
	Supplies vs. COGS & Inventory Methods
	You, Bookkeeper, and/or Accountant
	One Box Method or Your Own System?
Your System	If Designing Your Own System:
	Set up Collection Tools
	Proofs of Sale and Income Record
	Tracking Sales by Category
	Receipts for Expenses
	Tracking COGS and Tax Paid at the Source
	Mileage Tracking
	Bank Statements
	Choose Tracking Method
	Choose Rhythm

Introduction to Numbers

There are two major goals for this chapter—to explain how to earn enough money, and to help you to be ready for taxes.

In order to accomplish these goals, we'll need to look at several little parts—terms, formulas, concepts, and practices—and then put them all together. It might come naturally to you, or it might get overwhelming. Please hang in there. A lot of these things can feel really abstract, but once you start to work on them, they'll make more sense. Most of my clients say it all comes together after going through their first tax season.

All of this will result in two major actions:

- Choosing your prices or rates
- Deciding how you will handle number tracking

These two things affect each other, and like chicken-and-egg situations, sometimes it's hard to know where to start. It may feel counterintuitive, but learning about taxes is essential for earning enough money—because being ready for tax reporting also teaches you how to figure out what your profit actually is. Many clients started out charging lower rates or prices, but after paying taxes the first year, they usually raised their prices and felt great about it.

It's totally possible to do all of your accounting once a year, but if you can incorporate number tracking into your monthly rhythm, it will help you in other ways too.

We'll take a quick look at working with numbers and some terminology. Then we'll dive right in to what is probably top of mind for you: what to charge. After that, we'll look at number tracking and how to build your own system.

☞ Bottom line: You need to know your numbers to grow your numbers.

Know Your Numbers to Grow Your Numbers

Numbers are related to freedom, time, and energy. How many hours a week do you want to work? How many weeks a year do you want to travel? How much money do you need to buy the kind of food that you like?

Numbers reflect the health of your business. For example, they answer these types of questions: Are you making a profit? Is that profit increasing or decreasing over time? How many clients are repeating? How many clicks on your website each week?

You may be tempted to skip this section. Please do not! Numbers hold the key to making your business grow, and avoiding common pitfalls. Knowing them helps you to make decisions, like how much to charge, which services to offer, when to raise your prices, and which marketing efforts to use. You need numbers to make these choices, so this venture can be successful. Success meaning here that you stay in business and live the way that you want to live. Happily, all of the math involved is pretty simple; it's mostly addition, subtraction, division and multiplication.

This is what happens when people don't learn about the numbers of business. They:

- get surprised with a huge tax bill
- don't charge enough to cover business expenses and taxes
- think they're earning more than they are...and then spend more than they have.

...all of which lead to digging a financial hole. Don't let this happen to you! Often, people start to believe this is inherent to small business—that it's always hard for the little guy. While there are many challenges to being the little guy, falling into financial pitfalls is not required.

With a little knowledge and a few habits, you can navigate around those traps and give your business a chance to thrive and grow. The information in this chapter will help you to:

- pay the right amount of taxes, and not too many
- be ready for taxes due
- understand how much you're actually earning
- charge enough to get a good paycheck.

Profit, COGS and Other Terms

To work with the numbers of your business, it's helpful to know a few terms.

Gross Before taxes or deductions.

Gross Sales The total of all payments you've collected, NOT including sales tax. This is before any deductions or adjustments. (Different from *Gross Receipts*, which is the total of all payments including sales tax.)

Net The amount of profit you actually made. It is gross minus everything you spent on the business: expenses, supplies for materials (or COGS)

Profit The amount of money you actually earned. This is pre-tax. For our situation, *profit* and *net* are the same.

Expenses or Business Expenses any costs related to doing business, for example, your website, office supplies, and business license. This does not include supplies that go into making products. See COGS below.

Deductions Business expenses get subtracted, or deducted, from total sales, reducing taxes that you owe. These are also called *write-offs*.

Personal Property The property you use to do business that is movable (not real estate). This includes furniture, computers, printers, supplies, etc.

If you make products—

Cost of Goods Sold or COGS The cost of materials that go directly into the products—whether you change them or not. For example, if you are a painter, COGS include canvases and frames. These are different from the costs of running a business. We use the term COGS if you deduct them after they are *sold*, and use the COGS & Inventory method to take the deduction. Covered on page 161.

How to Earn Enough Money

Quite simply, you have to charge enough money.

Whatever you need to charge will feel like too much in the beginning. But remember, you're collecting payment for your business, not just your personal paycheck. You now have business expenses and additional taxes to pay. When you were an employee, the company did this for you. Now, it's up to you.

Think about buying a latte at Starbucks. Let's say you pay $3.74. You already know that this doesn't all go to the barista who's making it for you—that's why they have those tip jars after all. Maybe she gets $0.30 from the latte that you just bought. So where does it all go?

Here's what else that charge has to pay for:

- barista, the person at the register, other staff
- coffee grounds, milk, cup, the lid
- espresso machine, spoons, pitchers
- building—the counters, floors, leather furniture, signs, plants
- utilities: lights, water, heat
- manager, district manager, corporate officers, human resources
- taxes for city, county, state, and IRS
- sick pay, vacation time, bonuses
- marketing

In more streamlined terms, you have to charge for your:

- paycheck
- taxes
- cost of business
- benefits (time off, retirement)

Even without knowing these figures exactly, I hope this will help you feel better about charging more. Starbucks is likely charging twelve times what the barista is taking home. (They are also providing other things besides the drink.) Your charge needs to be *at least* two or three times what you want to take home, in order to earn enough.

What do You Need to Earn? / What do You Need Your Paycheck to Be?

Do you know what you need to take home each month? If you don't, it's okay. We'll figure it out together.

Some of you have to bring home the bacon for the family. For others of you, your earnings will be all gravy on top. Either way, it is important to have a monthly number goal. It gives you something to measure against, it motivates you to keep going, and it reminds you what the money is for—living your life in the way that you want.

If you know these amounts, write them here.

What do you need to make monthly, at a minimum? __________

What do you wish to earn some day? __________________

If you're not sure, there's a worksheet on the next page to help you find these totals. Even if your earnings are all extra, it still helps to allocate this money to a particular goal or bonus activities.

Remember, these figures are your net amount, after taxes and business expenses.

If you have a partner who contributes to the bills, or pays many of them, then just list out the things you would like to cover. For example, if you're married with kids, and your partner's salary covers all the bills, maybe you cover the extras—like summer camp, education for yourself, etc.

When filling out this chart, put in the amount that you know—whether it is monthly or yearly. Then, calculate the other one so you have totals in each column. It's okay to estimate.

		Monthly	Yearly
Housing	rent or mortgage (including tax)		
Utilities	water/sewer/garbage, electricity, gas		
Tech	cell phones, cable, internet		
Vehicle(s)	auto insurance, gas, average of repairs		
Transportation	parking, bus pass, bike repairs/gear		
Insurance	health, life, renters		
Food & Home	groceries, houseold items, alcohol		
Eating Out	dining out, lunches, coffee		
Pets	food, licenses, vet		
Wellness	fitness, therapy, doctor, bodywork		
Entertainment	Netflix/Hulu, Xbox live, etc., movies		
Personal Care	clothes, hair, make-up, jewelry		
Vacation	savings or pay off		
Debt Payoff	min. payments + any extra payments		
Investments	college funds, retirement, property		
Education	program, workshops, training		
Big Purchases	furniture, computer, TV, car		
Total			

Your Income is the Same as Profit (Your Paycheck is Different)

Income, profit, and *paycheck* are terms that often get thrown around and used interchangeably.

As a sole proprietor you and your business are the same entity. (As a single member LLC, you are generally treated like a sole proprietor.) So this means that your business profit is the *same* as your income. This matters to the IRS, to any banks if you're trying to get a loan, and to Washington State if you have Apple Care.

Profit is the money you actually earned. Here's how to figure that out:

Total Sales (This figure never includes sales tax.)
- Supplies to make products (COGS)
- Business Expenses
= Profit / Your Income

Example:

$12,000 Total Sales
- $3000 Supplies to make products (or COGS)
- $1200 in Business Expenses
= $7800...is your Profit / Your Income

A paycheck is what you take home after income and self-employment taxes. When you get a paycheck from a company, they've already done this for you. Remember to do the same for yourself! This means always transferring 30% into your business savings account whenever you make a deposit.

Working with the above figure:

$7800
- $2340 (30% into Savings)
= $5460...is your paycheck.

The Money Machine and Your Paycheck

Here's an overview of how profit and federal taxes are calculated, so you can know how to determine your paycheck.

(Washington state sales tax is never included in this formula.)

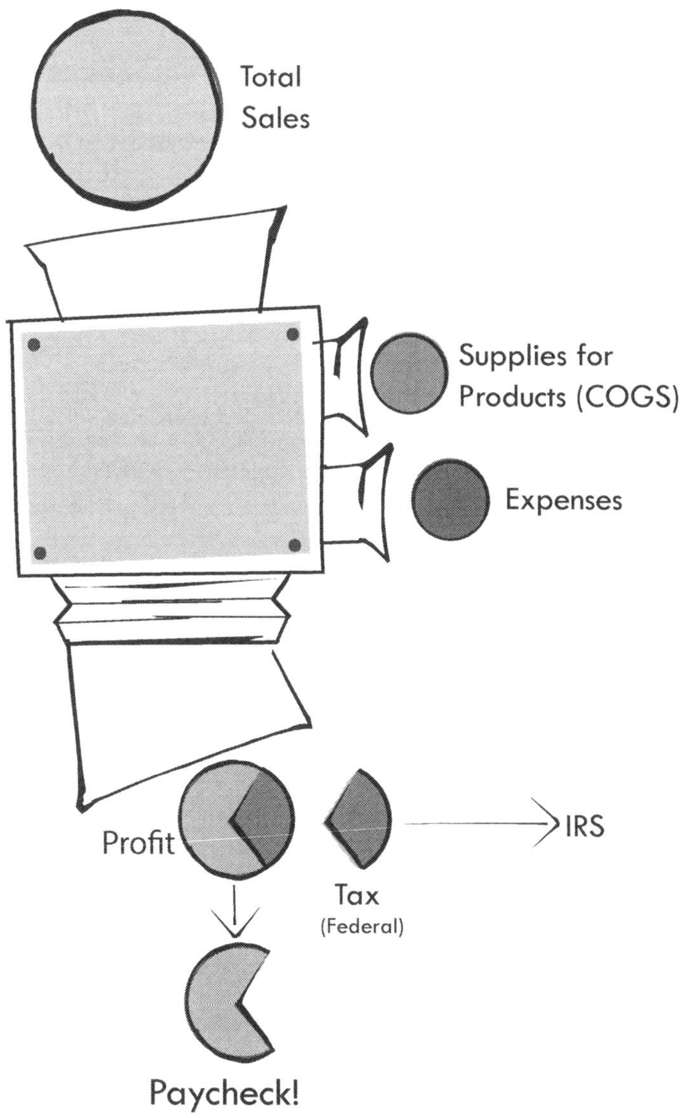

Work Hours—
Earning Hours vs. Admin Hours

How many hours do you plan to work each week? Please write that number here: ______. By any chance, did the number forty pop into your mind? Most people think of this by default; it's just so ingrained in our culture (even though many full-time employees work fifty, sixty, or more).

Whatever the number you wrote…how many of those hours did you plan to get paid for? Write that here: _______. It is very common to believe you will get paid for most or all of the hours you're planning to work. This is how jobs operate, after all.

Self-employment is different. Sometimes you'll be working and you can charge for it. Other times you'll be working but not directly getting paid for those hours. It's good to realize this early so you can plan accordingly. It also helps to name these two different work modes.

The hours you're charging for: when you're offering your service or making your product. If you charge hourly, you can call them *billable hours* or *billables*. If you offer packages or make products, you might call them *earning hours*. Or, you can make up any nickname you like.

The hours you're not directly charging for include all of the business tasks: marketing, selling, emails, scheduling, shopping, invoicing, bookkeeping, errands, etc. You might call these *task hours* or *admin hours*.

What do you plan to call these hours?

Hours you get paid for: ____

Hours for business tasks: ______________________________________

About Billable Hours—For Service Providers

If you're a service provider or artist-for-hire, you can charge by the job or by the hour. Many start out charging by the hour, and we sometimes refer to these as billable hours.

Two good rules of thumb:

- Generally, twenty billable hours is considered full time. It is typically the most you can plan to get in a week. This is because it takes time to run the business too—scheduling, invoicing, advertising, getting supplies, etc. (the admin hours).
- For every billable hour, it is likely you will work at least one hour that you're not paid for.

Note: These rules of thumb may not apply to you IF you regularly do contract work where you don't have to advertise, find your own clients, or do a lot of billing.

These may sound extreme, but they are based on accepted industry standards in many fields. And actually, these are a bit generous if you're new to being self-employed!

Often, in the beginning, you'll be working several hours for each billable. That's okay, considering that you're doing business development too. I would estimate that in my first year, I worked 3-4 hours for every one hour spent with a client. My goal was to get to the 1:1 ratio!

You can start with the above rules of thumb: a 20 hour limit, and a 1:1 ratio...or create your own. Just be sure to keep these in mind when choosing your rate and creating earnings projections.

Know Your (Earning) Work Hours

It's important to know much time you'll be working when you're able to earn money in terms of hours per week and weeks per year.

This helps to calculate your rates or prices and set paycheck goals, and it also reinforces the need for time off. The more realistic you are, the better planning you can do.

To calculate hours per week:

Use the week chart on page 297. Draw in your ideal schedule. Now, add time in for the admin hours. These usually take a minimum of 20% of your schedule. You might pick one day, or spread them out. Now add in time for lunch, driving, etc. Count up what's left.

For most people, twenty is the max for service providers. For product makers, it's twenty to twenty-five.

Your (earning) work hours per week: ______________

To figure out weeks per year:

Use the Year At-a-Glance chart on page 300 or find a calendar. Mark whatever time off you would like to have. Start with holidays, then put in vacations, trips for family, trips for work. Count up these weeks off and subtract from 52. Additionally, subtract two more weeks to cover illnesses.

Most people end up with about forty-two to forty-eight weeks. If it's fewer, that's fine. But I highly suggest forty-eight as the maximum.

Your weeks per year: ________________

Choosing Your Rate as a Service Provider

This is where we start putting together all of the ideas you've been exploring. Instead of looking at the typical rates in your field, start with what you need to earn and how much you actually want to work. You deserve to make a living.

Use this formula to figure out possible *Gross Sales* goals. (Gross sales are the total payments made to you by all customers.)

Weeks x Actual work hours x Rate = *Gross Sales*

Examples: 48 weeks x 20 hours x $80 = $76,800
42 weeks x 20 hours x $50 = $42,000

Then, and **this is crucial**, estimate how much of the *Gross Sales* becomes take-home pay. This varies so much. A good place to start is about 60%. This accounts for federal taxes and business expenses. (Once you've tracked your numbers for awhile, you can adjust this percentage to more precisely fit your business.)

Try it several times, changing the numbers to see what happens.

For example, using the above figures:

$76,800 x 60% = $46,080 (your paycheck)
$42,000 x 60% = $25,020 (your paycheck).

Rate		Hours		Weeks		Gross Sales	take 60%	Paycheck
	x		x		=		x .60	
	x		x		=		x .60	
	x		x		=		x .60	
	x		x		=		x .60	

Choose the rate that gives you the paycheck that you need.

Setting Prices If You Make Products

There's no quick way to find the right prices for your products. It's a process of trial and error and will take some time. There are so many variables to consider...e.g., what customers are willing to pay, how many products you're selling, the cost of materials, packaging, shipping, and your labor.

While there's no magic formula, the basic process is to pick some prices, monitor your earnings, and make adjustments.

Here are a couple guiding ideas and tips:

- Always put the season and year on your price lists—so if you raise them, it won't be a surprise. It'll be expected.
- Plan to raise your prices regularly for the first year or two.
- If you're comfortable with a price, it's too low. Try doubling it.
- Have a rhythm for reviewing these numbers—maybe monthly or quarterly.

Here are a few methods for picking your initial prices. Please note that all of these methods are very approximate. They are presented as a way to get you started. You'll need to adjust them for your situation and over time.

Weekly Income Method

Use this chart to calculate what to charge per product, based on what you need to earn. (Completed example on the following page.)

1	What is the paycheck that you need to earn each week?			*Paycheck*
2	Multiply that number by 3. This is the gross amount that you need to earn.	x 3		*Gross Amount*
3	How many products do you typically create in a week?	/		*Products*
4	Divide gross amount by product.	=		*Price to charge per product*

That is your charge per product.

Here's a completed example, filled out by a fine painter.

1	What is the paycheck that you need to earn each week?		$600	*Paycheck*
2	Multiply that number by 3. This is the gross amount that you need to earn.	x 3	$1,800	*Gross Amount*
3	How many products do you typically create in a week?	/	2	*Products*
4	Divide gross amount by product.	=	$900	*Price to charge per product*

Using this method, she would charge $900 per painting.

One caveat—this works if you're selling all of your products. If you sell a portion, then you can adjust your math by dividing by what you're actually selling.

Note: If you have different types of products, you'll need to divide the gross amount required into amounts for each group of products...then divide by product. For example, if you make both soaps and lotions, we would split the above $900 into two groups. $450 for lotions and $450 for soaps, then choose the unit prices.

Add 30% Method

1 Look at one to three competitors who are working at your level of quality.

2 Take their prices and add 30%.

Shop Owner Method

1 Identify two or three shops that could potentially carry your products. Request a consult with the owner/buyer. The consult could be informal, or formal, depending on the shop. If informal, offer to take the shop owner to lunch or coffee.

2 Bring in some of your products and ask what they would charge. Be sure to record their answers!

3 Send them a thank you card.

Keep in mind, if they sell your products in their store, they will take a cut, usually around 50%. But, you can use their prices to inform your own sales—if selling directly online or at fairs, markets, or through custom orders.

Heart Method

What prices do you *want* to put down? The key word is want, please ignore anything you *should* do, or what others would say.

Tune in to yourself. What would you feel thrilled about earning for your products? What price would make you smile?

Setting Your Prices High Enough

It can be tempting to underprice or offer lots of discounts when you're first starting. After all, you enjoy doing your work, your confidence is still growing, and you want more clients.

Be careful when doing this. There's a danger of getting stuck at a certain price level.

Find a way to set your prices at the standard rate, if not higher. Do whatever you need mentally/emotionally to do this. Perhaps look online at competitors' rates, and notice how the product or service that you're offering is better than theirs. Get a friend to talk you up. Maybe run some numbers based on what you need to earn.

Here are some things to consider:

☞ Setting the price too low hurts the industry. It can force other competitors to lower their prices too. This is not helpful for artists, service folk, and micro-business people. Help everybody earn a living wage by keeping your prices up.

☞ Price for the people who can afford to buy your stuff, and at a level that earns you a living. Don't price things for yourself or your friends. Remember, you can always give them a discount.

•

Next, we'll turn out attention to taxes. We'll look at all the pieces, some strategies and how to set up a system for collecting numbers.

The A, B, Cs of Taxes and Number Tracking

A is for Accounting. This is the story we tell about our numbers. This includes tax reporting (profit and loss), calculating growth, making predictions, creating budgets, and making goals. Accountants have professional codes of conduct and are responsible for knowing the current tax codes, etc.

B is for Bookkeeping. This is the practice of tracking the numbers. This involves making invoices, collecting payments, depositing, filing, and keeping records. This is required to do any accounting. Bookkeepers keep everything in order for you. Bookkeepers range in skills and abilities. Some are hired to simply follow a system already in place. Others work at a more involved level, perhaps creating your bookkeeping system and even doing some accounting.

These two roles can have a lot of overlap.

C is for Schedule C. Federal taxes require this form. It is a version of a *Profit and Loss Statement.* It is used for both sole proprietors and single-member LLCs. The actual form is pretty straightforward and not that scary. (More about Schedule C on the next page.)

This form shows you all of the numbers that you'll need to know for federal taxes and for calculating your income.

Schedule C

(Federal)

Before we proceed, I would like to introduce you to the Schedule C. It is the tax form used for self-employed folks, and it is friendlier than you might think.

Please—

1. Go to www.irs.gov
2. Search for Schedule C
3. Select the result
4. Open up the form and print

Some Things to Notice:

It's only two pages long.

It uses plain English. Look at Section II—Expenses. Categories are named things like Advertising, Car & Truck, and Office Expense. In addition, if you have some expenses that don't seem to fit a category, you can create your own in the Other Expenses section.

If you don't have any COGS or inventory to account for, you can skip most of the second page!

•

Taxes can feel like the monster in the closet. Many people dread and fear what they don't know or can't see. Taking a look at the actual tax form can be calming and empowering. You will know exactly what is required of you, giving you nothing to fear. Knowledge is power!

Even if you file online, it's important to know this form, so you are clear about what's actually on it and what you need to track.

The Numbers You'll Need Next Year For Tax Reporting

Starting next calendar year, you will need to make a report to each level of government: city, county, state, and federal. For some you'll owe taxes, for others, you won't, depending on your business activity. Here are the numbers that you'll for each one. Notice there is some overlap.

For the IRS:

- Gross Sales
- COGS (if applicable)
- Expenses by category
- Mileage
- Profit

For the County:

- Value of Personal Property

For the State:

- Gross Sales by category
  (Retail, Service, Manufacturing, Wholesaling, Royalties)
- Sales Tax Paid at the Source if you have supplies for products (or COGS)

For the City:

- Gross Sales by category
  (Retail, Service, Manufacturing, Wholesaling)

Please Note: These are the numbers needed for all businesses. It's possible that you'll need additional numbers if you have a special type of business. You can either check with an accountant or someone else in your field.

A Note for Product Makers—Supplies vs. COGS & Inventory

If you make products...then you have a choice to make related to taxes. It has to do with any materials you buy to make these products, or any services you pay for, related to your products. Strictly speaking, these are not considered business expenses—because they aren't part of running your business (such as your website, business cards, or file cabinets).

We will either call these costs either *supplies* or *cost of goods sold (COGS),* depending on which method you choose—either the Supply Method or COGS & Inventory Method. Generally speaking, product makers are expected to use the COGS & Inventory Method. In some cases, it is allowable to use the Supply Method.

Option A: The Supply Method

This is the simplest. All of these materials are considered *supplies*. The idea is to keep all of the receipts and deduct the amount each year in the *supplies* category under business expenses. If you hire anyone to apply a service to your products, you would record their costs under *contract labor*, also in business expenses section. (For example, imagine that Gabe has built some beautiful cherry wood bookshelves. He pays a guy to sand them all—this would be a contract labor expense.)

The Supply Method means taking the deduction as you go, whether or not you've sold the product. In general, this method works best for businesses that do commission work, do not build up inventory, or have a very small working budget.

Option B: The COGS & Inventory Method

For this method, you must have a system. In contrast to the above, you take the deduction of these materials and services *after* you've sold the products. This is why they are called cost of goods *sold* (COGS). The COGS must be calculated, and for this, one must keep inventory. There are a few different ways to do these calculations.

Systems and tools vary so greatly, that I will not be able to cover them in this book. My one tip is to find a system that you like that is easy to follow. Here are a few ideas to get you started on selecting yours: consult with a bookkeeper or accountant, utilize software such as Quickbooks which tracks inventory, interview other product makers about their system, check with Greater Seattle SCORE for a class or consult at www.seattle.score.org.

This method is more complicated, but it's created to be the most fair—it allows you to take the COGS deduction during the same year when you've actually sold the products. To give you a picture of this, let's look at Robyn and kale chips. Let's say that Robyn decides to start her business in December and purchases all her supplies late that month so she can be ready for January (when people are trying to get back to healthier eating). She buys a ton of kale, coconut oil, spices, containers, and stickers. She makes all the chips, and then sells them like crazy in January.

With using the Supply Method, she'd be deducting a hundreds, maybe thousands of dollars in materials that first year. But, since she'd no income yet, the deduction wouldn't help her much. With the COGS & Inventory Method, Robyn would deduct these costs after selling all of her delicious kale chips in the second year—the deduction would offset her gross sales giving her a better tax advantage.

•

ProTip: If you're not sure which method to use, write COGS on all of the receipts whenever you pay for materials or services related to your products. Later, once you know your method, you can handle these receipts as needed.

You Have Options!

When it comes to calculating these numbers, you have some options.

Do It Yourself

All of this stuff is doable. If you're willing to dive in, you can do your own bookkeeping and accounting, and fill out your own Schedule C, as well as your reports to the city, county, and state.

For filing taxes with the IRS, TurboTax takes you through all the business stuff. For reporting to the state and the city, just call them, and they will walk you through filing your form. It's their job!

Hire an Accountant

Another option is to keep your own books and then hire an accountant. For anywhere from $600 to $1200 a year (or more), this person can do all your federal tax reporting (including both business and personal), help you understand what to report, and inform you about any current credits or tax incentives. The price may be higher if you're using the One Box Method, page 123, and they're adding up all your receipts and/or if you want them to make reports to the city and the state. Many self-employed people find it very reassuring to have this person on their team.

Keep in mind that it's sometimes possible to earn the money to pay a professional in less time than doing it yourself.

Hire a Bookkeeper

An official bookkeeper can do all the minutiae for you—recording expenses, organizing documents, and sometimes billing and making deposits. They can also provide you with monthly reports for analysis of your business, and some will even file reports to the city and state. If you're using the One Box Method, a bookkeeper could also take all of your receipts and get them in order for you or an accountant.

It's possible to take their work and do your taxes yourself.

Hire Both!

The last option is to find someone to help with accounting and bookkeeping—whether it's the same person, or two different people.

Keep in mind, it's still up to you to collect all the required stuff for them to process. We'll cover this in a few pages.

A Cautionary Tale—Dread vs. Easy-Breezy

Imagine this scenario: You get started on your business in the spring and you think, "I'll figure out taxes later." You start getting some clients, and it feels amazing to do your work and to get paid! You forget about taxes. At some point in the fall, you hear the word *January*, and a sinking feeling moves into your stomach. A few months later, a little voice in the back of your head whispers...*April is coming*. This makes your stomach feel worse, so you quiet that voice and move on.

When March comes, the *shoulds* move in. *I should really get started on this. I should have gotten that app my friend told me about. I should have saved those receipts.* But every time you think about starting, you get overwhelmed. You feel guilty that you haven't started, and worried about what the tax bill will be. You stay up all night on April 14th. You do the best you can, but probably don't get enough deductions—meaning you paid too many taxes!

Oh well, you say. *At least it's done.* And then you remember that you're already almost four months into the current year. You wonder if you can handle self-employment....

This will not be you!

Instead...

Your experience is going to be easy-breezy. You'll sort of forget about taxes. If you hear someone talking about it, you might start to worry, and then remember, *I've got it handled. I've got my system, and dates on the calendar. I'm fine.* You'll sleep through April 14th without even thinking about the date.

So what's the difference between dread and easy-breezy? It's all about collecting stuff.

Option A: One Box Method

(Review from page 123)

The One Box Method is the simplest, most straightforward way to be ready for taxes. It's easy to use and accomplishes much of the work of tax preparation—to collect all the stuff you need! Please see page 123 for the full description.

You're welcome to stick to the One Box Method...forever, if it fits your style.

Remember, it works if you do ALL of these things:

- Set up a box with no lid
- Put all paperwork in there
- Always transfer money to savings—30% (40% if you collect sales tax)
- Write important dates on your calendar

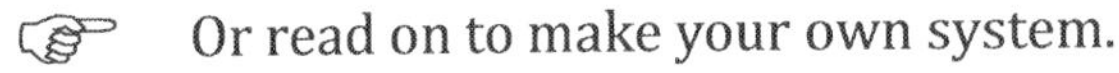

☞ Or read on to make your own system.

Option B: Setting Up Your Own System

What's the best system? Is there an app? Isn't Quickbooks what I'm supposed to use? This is really important: **The best system is the one that you'll follow.**

Our goal is to set up a system that is the right size for your business—not too complicated and not to simple—and that fits your style. In order to get this dialed in just right, I need to present some choices for you to consider. Unfortunately, seeing all the choices makes it look more complicated than it is. Please trust me—the end result should feel easy and streamlined.

The goal is to know all of the numbers you need for tax reporting. You need to collect stuff all year in order to calculate these.

Here's what we'll do together:

1 Choose your collection tools and set them up

2 Review categories for what you're collecting

3 Choose your tracking method—how you record and calculate totals

4 Define your rhythm

Even if you plan to use some sort of accounting software, you still need to develop your own system of collect, sorting, and entering numbers.

1. Start with Your Collection Tools

There are oh-so-many ways to do this part. Here are some ideas and choices for you. These are just to get you started. Of course, feel free to riff off of them! Whatever you do, make your system easy and fun.

ProTip: If you have multiple containers, be sure to LABEL them clearly.

1 First, decide: ___ One container for everything, or

___ Containers by category:

- Proofs of Sale
- Receipts from Expenses
- Receipts from Supplies for Products (or COGS)—if applicable
- Bank Statements

2 Choose which physical tools you would like to use:

___ Shallow trays	___ Shoeboxes	___ Other:
___ Baskets	___ Hanging files	
___ Large envelope	___ Accordion file	

3 Electronic Receipts—you will need a method for receipts that you get through email. Here are two strategies. Pick one and stay consistent.

____ Always print immediately and file in the physical inbox.
____ Create an electronic file, always transfer receipts to this folder, and then print when you work on accounting.
____ Go totally electronic. Transfer electronic receipts to this file, and scan all paper receipts.

4 Mileage record—plan to set this up after reading page 196.

____ Notebook ____ Excel spreadsheet
____ App for phone

2a. Income Tracking or Sales Tracking for the Gross Sales Number

Remember, the way to know your profit is this formula:

Gross Sales
- Expenses
- Supplies for Products (or COGS)—if applicable
= Profit

In order to know your *Gross Sales*, you'll need a way to keep track of all your payments from customers. This is often referred to as *income tracking* or *sales tracking*.

There are two important things to know:

- *Gross Sales* is the total amount of all the money that comes in to you from customers, before any deductions.
- *Gross Sales* **never** includes sales tax.

Note: If you plan to use software or a program to make invoices, it will automatically create a record and you can skip this section.

To track your income or sales, you have many options, ranging from informal to formal. Decide which ones you will use, and be consistent! If you collect sales tax, you'll need to find a way to record or calculate the total of all your gross sales without sales tax.

Whatever your system, be sure to include:

1 Date

2 Amount

3 Service or product

4 Customer name or information

Physical Options

___ Notes in calendar: write down the amount collected in your calendar, next to the appointment

___ Deposit slip from bank: write the customer and date on the slip

___ Carbon receipt slips

___ Carbon invoice copies—only include for invoices that have been paid

___ Make a copy of each invoice that you give to clients—only include for invoices that have been paid

___ Keep a list in a notebook or in Excel

Electronic

___ Notes in electronic calendar: write down the amount collected in your calendar next to the appointment

___ Email/text yourself with amount and customer

___ List in Excel

2b. Totals for Each Business Activity Type

The state and city want to know your gross sales total for each business activity: Service, Retail, Wholesaling, and Manufacturing. You can review definitions of these on page 72.

First, determine if your work falls into one category or more. If it's in just one category, then you will skip this step. There are only a few types of jobs where you work in only one category.

Here are two examples:

> Tavia is a consultant for nonprofits. All her work is in the *service* category with no sales tax collection required.
>
> Mike buys antiques at wholesale prices and sells them in a shop. He is doing *retail* only.

Be aware, sometimes even service-type jobs can fall into two categories. For example, Sally-Anne is an amazing plant designer. She offers consults for homeowners who want to create beautiful yards with edible and native plants, utilizing organic methods. When Sally-Anne is consulting, she's offering *services*. Sometimes, Sally-Anne and her crew will do some of the landscaping and even provide pots and yard elements (usually re-purposed or found). In those cases, Sally-Anne's work is considered *retail*. Sally-Anne is working in both *service* and *retail*. She'll need to track her *gross sales* in each category.

If you are unsure, then call the state's Department of Revenue at 800.647.7706.

Two or More Types of Business Activity

Many types of businesses work in two or more categories. If you make products, then you are automatically in this camp. You are *manufacturing* and either *wholesaling, retailing*, or both.

You will need to report the *gross sales* totals in each business activity you're engaging in. It's easiest to explain using examples.

Let's say that Gabe makes bookshelves and then sells them directly to customers. He is both *manufacturing* and *retailing*. If the total gross sales were $4500, he would report:

Manufacturing—$4500
Retail—$4500

The next year, a store wants to sell Gabe's bookshelves. Gabe makes the same number of bookshelves, valuing at $4500. He sells half of them directly to customers and half to the store. He would report:

Manufacturing—$4500
Retail—$2250
Wholesale—$2250

Note: There is a B&O tax credit available when you report the sales amount in two separate categories. For more information, call the DOR at 800.647.7706. Be sure to claim this credit so you don't over pay taxes to the state!

2c. Receipts for Getting to Your Total Expenses

Expenses are all costs related to running the business, including any licenses required to work in your profession. They get subtracted from your *gross sales* in order to figure out your actual profit. Tracking and reporting these will reduce the amount of federal taxes that you need to pay. They are commonly referred to as *write-offs* or *deductions*.

The official categories from the Schedule C are below. For a user friendly list/worksheet, find Business Expenses by Category on page 374.

Notice that the line is Other Expenses. If you have a business cost that doesn't seem to fit any of the named categories, you may add your own in the Other Expenses section. Two common "other" expenses are: Other-Bank Fees, and Other-Professional Development.

Receipts are required to prove these expenses for your business.

Part II **Expenses.** Enter expenses for business use of your home **only** on line 30.

8	Advertising	8		18	Office expense (see instructions)	18	
9	Car and truck expenses (see instructions)	9		19	Pension and profit-sharing plans	19	
10	Commissions and fees	10		20	Rent or lease (see instructions):		
11	Contract labor (see instructions)	11		a	Vehicles, machinery, and equipment	20a	
12	Depletion	12		b	Other business property	20b	
13	Depreciation and section 179 expense deduction (not included in Part III) (see instructions)	13		21	Repairs and maintenance	21	
				22	Supplies (not included in Part III)	22	
				23	Taxes and licenses	23	
				24	Travel, meals, and entertainment:		
14	Employee benefit programs (other than on line 19)	14		a	Travel	24a	
15	Insurance (other than health)	15		b	Deductible meals and entertainment (see instructions)	24b	
16	Interest:			25	Utilities	25	
a	Mortgage (paid to banks, etc.)	16a		26	Wages (less employment credits)	26	
b	Other	16b		27a	Other expenses (from line 48)	27a	
17	Legal and professional services	17		b	**Reserved for future use**	27b	

From the 2016 Schedule C, found on www.irs.gov.

Eventually, you'll need totals of expenses in each category. You're welcome to figure that out later unless you want to set up a way to track them now. These totals will include any sales tax that you paid.

Sometimes, it can be unclear which category to use for an expense. For example, does a monthly website fee go under Advertising or Utilities? Here are two strategies: 1) pick the category and stick to it or 2) file it under *Ask Accountant* to figure out later. The important thing is that you do claim the expense, and that you claim it only one time.

ProTip: Whenever you get a receipt that's for a business expense, write your business name on top.

ProTip: For meal or entertainment expenses, also add the name of the person you were meeting and the purpose. If it's for travel, write the trip name and purpose.

2d. Total COGS or Supplies

Remember, if you make products, you'll be deducting the cost of materials and labor that go into making your products. There are two methods—the Supply Method and the COGS & Inventory Method. (See page 179.)

Let's review COGS, which refer to Cost of Goods Sold. In general, these are used to describe materials and labor that are specifically purchased to make a product. For example, if you're making custom chairs, material COGS would include the wood, fabric, stuffing, and any hardware. Labor COGS might be a subcontractor who stains the wood used on the chair. (Things like tags on the chair, invoices, printing a photo of the chair to run and ad in a magazine would all be considered *business expenses.*)

Review of the Methods

The Supply Method—If you have chosen to use the Supply Method, then all of your receipts that say COGS need to get totaled up, and they will be added to your other *supply* receipts. If you paid for any services related to your products, then these get filed under *contract labor.*

COGS & Inventory Method—COGS are only deducted after products are sold. This amount must be calculated and includes keeping inventory. If you have chosen this method, you need to keep all of your COGS receipts, but you won't need to total them up. Instead, you'll be working with your accountant, bookkeeper or software to do some calculations.

If Using the COGS & Inventory Method—Fuzzy Areas

Sometimes things fall in between COGS and business expenses, and you might not know where to report their costs. Consider the glue and nails used to make the chairs. These could go either way—you could file them under "Supplies" in Expenses, or under COGS. In this case, just pick a category and stick with it. Or file under *Ask Accountant* to get their guidance.

2e. Tax Paid at the Source

Important Note: For this page, I'm using the phrase materials-supplies, to refer to supplies used to make products. These DO NOT include supplies for your business, such as books or thank you cards.

If you ever paid sales tax when buying COGS or materials-supplies, you can take a deduction with on your state tax form. It is called *Tax Paid at the Source.* Why? Because your customer is the one who ultimately needs to pay sales taxes on the products they're purchasing. Since COGS and materials-supplies are essentially bought on behalf of the client, you're essentially paying their tax for them...ahead of time. (See Reseller Permit, page 143.)

You will still charge them for the full sales tax owed on your products. You will report all of this to the state, and then take a deduction so that you keep the portion of the sales tax that you already paid.

Here's an example. Let's say that I buy a folding chair at the store. It cost me $11—about $10 for the chair and about $1 for the sales tax. I transform this chair into a yoga prop—I take out the back and paint some designs on it. I then sell it for $40 + sales tax. The customer pays me about $44 total. $40 for the chair and about $4 for the tax.

Here's where it gets interesting. Think about that chair. I paid $1 in sales tax, then my customer paid me $4. I never used that chair for myself, it was a materials-supply, so it's not intended that I pay sales tax on it. I was paying $1 on behalf of my customer out of the $4 they owe the state.

When I take the *Tax Paid at the Source* deduction, it allows me to subtract that $1 from what I owe the state, meaning I only send in the $3.

You Need Subtotals in Order to Take the Deduction

In order to take this deduction, you'll need the grand subtotal of all the COGS or materials-supplies that you paid sales tax on. The subtotal means here the amount you paid *before* tax...the subtotals...on your receipts.

For example, if I bought the following items throughout the year, my grand total, before sales tax would be $7000.

Total Fabric Purchases: $4000 + $384 tax = $4384
Total Hardware Purchases: $3000 + $288 tax = $3288

The $7000 is the number that I will need to get the deduction.

2f. Auto Expenses—Two Choices: Track Mileage or Actual Costs of Vehicle(s)

There are two ways to report expenses related to your vehicle:

1 Mileage

OR

2 Costs of gas, repairs, insurance, registration, etc.

For each vehicle, you have to pick one method and stick to it for the entire year. If you choose the mileage method, it's possible to switch to the actual cost method. However, once using the actual cost method, it's not allowable to switch back.

It can be hard to know which deal is better. Sometimes it's tracking mileage, and sometimes it's deducting all of the costs related to the vehicle.

Not sure which to use? I find that tracking mileage method is the simplest method. If you want to get the biggest deduction, track both mileage and all the costs of that vehicle, and then compare the write-offs. If your car is older and needs a lot of maintenance, then it might be better to track actual costs.

The easiest way to track mileage is to get an app. A favorite among clients is MileIQ. Find at www.mileiq.com. You can try it with a free plan, and then upgrade if you like it.

The other option is to keep your own record—either on paper or in Excel. The IRS asks that you keep very specific information. If you set up your own system, include the required headings: date, purpose, odometer start, and odometer end. You can also buy mileage notebooks at most office stores.

In addition, you'll need to know the total miles for the year. For this, you would record the odometer reading at January 1st and December 31st.

It might feel like a burden...but it is usually worth it! One year, a client of mine saved $1600 because of mileage. Pretend that every time you write down mileage notes, you're saving between one and six dollars. That's enough to buy a latte or beer.

2g. Bank Statements

Please note: I'm using the term *bank statements* whether you use a bank, credit union, or credit card. Remember, the strategy is to have one business account that you use for all purchases. If you've been using more than one, you'll need to collect statements from each account.

Each month, print and store all bank statements that include business purchases and deposits. And/or collect and store PDF versions of statements in one file on your computer.

Bank statements are so useful!

- They help you to catch purchases you might have forgotten about, such as parking, or coffee for meetings.
- They are a secondary source of proving expenses—so that if a receipt was lost, you can still demonstrate that purchase.
- They can serve as a reminder to work on your bookkeeping.
- When you look at them, they might seem dry and full of indecipherable code, but look closer! They tell the story of your business, which can offer an opportunity for reflection and/or feelings of accomplishment.

Just last night, I was working with Tavia, a musician and fundraising consultant, on tax preparation. We were double-checking her records using her bank statements. We noticed how one day, she had four different parking receipts.

"Whoa, that's a lot of parking! What were you doing that day?" I asked.

"Oh, wow. I had a lot of meetings that day. I met with ...."

"And look here, you were in three different restaurants in one day."

"Oh yeah, I was meeting with [three nonprofits]. That really was such a busy time! I can't believe I was working on all of those events at once, and that they all turned out so great." She smiled.

Reviewing these statements prompted Tavia to think back over her year and to remember all that she had accomplished.

3. Tracking Methods

In order to know all of your important numbers and to file taxes, you have to do two things:

1 Have a record of transactions

2 Have a way of adding them all up

Those two processes can be separate, or they can be combined into one, depending on which method you choose.

Again, the best method is the one that you'll follow. Here are some options:

☞ Paper and Calculator

- Receipts and copies of invoices. Sort by category, staple together, and add up with calculator.
  OR
- Notebook—with pages dedicated to *Income*, *COGS* (if applicable), *Expenses*, and *Mileage*. Use a calculator to add it up.

☞ Spreadsheets

- Set tabs for *Income*, *COGS* (if applicable), *Expenses*, and *Mileage*. Enter all transactions into a table, and set the program to do the adding for you. You can put in various formulas to collect data, if you know how to do it, or, you can get a friend to help you.

☞ Software on computer

- Look for programs such as Quickbooks or Wave.

☞ Apps on your phone or iPad

4. How Often?—Choosing Your Rhythm

How often you work on bookkeeping is totally up to you. It's about what fits into your rhythm and works with your tools. I have some clients who enter every single transaction into their phone right after it happens. I have some who add everything up in January. Since they always transfer money into savings for taxes, they can generally trust what their paycheck is.

The important thing is to pick your rhythm, name it, and stick to it. If you get behind, then you have two choices. Get caught up, or change your rhythm to match what you're actually doing. It's stressful to have a plan and not follow it. So be real with yourself.

It also helps to have a cue to work on bookkeeping. Some ideas are:

- Put time into your weekly schedule, maybe *Money Mondays*, or *Financial Fridays.*
- If you're in a monthly rhythm, pick the same day each month and write it on the calendar.
- If you're working quarterly, line up a bookkeeping work day with the solstices or the business quarters. Write these on your calendar.
- Work on bookkeeping whenever you get your bank statements.

Here's the rhythm I use: every Friday, I update my income record. I like to see what I've been earning! Then, once a month when the bank statements arrive, I enter all my expenses into my spreadsheet, both from the statement itself and any receipts I have in my basket.

In some ways, doing things less often can actually be more efficient. The benefit of working more often is that you don't have a big job looming over your head, and you have a better sense of what you're actually earning.

Pick what works for you.

Why Do I Need to Track All These Numbers?

Tracking and knowing your numbers will help you in three important ways. I like to think of them in layers, starting at the surface and moving deeper:

First Layer: To Pay the Correct Amount of Taxes

If you only tracked income, you'd pay too many taxes. You have to track all of your expenses in order to take the deductions, so that the tax can be calculated based on your true profit. It's a system based on a spirit of fairness. This is the first layer and the only required one.

Example: Shawn is a photographer. In his first year doing business, he collected every single receipt and put them in a shoebox. We sat at Phinney Market Pub, straightened them all out, and added them to a spreadsheet to claim as his business expenses. Thank goodness! Without that box, he would have had to pay about $3000 in tax. With the deductions, his income was low enough to owe only a few hundred dollars.

Second Layer: Health / Reality Check

Usually, when you go to the doctor, they check your vitals—height, weight, blood pressure, and heart rate. This doesn't give you a complete picture, but it does give a lot of information. Generally, it can tell the doctor if you're basically healthy or not.

Knowing a couple important numbers can do the same for your business. You might feel that you're earning a lot or not earning enough. The feelings aren't always accurate in the beginning. For example, I've witnessed clients thinking their earnings have dropped, when in reality, their earnings are up. They've just been spending more.

If you track one thing, track your actual profit each month. Make a simple chart, or use the one from Appendix 5. This will give you the best health check and a reality check as well.

Third Layer: Predictions, Trends, and Motivation

Is your profit growing? Are you business expenses going down? How many initial clients turn into regular ones? Going back to the physical health analogy, changes are important to doctors too. It's one thing if your weight is 162 this month. But what if it last month it was 145? Changes in weight, blood pressure, or blood sugar can point to issues or trends.

Watching the changes of your business helps you in the same way. It can tell you if you're on a healthy or unhealthy path and how fast you're traveling. This helps you to know if you should carry on or make a course correction. It's the best way to make predictions and bigger decisions.

Here's an example. One client was encouraged to see her monthly online sales going up until she noticed that her COGS were going up as well. So, her actual profit was staying the same. She needed to work on getting those COGS down, and she did (by buying in bulk and switching suppliers).

Here's another example. A client felt great—he was working a lot and getting some nice big checks. He was charging $75 an hour, which was below industry standard, but he was happy to be working. Then, we did some math and realized that he was only pocketing $35 per actual hour worked. Also, he didn't have enough time for other important projects. Seeing the numbers helped him raise his rates and bid future projects more realistically.

After you've collected some basic numbers, find and track a few statistics that you care about. Some ideas are rate of growth, cost per hours worked, or advertising dollars per new customer. Most software programs can provide these for you.

Believe it or not, numbers are your friends. They tell you the truth and help you to make decisions. They help you to feel the success of all your work. They help you with motivation and goal setting, and give you the confidence to raise your prices when you realize how much you're actually earning.

In Summary—Numbers

You need to know your numbers to grow your numbers. You may find yourself asking, "How do I earn enough money?" To answer that question, you need to figure out:

- what you need to earn
- how to calculate your paycheck
- how to calculate profits and taxes.

This requires knowing how to find gross sales, total COGS, and deductions by category, including mileage.

To know what to charge, you need to know:

- how many hours per week you can be earning
- how many weeks a year you'll be working.

In order to have the numbers required for tax reporting, you have to collect and track:

- proofs of sale
- receipts for COGS
- receipts for expenses
- mileage
- bank statements as a back up.

You also have to keep a record and come up with totals, whether by paper and calculator, spreadsheet, or software.

Doing this work helps you to be ready for taxes, and more importantly, it helps you to check the health of your business and meet your income goals.

Marketing

Things to review, choose, and do. Check when complete, or mark NA.

Foundation	Foundation, Marketing is Matchmaking
	Define Ideal Clients
	Determine the Problem / Pain of Clients
	Clarify Your Offering
	Define the Why of Your Work
	Create Your Story
Brand	Define Your Brand Personality
	Brand Elements
	Logo
	Collect and Post Reviews / Testimonials
Advertising Options	Define Advertising Pathways
	Tools for Word of Mouth
	Networking—Formal or Informal
	Social Media—Yes or No
	Newsletters / Group Emails
	Ways to Advertise
	Practice Elevator Speech
	Set up a Website
	About Domain Names
	Email Address
	Order Business Cards
	Make Gift Certificates
Putting It All Together	Marketing Snapshot

Introduction to Marketing

Sooner or later, you'll be asking yourself:

How do I find clients?

How you answer this question is up to you, and it is what marketing is all about. It looks different for each self-employed person and it can be simple or complicated, depending on a lot of things.

Generally speaking, marketing includes all the efforts you do to keep current clients and to get new clients. Marketing is the umbrella term. It's the system of making and managing these efforts. It includes branding and advertising as well as being excellent at what you do. (More on those later.)

Marketing is a lot like gardening. Sometimes people get lucky—they throw a few plants in the ground and they take off. More often though, creating a bountiful garden takes soil preparation, plant selection, cultivation and then later, regular watering, weeding and making adjustments.

In this chapter, we'll start with the groundwork—your central story and brand—and then work our way up. Your story is based on what you have to offer + who your ideal clients are + why you do this work. It is at the heart of your business and all your marketing efforts. Brand is about creating a quick impression that is appealing to your desired clients and is true about you. It helps to build your reputation. Once the soil is prepped, you can start thinking about how you want to advertise. What efforts will get the attention of your desired client? Once you know these, you can start developing the tools you'll need, such as business cards, a website, or a Yelp review page.

Although I present these steps in a specific order, the truth is you're likely to cycle and swirl between all of them. Sometimes making a tool, such as a business card or flyer, will help you to discover more about the brand you're trying to build.

Whatever order you work in, I invite you to capture your ideas and choices on one page. You might use the Marketing Snapshot on page 257 or make your own. It's important to feel that there's a limit to this work.

ProTip: Almost everybody needs a website, even if it's one page. In this day and age, websites are like the new storefront. They give a sense of legitimacy to your business offering. Building a website is a great project to start with, as the process will help you make choices about both the design and the business itself—rates, policies, schedule etc.

•

Developing your way of marketing is a process and will take some time. It will include soul-searching, making decisions and learning through trial and error. It's important, and also easy to put off. It's personal. It can be scary. It can also be really fun and rewarding. It's so pleasing to see a new flyer or business card that truly reflects your business. It's even more pleasing to have someone find you for the first time through your advertising.

Here are a few tips as you navigate through the process.

- Put time in your schedule for this important work! Now, and in the future—even established gardens need a little attention. As a general rule, I suggest 2 – 5 hours a week. In the beginning, it might be even more as you're developing your brand and advertising tools.
- Do some groundwork. I would submit that knowing your story is 80% of marketing. A lot of businesses skip this step and instead focus on making cut-and-paste ads or getting people to Like their Facebook page. Diving deep into the questions around your story is the only way to create marketing that is cohesive and effective. When it's authentic, the heart of the story will still ring through any imperfect speech or visuals. In addition, having a story and brand provides direction when making choices about marketing. It makes decisions go easier and faster.

- Pick a handful of advertising methods. There are unlimited options on how to market—especially now that we live in such a digital world! There's no way to do them all, and no reason to. When we start talking about advertising ideas and tools, select 3 – 5 methods to try. Put your efforts into those, and ignore the rest. After several months, reevaluate and adjust as needed.

- Most importantly, work with your natural style. Efforts will be effective when you feel comfortable. If you're a more shy person who likes to write, then blogging and commenting on social media might be better for you than attending conferences and networking. If you're outgoing, then speaking to baristas and friends constantly might do the trick. You're more likely to do the work if you enjoy it, and people will respond to you when you seem happy.

☞ Bottom Line: Take the time to define your story and your own way of marketing. Work on these efforts weekly.

Marketing Tools Work Better with a Strong Foundation

How do I find clients?

This question is the beginning of all marketing efforts. It is common for new businesses to start out with some word of mouth advertising, a website, and business cards. In addition, some create print materials or perhaps a Facebook page. These are all essentially tools of marketing. They are mechanisms that let others know your business exists. Many self-employed people struggle with building these marketing tools. And once built, questions arise. *Are these the right tools for the job? Are they the best ones? Should I use different ones?*

This is where having a good foundation for marketing comes into play. It can fill in the important ideas and parts behind marketing efforts—like a back story for a movie. Once you have a solid foundation, it's easier to make choices and build tools, and they usually work way better.

People often skip these steps because they don't know about them. They are invisible and behind the scenes. And yet, they have huge impact.

The next few sections will help you build the foundation of marketing for your business. You don't have to do it all at once, but it helps to do a little foundation work, and to just know that it exists...so you can circle back and keep working on it.

It starts with defining what you have to offer, the ideal client, and a central story that connects you both. Next is the brand or reputation you want to build. This reflects the style and values of your business and appeals to the clients you're looking for. Once you define the brand, you can then choose the elements that communicate this feeling.

On top of these efforts are the tools and advertising strategies you need.

This chapter will work from the ground up. (If you're ready to get started with advertising, you can skip to page 235.) You will get better plants with better soil. This view is to give you the concept of how the three work together.

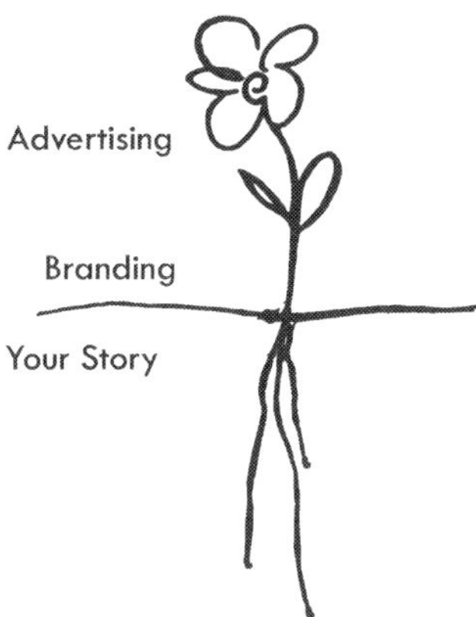

To get more guidance in building the layers, it helps to split each into two parts.

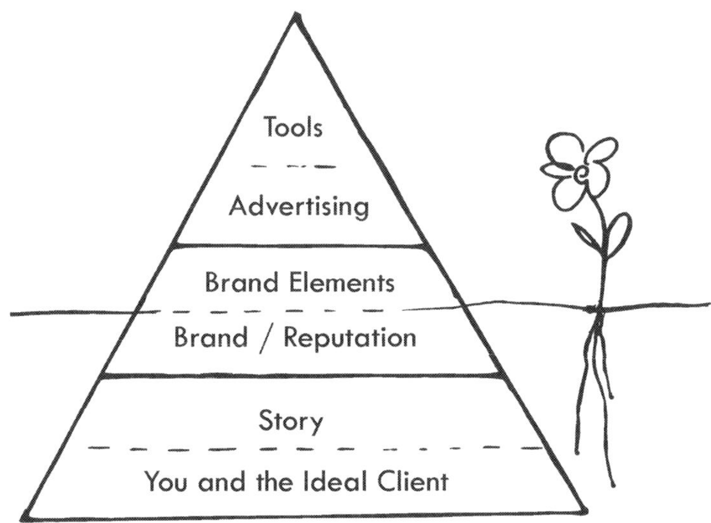

While you can build from the bottom up, you don't have to. Sometimes working on tools and advertising will actually teach you about the brand. As you make choices thinking about you and your ideal client, the brand starts to emerge. Once you've got it, it clarifies further choices.

Marketing is Matchmaking

I like to say that marketing is matchmaking. It connect two parties who are looking for each other.

This idea guides you through building your marketing strategies, brand, advertising and tools. It gives the basic foundation. The more you can understand the parties involved, the more effective your approaches will be. With every choice, ask yourself, *Does this reflect me?* And, *Will my ideal client like this?*

Your first job is to really understand yourself: precisely what service or product you're offering, why you're doing this work, what makes you special, and your style.

Next, define your ideal client. What are they like? What do they need? Where are they? What will catch their eye? Once we know more about them, we can choose marketing approaches that will find them, and appeal to them.

Without clarifying your ideal client, you're marketing blindly. Although businesses can sometimes get lucky, it usually leads to finding customers you don't want or efforts that flop.

The clearer you are about yourself and your ideal client, the better the match. When done right, the result is a love story. You'll feel lucky to have your clients, and they'll feel lucky to have found you!

We'll explore both you and your ideal clients within the context of telling your story.

What's Your Story?

What is the work you are doing? + Why are you doing it?

Your first marketing task is to create a simple story about your work that answers those two questions—for yourself, your friends and family, and for your potential clients. The beginning of this chapter will help you with this task. We'll put it all together on page 246 in your Elevator Speech.

Knowing your story will help you in a variety of ways. It gives clarity and direction for your venture, and it affects your self-perception, which is important and strongly affects your attitude and approach to daily life.

This story helps friends and family understand what you're doing. If you're confident and can explain your new path, they're less likely to doubt and critique.

Most importantly, this story is how you'll find the customers that you want. It helps you and others talk about you and your work, which is essential for getting more business, and it'll inform any marketing materials.

The more you can tell a story, rather than reciting a list of facts, the better. A story has a beginning and end and a change of some type. If it includes any values, ideals, or movements, it helps connect your work to something greater.

Compare these examples:

I'm a massage therapist, with a specialty in ATMAT®.

(Not bad, kind of boring. An inquisitive person might ask more.)

I work in the healing arts. I love my clients and also the flexibility of my schedule. It allows me to attend more classes and travel more.

(This one is all about the speaker. Only personal friends would want to know more.)

I love my job. My specialty is Pelvic Bowl Well-Being, especially for women, the LGBTQ+ community, and their families. People don't always think about the abdomen and pelvic bowl, but that's truly the root of the body. Everyday stresses, life changes, and traumas affect our organs in profound ways, which leads to all kinds of symptoms. I offer ATMAT® and other therapies which bring relief and vitality to the whole person.

(Much better—It's more interesting, and it describes the services in more details as well as the desired clients and what they need.)

A short story with a punch can be hard to craft sometimes. First, we need to come up with all the elements that need to be in there, and then we need to pare them down and put them in order. The ideas and exercises on the next few pages will help you to do just that. The Elevator Speech exercise on page 246 will help you put it all together.

Pro Tip: Writing things down in this book or a journal will open up more thinking and insights. I invite you to find a pen or pencil right now.

Before we dive in, let's warm up with answering the two questions from above:

What is the work you're doing? Who is it for?

Why are you doing this work? Why is this important for you and for your clients?

Who Are Your Ideal Clients?

Who are the people you want to work with? Thinking deeply about who they are will help you figure out what they need, where to find them, and what language and design will get their attention. It will also help you decide when to accept work, and when to politely decline.

It's hard to describe an imaginary group. To help you out, work through the following exercise.

Create three ideal clients that you would love to work with or to sell products to. Sometimes these are called avatars. Choose them so that they represent different types of clients/buyers. Really think them through; flesh them out. Name them, describe them, build a picture of them in your head.

For each one, fill out the following:

For Individuals:

- Name
- Age
- Religion/politics
- Where they live
- How they dress
- Family
- Career
- Aspirations
- Hobbies
- Everything you can think of!

For Companies/Organizations:

- Name
- Size
- Services/Products
- Location
- Design/Look/Brand
- Who they work with
- Company values/causes
- How long in business
- Community connections

Use the workspace on the next page to bring your ideal clients to life. Afterwards, we'll make some observations.

Name: ....

Description:

Name: ....

Description:

Name: ....

Description:

Observations

Now, look at your three clients. Let's make some observations:

What do they have in common?

Where do they hang out?

What do they like?

What do they need that they're not able to get?

What ideas, images, and values do they have in common with you and your business?

Use this knowledge to help you when choosing words and tone in your marketing materials, such as colors, design, and imagery. Think about them by name. For example, *Would this make sense to Sally, the Florist in Ballard?*

Continue to refine these three imaginary clients. Carry them with you as guides.

The Problem / Pain

Guy Kawasaki, business author, talks about the *pain* of the customer or client. The more you can understand and articulate this pain, the more you can meet their needs, and the better you can get people to understand your work. In my experience, this concept gives the most guidance in marketing.

I like the word *pain* because it is evocative. It speaks to a need that hurts a little. This makes your service or offering the antidote. This gives your work real purpose. It also provides a reality check. If you can't figure out a pain, then you might need to rethink your services.

Sometimes you can refer to the pain in your advertising. This is a common technique that you've likely seen before. "Winter blues got you down?" Or remember from the '80s: "It's 4:00pm. What am I going to cook for dinner?"

You can describe your services in light of solving the pain. *Therapeutic massage for injury recovery—so you can feel relief and prevent further injury...and get back to your active life.*

Sometimes the pain of the customer is hidden or private. They think they want one thing, but they want something else too. It could be a pain that's darker, like embarrassment or guilt, or, it could be related to a secret desire. Referring to this hidden pain directly will not work. In this case, the customer is too vulnerable. However, identifying it for yourself can help you immensely—you can figure out what outer needs relate to this inner pain and attend to those.

For example, I sometimes run a flyer that says, *Need help with taxes? Shoeboxes and crumpled receipts are all welcome.* My thinking is this—many people are sheepish and embarrassed when they haven't done any tax prep. I want to help those people feel better with their taxes. To that end, I'm trying to normalize their experience and show acceptance. Identifying the deeper pain helps me both with advertising and being ready for any emotions that come up in work sessions.

Knowing the pain really helps when I'm talking about my work with folks. I've found that when I can describe in detail the pain and needs of my clients, the listener never even asks for my credentials or background! It's as if this understanding is all the credential that I need. Having said that, it follows that I can likely solve these pains because I have identified them.

Compare:

I help self-employed people. There are a lot of pressures on these folks.

Many listeners would be done at this point. They might ask me about the pressures though.

I help people who are self-employed. They have some unique challenges. They have to wear a lot of different hats: taxes, licenses, marketing, bookkeeping, paperwork, organizing and more. This can be challenging and lonely. When they try to get help, many of the books and online resources are very confusing. The worst part is, if the business side starts to fail, then their dream fails.... This is where I come in.

Usually, at this point, the listener is asking for my business card or web-site address.

Think about your ideal clients. What is the pain that they feel? If it's not obvious, keep thinking. There's one there. (Or, if there isn't one, you may need to rethink your service or product!)

How you describe the problem or pain of your ideal clients?

Get Clear About What You Have to Offer

It's essential for you to be able to describe what you have to offer, both verbally and in writing. This is the only way for you to get work! (Even if you hire someone to do your marketing, you will have to provide them with the description of what you're selling.)

Many self-employed people feel shy to talk about themselves. This is understandable. So let's make a shift and say, we're figuring out how to talk about your work. In order for potential customers to hire you, they need to know what they're getting. This includes both what your services or products include, as well as what makes them special.

The more clear and interesting the description, the more you serve your clients and help yourself. You will get people's attention, educate them to make the best choices for themselves, stick in their minds for the future, and enable them to talk about you to others.

What if you saw a sandwich board that said, "Massage Services". It would probably pass right through your brain. There's no reason to take notice. Even if you were looking for a new massage therapist, you might not remember it. Vague descriptions get vague results.

Compare "Massage Services" to: "Nurturing Therapeutic Massage for Injury Recovery. All treatments include hot stones. "

This is more likely to get your attention. If it applies to you, you'll remember it. If it doesn't apply to you, you still might think, *I need to remember that for so-and-so.*

It works the same in conversation. Imagine my client Sandy at a party. If someone asked her, "What do you do?" And she said, "I'm a designer," that might be the end of it. Instead, she might say, "I do graphic design for local businesses. My specialty is packaging that has surprising little touches."

It's not bragging or "selling yourself" to describe what you have to offer. It's the truth, and it helps your potential customer to make the best choice.

Use the questions below to clarify these ideas for your business.

What are your services or products, in general?

What are some details or special features?
(For example, "all organic ingredients" or "sterling silver".)

How would you describe your style?

What is unique about your offering?

What are some of your ideals or values? Is your work part of a bigger cause?

Why Are You Doing This Work?

How does your work contribute to the world? How does it make the world a better place? If you know the answer to this question, this sense of purpose will give you extra energy and drive. Additionally, it will help others cheer for your efforts, and give them a reason to hire you.

Usually, making the world a better place means you're helping with a need or problem. What's the problem that you're solving or pain that you're relieving? It's important to understand this for yourself and to be able to articulate it for others...even if it feels kind of dramatic.

Consider how these roles make the world a better place.

Screenwriters: People need entertainment and information. The modern day world is stressful; it's full of working and driving and thinking about work. Getting a mental break and laughing or learning helps to balance things out. Humans have always shared stories. It's in our nature. Screenwriters help people to get a break, feel better and stay mentally well.

Massage Therapists: You know what you do! Everyone could use massage—whether it's to relieve stress, manage pain, deal with an injury, or boost the immune system. Healthier people function better.

Beekeepers: The bee population is dwindling. We need bees to keep making food! Beekeepers are literally helping to save the human race by making sure enough food is produced.

Jewelry Artists: Handmade jewelry helps us to feel special. When you put a piece of special jewelry on, you feel enjoyment that takes you through the day. Beautiful jewelry invites conversation and connection. It is also one antidote to a throwaway society. Jewelry artists make pieces that last, can be keepsakes and are handed down through generations.

Your turn!

What are your reasons for doing your work?

Why do you like it?

How does your work make the world a better place?

Your Story

Now it's time to put your story together. It is some combination of the ideas we've been exploring, and it is the foundation for your marketing as well as your business.

First, capture a few thoughts under each section. Then, try stringing them together in various combinations. You might try talking it through with a friend or writing it out a few times. Aim for two to five sentences in length.

What you do:

Who you serve, what they need:

How you're different:

Why you're good at it/why you like it:

Now, try putting it all together:

Your Brand, Part One: Personality

Once you know who your desired clients are and what you want to say to them, it's time to answer these questions:

> How do I get their attention?
> How do I quickly communicate my message?

If we're using the matchmaking analogy, this would be similar to, "How do I make myself look attractive to my date in a way that reflects me and what I value?" For a woman who's very outdoorsy, a red dress, heavy make-up and heels might not be the answer for making the first impression. And neither is a downtown bar. A better solution might be for her to go to an event at the Mountaineers Club, wearing a favorite hiking skirt with her hair up in a ponytail.

Attracting others involves giving a very quick impression that makes others want to know more. Usually, it involves some combination of words, visuals, context, and experience. It's an impression that establishes a mood, feeling, or expression of value that creates chemistry. The recipient feels understood, validated, and curious. And they are excited to create a connection with you.

That's what a brand essentially is. It's the style or personality of your business, chosen carefully to represent your values and story. A clear brand attracts the clients you want and sorts out the ones that you don't.

For self-employed people, this brand reflects both your business and you as a person. It only works when it's always true. So it's good to take some time with this and to be really honest with yourself. Anything you include must be true about you all the time, without extra effort. For example, if you value promptness and are always, *always* on time, you can include this in your brand. *Deadlines met, 100% of the time.* If you value being on time and usually are, but sometimes you're late, this could backfire on you.

In my case, I considered having *energy* as part of my brand. People tell me I'm energetic and that they appreciate my enthusiasm. However, I realized, even though this is usually true, it's not always true. Once in a while, I'm in a more contemplative mood. I'm still engaged with my work, but not as energetic. Furthermore, some clients don't need outside energy. Some are so energetic themselves that they actually need a calming agent to balance them out.

This brings us to our next point. Your brand works best when it answers the need of every client. In that case, I chose to make *individualist* the leading attribute of my brand. I also think of it as quirky or unique. I'm always this way. I don't have to try, it's just true. And it meets the needs of my clients. They are people who want to do things their way, and that's my promise.

Developing a brand takes some time and effort, and it can sometimes feel messy. I liken it to making whiskey. You throw a whole bunch of grains in water. It sits and bubbles, looks messy and probably tastes terrible. After a time, you strain it and then run it through the still. The water is cooked out, and the liquid is condensed and drips down the spout into a jar. It's transferred to a cask where it sits and matures for a smooth, beautiful result. Branding is like this. It includes a lot of self-reflection, brainstorming, trial and error, then waiting, and finally narrowing ideas.

The work is worth it, and it will get better with time.

For now, you can get started with thinking in terms of style or personality. It's what makes you stand out from the crowd and relates to the clients you want. You've already started the process by creating your story. The next step is to pick one or two top attributes or promises.

Ideas for brand personality: Part of your style
Related to a value or movement
Unique part of your service or products
A specific ideal client you're hoping for

Some examples of brand personalities—

Roxie, How-To Hair Girl—

Website with blog and online store, offering hair how-tos, natural products, inspirational photos

Leading Attributes: Radical beauty

Feeling: natural, DIY, empowerment, freedom

Charles, Seattle Qwik Tour with the Chuckster—

90-minute city tours of Seattle

Leading Attribute: Entertainment in the form of a tour

Feeling: Tongue-in-cheek, funny, classy, informative, lively

Sadie, Sadie Accounts—

Bookkeeping services for nonprofits, schools, and wellness businesses in Downtown Seattle

Leading Attributes: Always complete, always cheerful

Feeling: Professional, thorough, smiley, easy to work with, local

Heidi, Root Down Healing Arts—

Pelvic Bowl Well-Being with ATMAT® and Other Therapies, for women, the LGBTQ+ community and their families

Leading Promise: Untwist and be

Feeling: Ancient wisdoms, skillful and intuitive healing, accepting of every body

Jeff, 320 Sycamore Studios—

Quality read aloud stories for kids and their caregivers

Leading Promise: Tonight at bedtime, read your kid something with daring

Feeling: Silly, clever, connection, stories

Your Brand Part Two: Building Your Reputation

Another way to think of having a brand is to think of building a reputation. What do you want to be known for? How do you want people to talk about you?

Hopefully, your service or product will be so great, that clients will naturally want to talk about you. However, without any direction, they are likely to say different great things about you. This won't build much of a reputation.

A reputation builds when the story about you is the same, and your name becomes associated with something that the client wants. For example, two different people told me about the same accountant, "She's very friendly and good at explaining things." I was all ready to hire this accountant before even meeting her!

A strong reputation sticks in the brain and gives you a head start on earning trust with potential clients.

A reputation builds when the message is true, concise, sets you apart, and meets a need.

To build a reputation, you need to get clear on what you want it to be, and then be consistent in your materials. When I looked on this particular accountant's website, she was smiling warmly in her pictures.

Doing brand work means taking control of your reputation, so that it is focused on what you want. In this light, it is really very exciting, as you're working to make clear what you value the most.

Elements of Your Brand

Once you know the personality of your brand, use it to guide you with building your marketing tools. Language, design, and even policies need to illustrate the feeling or mood you're trying to create. Here are some elements to think about. Once you decide on these, I suggest putting all your choices into a document for you to reference, or to share with a designer if you hire one.

Colors

Colors have a strong effect on us. Many come with associations or symbolism, such as green for go and red for stop. Others actually activate our brain. Orange gets people thinking, and blue or green can be calming.

Color combinations do the same. Yellow and black mean caution. Red and green symbolize Christmas.

Sometimes you'll intuit the colors that fit your brand. If not, you can either read about color theory, or, you can collect a whole bunch of designs you like, and notice which colors are present.

Record color ideas here:

Fonts

Fonts have personality. They communicate a lot, even though most people don't realize it. It's nice to pick two or three fonts that you like and use them in all your materials. This will give your materials a consistent look. Check out fontsquirrel.com to get ideas.

Record font ideas here:

Imagery

Imagery includes photos, symbols, illustrations, and design elements such as borders. They also include your logo. Read more on that in the following section.

Choose images that create the mood or feeling that you want. Find images you like, and see if there's a connection to the brand you're building.

For example, Heidi uses botanical illustrations in all of her print materials and on her website. These images are calming, medicinal, and historic—a great way to set the tone for her mix of healing arts which include bodywork, ATMAT®, and herbal remedies.

Record imagery ideas here:

Words

Be thoughtful toward your clients and brand when choosing words. There are many ways to say the same thing, each with different connotations and tone. Select words that appeal to your clients.

Additionally, identify words and phrases that describe what you do which will get the attention of your clients. Make a list of these. Pick a few of them and use them regularly in all of your materials.

Record important words and phrases here:

Special touches

Special touches can be policies, little surprises, gifts…anything you want to include in your services that fit you, your brand, and serve your client.

For example, Nikki Jacoby makes jewelry to last a lifetime. They are treasured pieces to be enjoyed and passed down. When I purchased from her last, they came in a sweet little drawstring bag, stamped with one of her designs.

Record ideas here:

Logo

A logo is a symbol associated with your business. It is a great way to illustrate your brand. It can be a picture, a design motif, an icon, or letters designed in a unique way. Having a great logo is wonderful, but not necessary. If you have the time or can afford a designer, go for it!

If you're struggling to make a decision, or don't have a lot of funds right now, don't worry. You can still get started on your marketing materials. Remember, you can change your logo later.

Here are some ideas for a starter logo:

☞ **Cool Font:** Do your trade name in a cool font. Maybe in a signature color too. You can find free downloadable fonts on websites such as fontsquirrel.com.

☞ **Initials:** Use your trade name initials in a larger size, in a cool font. Maybe with a dot or symbol between, maybe not.

☞ **Logo Contest:** Use www.designcrowd.com. You share what you need, and designers submit designs. You pay a fee to the winner.

☞ **Use Online Logo Makers:** Try tailorbrands.com. After answering a few questions, they present different logos to you within minutes. You can make adjustments and then purchase. They are surprisingly affordable.

☞ **Find a Designer on Etsy:** Go to www.etsy.com and search for logo design. Look at their profiles, examples and prices. Some are quite affordable.

AmyLeah and Catherine are a mom and daughter shop who make fun jewelry and textiles. They purchased a custom logo with hand lettering for $200 on Etsy. It was beautiful and fit their style perfectly.

If you're not sure what you like, or what look to go with, that's okay too. Give yourself some time to figure it out. Set out a basket, a bulletin board stocked with tacks, or a board on Pinterest. Start collecting anything that you like the look of—wrapping papers, ribbons, pictures of furniture, logos, fonts, cards, book covers, anything. It doesn't have to be business related. Just collect, and collect…anything that makes you happy.

After some time, you can look at the pile and notice some things. What colors keep popping up? How about images or themes? How would you characterize what you tend to choose?

If you hire a designer, take the images to show them. If you're going to design the logo, use this imagery to inform your work. After you have some ideas, ask yourself, the following: which logos would appeal to your ideal customer? Which help convey the story that you're trying to tell about your business?

Testimonials and Reviews

Do you find it hard to talk about your work—and how you're great at it? Invite others to do it for you! You can start collecting testimonials and reviews at any time.

In this day and age, many people need social proof. They might be reading your website and thinking, *Wow, she sounds great, but can I trust her? Is she sharing the truth?* This is where testimonials and reviews come into play.

The term *review* is usually used when a customer leaves comments or ratings on a third-party site such as Yelp, Amazon, or GooglePlus. *Testimonial* generally refers to a statement that the happy customer gives to you, so you can use it on your website, on a flyer, or in a brochure.

Help your clients help you. Ask for these in the form of an email and provide links (if applicable) and give some prompts to make it easier for them to write about you...and guidance so that their comments fit your brand. For example, let's say a client has agreed to write a testimonial for you. You might say, "Wow, thank you! I'm hoping to get a statement from two to six sentences. My goals with our work were...[give four to six goals]. If I met any of those, can you please speak to them."

For a review, you might send a follow-up email with a link to the reviewer's site. "Your happiness is my goal! I hope that you are 100% happy with your product and that shipping was very fast. If so, would you be willing to share your experience on Amazon? Click here."

It also helps to ask clients to speak to a change in their lives from your service or product. In which case, you might ask, "What led you to find me in the first place? After our work, what was different for you?"

In addition to bolstering your cache online and in print materials, having testimonials and reviews will help you with talking to people about your work. You can say things like, "One client told me that our work..."

Advertising: Find the Pathway to Your Ideal Clients, Then Build the Tools

Where are your customers? What is the best way to find them? Once you find them, what do they need from you in order to hire you? It's important to think through these questions first, and then build the tools you need to do this well.

So many new businesses get this backward. They build the tools, but they don't know how to use them. Business cards don't do much if you're not talking to people and handing them out. Websites just sit quietly if you're not directing traffic to them. Take time to think through the pathway of attracting and acquiring new ideal clients.

1 They need to see or hear about you in some way. What is the best way to get their attention—is it a bulletin board, online search, or referral?

2 For that route, what tool is needed? For bulletin boards, it could be flyers, coupons, or business cards. Online searches use Google AdWords or links from other related sites. For a referral, it could be a link, a verbal statement, or maybe a brochure that tells about you.

3 Refine. How can this tool get the desired client's attention? Perhaps you can add some pizzazz—some great design or something noteworthy—or maybe a promotion or discount.

4 Be memorable and make a connection. You've got the client's attention, how can you get them to remember you and/or decide to hire you? Direct them to your website, online reviews, or a Facebook page, or perhaps offer a free consult or incentive.

Build tools to fit the pathway that makes sense for you and your potential clients.

Word of Mouth

Word of mouth means that people are talking about you—whether it's friends and family or happy clients sharing their story—and this talk is leading to more business for you. It's the dreamiest of all paths because others are doing your marketing, it's a compliment to you, and it's free or very inexpensive.

Word of mouth goes much, much further when you help people talk about you—by giving them both invisible and tangible tools.

First, let's review that, for good word of mouth, you need to provide excellent, remarkable service or products. The word *remarkable* means that there's something worth making a remark about.

Next, help your clients know what to say about you. This is where your brand description comes in. Have you ever experienced really great service, and you want to share it, but you don't know what to say? This has definitely happened to me. I really loved my first dentist. People would ask why, and I wasn't sure. "I don't know, he's just great, and you should try him." This wasn't specific enough to make a memorable impression.

Give your clients the words or ideas. If this is already in your marketing materials, it will be easier. They might pick it up by osmosis. And/or, you can also share verbally what you're trying to do or what you're looking for. You might say, "I have room in my schedule for a few more clients. If you know anyone who's dealing with low back pain, send them my way! Most people feel relief after one or two sessions."

Perhaps give an incentive. You might offer a referral bonus, or two-for-one deals for a client and a friend.

Provide some tools. Give people business cards, postcards, or brochures to spread the word about you. Perhaps there's a small item to give away that invites conversation. For example, a soap maker could make little sample-sized soaps and ask clients to hand them out to see if people like them.

Networking

"Networking" sounds fun to some folks and strikes fear in the heart of others, and with good reason! The word usually brings up the image of people in a basement, wearing nametags, shaking hands and having to introduce themselves with their 'elevator pitch'. Ugh. Good news! There are so many ways to network these days! There's something to suit everybody's style. Networking can range from casual and organic to structured and formal. And while you don't have to embrace networking, it's worth looking into. It can be both very effective and quite fun!

Networking is simply making connections with other folks that may lead to business or support in either direction. It works when it's authentic and can happen when you least expect it. It's common to be talking with a neighbor, family member, or barista, and suddenly they say something like, "I should put you in touch with my friend. She's been looking for a photographer to refer people to."

Formalized networking includes joining a referral group. They can be tightly or loosely structured. Fee structures and membership requirements vary greatly. One popular choice in Seattle is Business Networking International (BNI). It is an example of a more structured group—each chapter holds a weekly meeting, with an attendance requirement. Building business through referrals is a major focus. The Greater Seattle Business Association (GSBA) offers a different experience. As a member, you have access to a variety of events and are listed in the directory, among other benefits. The GSBA is an example of a group with a social mission—advocacy and business support for the LGBTQ+ community and allies.

Semi-formal versions of networking involve finding ways to be around other self-employed folks that support community and connection. Here are three ideas:

1) Join a co-working space. This gives you a chance to work around others, slowly getting to know them. Many offer programming and events,

which offers a natural way to be around others. The Riveter is designed for women, and even offers meditation rooms, yoga classes, a kitchen and more. Both locations are modern, bright, and gorgeous. The Inc.: Coworking and Playspace serves parents and children in one handy location. You have the option to work alongside your child, in one of the playrooms equipped with desks. Or, if want to work kid-free, you can drop your child off at daycare or preschool, and use one of the adult-only office areas.

2) Join a community or meet-up group. One I attended recently is called the F Bomb Breakfast Club. It was super fun! It's created for women who are ready to be real (including dropping F bombs), to connect, dream, laugh, and offer support. The club meets once a month at breakfast time in Pioneer Square, and it hosts Facebook discussions throughout the week.

3) Take business classes or attend events, where you likely have things in common with the other attendees. Last year, I was thrilled to go to Camp Thundercraft on Vashon Island! It's put on by the Urban Craft Uprising folks. It was easy to connect with other self-employed people and small business owners over meals, attending classes, and doing fun activities.

Another great option is networking online. This can include building LinkedIn connections; commenting on other websites, Facebook pages, Twitter or Forums; linking to websites and asking for links back to your page; or joining online webinars or discussion groups.

Do what works for you! It's best when you enjoy what you're doing.

Keep in mind, that part of building a network means you can reach out to people when you need some help. Maybe you need some information, advice, or a referral for a support person. These kinds of requests are natural and build your relationships. In this way, finding clients through networking is often the secondary goal.

Social Media

Social media is a choice; it's not a requirement. If you like social media and already use it, it can be a great option for you. If it sounds like a big chore, then it will be. Using social media works best when you engage with it naturally, regularly, and with joy.

There are lots of options. Here's a list of the most commonly utilized.

Facebook is best for maintaining relationships with customers.

Use Facebook if you plan to post daily or at least weekly. (If you set up a page and never update it, it feels dead...you might as well add cartoon tumbleweeds to roll across it.) It's a great way to remind clients that you're there for them and to develop your connections and customer loyalty. This might be through quotes, information, helpful resources, or fun pictures. Sometimes, these connections can turn into new clients. If your followers feel engaged with you, they might share your posts.

Instagram is all about pictures and building your brand.

This is a great way to develop the awareness of your brand—since pictures set a mood and tone—and perhaps get people to your website. If people like what they see, they will follow you and perhaps make their way to your website to learn more. This works best if you have remarkable photos and you're clear about the mood and feeling that you want to build.

LinkedIn is a great way to build credibility and/or your professional network.

Many consumers go to LinkedIn to see if a seller or service provider is legit, since resumes and work backgrounds are often posted. LinkedIn also offers a way to build connections to other professionals. One client regularly posts articles and inspirational quotes as a way to show that she is approachable. She will also reach out to invite people to coffee, either to connect as referrers or for informational interviews.

Twitter is for staying in the loop and connected...by sharing and reading quick, concise messages.

Twitter helps to build relationships in a different way than Facebook. Usually people follow or make posts related to an area of interest, whether it's a topic or a person. This visibility helps to build familiarity and, therefore, credibility. You can also use Twitter to direct people to your website.

•

If you decide to use social media, be sure to have a plan and to dedicate time for this work. You might consider hiring a consultant, looking at a book, or interviewing someone who's very good at this type of marketing.

Group Emails and Newsletters

It is very handy to get in touch with all your clients from time to time. You can either use group emails or newsletters to do this. The frequency and formatting are up to you and will depend on the purpose. Some of my clients send a group email once a year as a holiday message combined with updates for the coming year. Other clients send out a regular newsletter once a month or even once a week.

In general, there are three major purposes:

- Client relationships and retention. Messages and newsletters remind clients that you're there. You can offer value and support through providing inspiration, educational content, tips, resources, and/or personal sharing.

- Marketing to your clients and to others via your clients with special offers, such as: new bonuses, special deals, discounts, promotions, and invitations to events. Clients can forward this sharable content to others.

- Updates on nitty gritty stuff like prices, policies, vacations, changes in locations, schedules, etc. Even these updates act as a marketing effort as you're getting the attention of clients for a moment.

Group Emails

Often, we think of group emails when the messages go out less often. They are usually for a specific purpose and for smaller groups. They are a bit less formal.

- Be sure to use the BCC to protect client privacy

- Make these easy to read. Put spaces between sections, use clear headings and possibly different colors.

Newsletters

Consider using the newsletter format when you plan to send out regular messages and your main goals are related to marketing. You may send these as a group email, though it's more common to use a newsletter program in order to create more visual interest and use extra features, such as videos, graphics, and links.

- The gold standard is MailChimp, at www.mailchimp.com. There are other options, of course.
- You need to get your clients' permission to add addresses to a newsletter list. With most programs, you can do this via a sign-up spot on your website that links to your account, giving permission through email, having people sign up on a paper list, or by including a permission question on your intake forms.
- Newsletter programs take some investment. You need to create some standardized messages, such as the welcome message and unsubscribe message. It also takes a little time to set up the visual look and to choose your formatting options.
- Test out your messages with some volunteers.

Tips for Both Group Emails and Newsletters

- If you plan to do a regular newsletter, set a schedule and stick to it.
- Send out in the morning when people are most likely to be checking email.
- The message and format needs to match your brand. If your brand is funny, be sure to include jokes every time. If it's inspirational or empowering, include quotes. If educational, add links or resources. Be sure to choose fonts, colors, and graphics that match the mood of your brand, too.

- Add personal element(s) to build a sense of connection. Share favorite things, such as pictures from trips, or current things you're reading or especially enjoying. This helps to build your relationships with clients.

Some Other Ways to Advertise

Here are some additional ways to advertise. There are many more options, these are the most common for self-employed folks.

☞ Make flyers for bulletin boards around town. Perhaps add a QR code (the black and white square) with your web address. To get the most out of flyers, you need to put them up regularly—perhaps once a month. (One place to get a QR code is www.qrstuff.com.)

☞ Write letters to potential partners or referrers in the area. Introduce yourself and include a menu of services or price list and business card. Perhaps invite the person out for tea or coffee to see if you're a referral match.

☞ Make donations to auctions for local charities or schools. In addition to the offering, include a mini-poster to add to the display and something that people can take away with them, such as business cards, book-marks, or any little token.

☞ Use Google Adwords. You only pay when people click on your ad, and you can set a limit.

☞ Make videos to put on YouTube. These can be how-tos, walkthroughs, or behind-the-scenes looks. I know of one local artist who makes wooden rings. He posted a 3-minute video showing his process. This sent people to his website, and, it earned some advertising dollars!

☞ Walk into stores with some of your products and ask if they want to sell them. JaLynn, a friend of mine, made some fun cards using photos of her new puppy, Scout. She walked into local gift stores in Ballard, and two of them made an order.

☞ Make a sandwich board with a chalkboard area. Set it out near the road or a busy sidewalk. Post quotes, tidbits, and any discount offerings. Change what it says every day or two.

What other ideas do you have?

Elevator Speech or Barista Speech

An elevator or barista speech (as I like to call it) is basically a very short version of your story. The best elevator speeches respond to the person in the moment. They sound sincere and natural. They are suited for the audience. So, instead of memorizing a speech, develop the parts and practice putting them together in different ways. Please remember, it's likely to feel awkward with friends, but it usually feels more natural with strangers. I like to call it the barista speech since this is where the opportunity comes up for many of us. When done right, it will invite conversation.

Tell what you do + one special thing

For what you do, include one or two of the following:

- your services
- who you serve, what they need
- a specific niche.

One special thing can be one or two of the following:

- how you're different
- why you're good at it/why you like it
- a specialty focus
- how you're making the world a better place.

Here's a good way to try this out. Write one or more answers to each of the prompts above on an index card, and put them into two piles: what you do and one special thing. Draw a card from each, and practice making a statement that includes them both.

Pro Tip: Use phrases that invite more questions from people.

Examples: *I'm sort of like a consultant.* Or, *I do whatever they need to move forward.* The words "sort of" and "whatever" make people wonder what you mean and ask to know more.

Here are some examples:

I help self-employed women with the business side, so they have more time for the work they love.

I specialize in family photography where people actually look like they're having fun and enjoying each other.

I make jewelry that will last a lifetime, and will hopefully get handed down through the generations.

The more you practice, the easier it will get. Give yourself room to get it wrong sometimes. Tell yourself that you need to practice it fifty times before you can judge yourself. Try all kinds of different ways and see what works.

Websites

Websites are the new storefront. People trust that you're a legitimate business when you have one. (Conversely, no one seems to believe that you're really in business unless you have a website!) They are both the storefront and the welcome mat that invites potential customers to "come in and look around" to see what you have to offer.

If you're not ready to build a whole website, I suggest that you at least start with a landing page. Include your business name, your name, your services, and contact information. Maybe add: *Website coming soon!*

There are lots of great website builders out there. Many have templates set up for specific professions, so the layout matches the services usually provided.

Many website builders offer free hosting. Be aware that the free plans usually include advertising for the host and are limited with pages and functionality. Many people eventually upgrade to get what they need.

Of the many website builder options, here are two to look at:

Squarespace: This is my hands-down favorite. By default, Squarespace sites have a design-y, classy look. They cost about $12 - $16 a month for a starter site, and include 24-hour help via email. For online stores, pricing starts at $26 a month. They are set up for pictures and automatically adjust the sizes for devices. I love that they have only 20 or so templates to choose from. You can import fonts.

Weebly: This website builder has lovely templates and various pricing structures. There are a few hundred templates to choose from, which can be a danger for some personalities.

There are a lot of other providers. You can put *web builder* into search to see more. Just be careful...it's easy to get lost down the rabbit hole of looking and comparing. One idea is to give yourself a time limit—maybe sixty to ninety minutes to peruse. Then pick one and start.

If you're looking at other web builders, check for these things: Can you change the theme or template after building your site? (Wix does NOT allow you to change.) Does it resize picture and layout for different devices? Will it put advertising on your site? Is support provided?

I encourage you to try building your own site. Below are some reasons.

- Filling out your website forces you to think through the business, and make some commitments. When you create your services or products page, you have to decide on prices. As you pick the theme or template, you think about the mood and who your clients or consumers are. Just follow your instincts in the beginning. You can refine the site later. *Do I like it? Will my ideal clients like it?*

- Everyone I know goes through several revisions before getting it right! If you're paying a designer, this can cost you a lot of money. Learning to do this yourself allows you to make changes as often as you want.

- Websites are also a great way to try things on for size! Put up taglines, prices, and policies, and see how they look. You get a chance to try them on like trying on various outfits in front of a mirror. You can change the wording, images, and colors until they look right to you. Remember too, in the beginning, no one knows you're there. So play with it.

For a starter website, I suggest the following pages. If you feel stuck, find a friend who's good with words or computers to work with you.

1 Welcome or Home

2 Services or Products

3 FAQs

4 Testimonials

5 About or My Story

6 Contact

Domain Name

Your domain name is your web address, also known as your URL. Once you find one that you want, you have to register that domain and pay for it. This is a separate step from building your website.

There are two ways to get a domain name:

1 Register the domain name with your website host.

Example: You sign up with Squarespace to build your website. You pay an extra fee to register your domain through them.

OR

2 Use a separate company for registering your domain name.

Note: You will then need to point it to your website.

Personally, I like to keep my website and domain name registry separate. That way if I change web hosts, my domain registration isn't disrupted. My current favorite is namecheap.com for registering domain names. However, there are many other options. Search for "register domain name" to see more.

ProTip: You can point different domain names to the same website. Currently, both of these addresses will get you to my site: jennymacleod.com and jennygirlfriday.com.

ProTip: You can change your domain name later.

How to Research Domain Names and Register with a Separate Company (if Applicable)

Selecting and registering your domain name is such a fun step! Follow these steps to research available names, minus the checkout step, of course.

1. Go to a domain registration site such as namecheap.com or iwantmyname.com.
2. Put the name you want into the search bar.
3. Within seconds, they'll tell you if it's available and how much it costs. They will also offer variations with different endings, such as .net and .me. If the domain name you want is not available, they will offer alternatives.
4. Keep trying until you find one that you like. Select it and go to the cart to check out.
5. Often as you go through checkout, they will offer lots of other services, such as email, privacy settings, and additional websites. Unless you know that you want these, you can skip them all for now.

If your name is taken, try a *.org* or *.net* address...or a custom ending such as *.photo* or *.massage*. Or add a word or phrase to your company name. Ideas:

welcome to	services
seattle	products
[your neighborhood name]	shop
LLC	

It's a good idea to research this when choosing your business name; it might affect your final choice.

If you register your domain name separately, you'll need to point it to your website. Usually, your website host will have a wizard to do this, or will provide tutorials. If you don't like this stuff, ask a friend to help you. Sometimes a second set of eyes is all you need.

Email Address

Part of looking professional is getting an email address that reflects your business. This also gives you the option of keeping work email separate from personal email, if you want that.

If you do want them combined, you can either use your work email for everything, or, you can route both personal email and work email to the same mail viewer. For example, Jane Doe could have both jane.doe@gmail.com and jane@janedoeconsulting.com routed to her Outlook inbox.

Here are some options for addresses, starting with the simplest.

Sign up with a free web-hosted email server, such as Google or Yahoo.

> yourbusinessname@gmail.com
> *example: howtohairgirl@gmail.com*

Sign up with a paid email provider that you're already using.

> yourbusinessname@mac.com
> *example: lizamodernartmedia@mac.com*

Get an address attached to your new website.

> yourname@yourwebsite.com
> *example: alex@rabbitstewstringband.com*

This last method takes some tech savvy. If you need help, you can try consulting with YouTube or a friend.

Business Cards

There are so many places to order business cards. If you want to look at all of the options, limit your research time to sixty minutes. Then, pick a supplier and start designing your cards. You can change them later. I'll offer two suggestions.

Moo.com

These are classy but a little spendier. They use thick paper that feels good in the hands. My mother-in-law says that every time she passes hers out, people rub their thumbs and fingers over it, flip it over, say *Ooohh, where did you get these?* They can makes a strong impression, which helps to make you memorable.

They have lots of lovely templates to choose from. You can change the fonts, colors, and type sizes, within limits. Or, you can upload complete designs.

Vistaprint.com

They have free cards, and very affordable cards. This is a great choice if you really don't know what you want or need tons of them. There are lots of options. When you put your info in and select a design, they'll show what the cards will look like right there on the screen.

Gift Certificates

Gift certificates are a great way to help others help you!

Gift certificates are a form of advertising that is nearly free. When a client or friend gifts one, the receiver is a new potential client that you didn't have to find or pay much for (just the cost of printing the gift certificate).

In addition, gift certificates expand the number of people who can make a purchase from you. For example, Claire is a fashion designer and dressmaker. Her clothes are handcrafted, beautiful, and made for women. When she added gift certificates to her table at the street fairs, suddenly men were able to make purchases from her as well.

Even very basic gift certificates work. You can make homemade ones, get them printed, or send them electronically. Go to www.vistaprint.com to find templates. Or, if you have a complete design, you can upload it on Moo.com as a postcard. I like to buy envelopes at The Paper Source in University Village. There are a few dozen colors, and they come in lots of different sizes.

If you have time, adding special touches is a nice way to demonstrate your brand personality and commitment to quality and care. You can find beautiful papers and interesting envelopes—either at the Paper Source or at an art store. You might also consider adding a special item that's related to your work. For example, if you're a massage therapist, you add a little packet of soaking salts for the bath.

Tangible items like this help to make your business feel really real— especially if you're a service provider.

Putting it All Together—Marketing Snapshot

One of the biggest keys for effective marking is to make some choices, and then do the work. It is very easy to stay in the idea stage with advertising. *What if I do this? Everyone says I should do that!* There are so many cool options that it's fun to picture all of them...and people get stuck in the imagination phase. The only strategies that work are the ones that exist.

This is why you need a plan...I like to call it, a Marketing Snapshot. It is a description of your brand plus a *limited* list of your choices for how you intend to find clients.

My suggestion is to develop your story and brand to the best of your ability right now, and then to select and commit to three to five advertising methods. For example, weekly activities might be making posts on Facebook, putting up flyers, and sending cold emails to possible referrers in the neighborhood. Choose ones that you would enjoy, reflect your style, and fit your budget, time, and energy. Schedule time on your calendar to develop your tools and create deadlines. In addition, build time into your regular schedule to maintain these efforts.

Committing to a few methods means saying *no* to some. Be ready to table good ideas for later.

Give yourself a time period for this current plan—three, six, or nine months. Don't second-guess it; just apply time and energy to it. At the end of the time period, assess what worked and what didn't work. Ask clients how they found you. Which methods were easy to maintain, and which did you avoid? If you have access to Google Analytics or Facebook Analytics, which referrers and search terms are working? Make a new, updated plan.

This plan can be formal or informal, written or just in your head. The key is that it is finite and manageable.

Example of a Marketing Snapshot. There's a blank form on the next page.

Marketing Snapshot: Seattle Qwik Tours

Foundation	Charles • entertainer/improv-er • hilarious • classy • loves Seattle	Customer • smart, good sense of humor • active • interested in seeing, then exploring the city • wants to make the right choice
Story	*I love Seattle and I'm an entertainer. I can show you the essential Seattle in 90 minutes - so you have more time to explore the city on your own. It's a high energy, no-snooz'n romp through the city. Cowbells, bubbles, and facts guaranteed. I can also customize tours for groups. I'm known as the Chuckster.*	
Brand	• tongue-in-cheek • entertaining *Everything should make people chuckle and be informative* *The Chuckster is the person you want to help you discover Seattle*	• classy • informative
Brand Elements	font(s): Futura colors: black, grey, white with two colors imagery: people having fun, the Chuckster, Seattle icons	keywords: the Chuckster, 90 minute high energy, upbeat special touches: cowbell, bubbles
Advertising	Where are customers? *Searching online* *Searching reviews* *Seattlites hosting visitors* *Going on cruise ships*	1. Top search results > web site 2. Rack cards 3. Reviews on Yelp, Viator 4. Referrals through concierges, downtown businesses 5. Flyers for Seattle hosts
Tools	• website • rack cards • signs requesting reviews, keychains as thank yous	• flyers • SEO

Find Charles at SeattleQwikTour.com

Try it for yourself! (There's another blank one on page 380.)

Marketing Snapshot

Foundation	You • • • •	Customer • • • •
Story		
Brand	• •	• •
Brand Elements	font(s): colors: imagery:	keywords: special touches:
Advertising	Where are customers?	1 2 3 4 5
Tools	• • •	• • •

Some Client Approaches

Carlie offers nurturing therapeutic massage that gets results. She currently works above The Dish in Ballard. You may have seen her sign on the sidewalk. It's yellow with flowers and a bird on it.

Carlie used to work for an employer and had a dedicated following. When she left to run her own practice, she wasn't allowed to advertise to her current clients so had to build from the ground up. She made a logo and business card and a matching sandwich board for the street. Carlie identified her ideal clients as people in the neighborhood who were active and needed and valued bodywork to be healthy and happy in their lifestyle.

Carlie's a friendly, engaging person, so she frequented neighborhood cafes and bars and struck up conversations with servers and bartenders. She mentioned her new location to everyone and often handed out cards. In addition, she joined the Ballard chapter of BNI (Business Networking International) where local business owners connect and offer referrals for one another. Lastly, she posted regularly on Facebook—inspirational quotes, articles, and last-minute openings. She decided to skip a website, since she uses her Facebook page and Schedulicity.

Advertising Summary: conversations in the neighborhood, BNI, Sandwich Board, Facebook page, Schedulicity

Sadie offers bookkeeping services to nonprofits, schools, and wellness businesses. Her tagline is "always complete, always cheerful!" Sadie's client load is usually full, but her schedule occasionally has room for one or two new clients. In order to fill those spots right away, and with best-fit clients, Sadie continues to do marketing work. Right now, it's the more subtle, behind-the-scenes stuff—refining the vision of her business, and working on her brand and materials.

Recently, Sadie's had two changes with her business that she's highlighting in her marketing work. First, she's offering a new service: bookkeeping consulting for people who need just a little, potent help. Second, that she's now committed to living and working in her own neighborhood, the Downtown/Belltown area. (She sold her car and walks, bikes, or uses public transportation.)

So far, Sadie's business has grown through referrals from happy clients. To keep these referrals going, Sadie uses group emails to stay in touch. In a recent email, she announced her new consulting service and downtown focus. In addition, Sadie's built a website for prospective clients to explore. Lastly, Sadie made rack cards that she will share selectively with any local businesses that she really likes. These include a graphic of the downtown Seattle skyline.

Advertising Summary: group emails, client referrals, rack cards, website

Anne is a color consultant and fine arts painter. She helps you find the right colors for your home, so it can be a nourishing and beautiful environment. She understands how to pick the right combinations to match the owner or designer's desired mood and the style of the home. Anne got her start by teaming up with an architect. When the architect made a proposal, he included Anne as a part of the project. This was a win-win as Anne helped his work look amazing at the end, providing a strong finish. Of course it was great for Anne to get clients without having to advertise.

Currently, Anne uses a combination of partnering with architects, builders and real estate agents; rack cards in paint stores; donations to school auctions; and word of mouth referrals. Anne told me, "I find the key is to build personal relationships. Even though websites are great—my best client referrals come from people that know me or know of my work. A qualified referral is preferred if you can get them!"

Advertising Summary: referral partners, bulletin boards, auction donations, website

In Summary—Marketing

Marketing is just this: all the efforts you do to keep current clients and get new ones. Marketing is the umbrella term; it's the system of making and managing these efforts. It includes branding and advertising as well as being excellent at what you do.

Really, marketing begins with being amazing at your job.

As you think about marketing, take some time to understand your story. Then build your marketing efforts as needed. Your central story incorporates what you do, for whom, and why you're doing it. Understanding the *pain* of your client brings clarity and focus.

The next layer is branding. This is the style or personality of your advertising and messaging. It helps you to make choices in language and design. When done well, it attracts the clients you want, and sorts out the ones that you don't.

Advertising works best when built on a solid foundation. Decide on advertising methods, and then build your tools. Common advertising efforts include: using word of mouth, networking, and social media.

Most people need:

- a website (including a domain name)
- an email signature.

Many like to have:

- business cards
- gift certificates
- an email address with the business name
- a social media presence.

Nitty Gritty

Things to review, choose, and do. Check when complete, or mark NA.

Payments and Billing	○ Payment Options ○ Make an Invoice and Receipt ○ Billing Schedule ○ Revise Price Sheet / Menu of Services ○ Plan for Increases ○ To Offer Discounts or Not?
Insurance	○ Determine Insurance Needs ○ Check to see if your Auto Policy Covers Business Use of Vehicle(s) ○ Check with/or Purchase Homeowners / Renters' Insurance ○ Professional Insurance
Office and Tools	○ Set up Physical Space (Office) ○ Collect Tools and Supplies
Working With Others	○ Policies ○ To Charge for Travel Time or Not? ○ How to Handle Barters ○ Working for Less - When and How ○ Contracts / Agreements ○ If and When to Accept Free Help
Time	○ Plan Time for All the Business Tasks ○ Create a Weekly Flow Plan ○ Create a Year At-a-Glance Calendar

Introduction to Nitty Gritty

Some people say that the devil is in the details. I prefer the saying the *delight* is in the details. Staying happy in your job is greatly enhanced when you enjoy your work, transactions with customers are going well, and you're earning enough money. This is where the details of doing business can make a big difference.

Operations include all the tasks and tools you need to deliver your service or product. *Operations* is the official term; I prefer *Nitty Gritty*. Managing them well directly affects your take-home pay.

Nitty gritty includes:

Tangible tools *such as* invoices, receipts, calendars, hardware, software, furniture, and supplies
+
Intangible tools *such as* policies, schedules, protocols and etiquettes
+
Methods of organizing them

This chapter presents many of the tools and policies that you're likely to need once in business as well as some strategies for organizing your space and time.

It is impossible to have all of these details down from the get-go. The best way is to develop them is through doing business. Give yourself a year or two as a learning period. Think of everything you do as a prototype, and then adjust through experience. For example, if a customer asks you what your late payment fee is, but you don't know, decide on the spot or say you'll get back to them. If you change your mind, or realize partway through a transaction that you're missing something, apologize and offer to make it up to the customer. Be sure to *resist feeling badly*. You're learning. Think of everything you're doing as research and development.

Your biggest allies are imagination and reflection. Before each client interaction, imagine how it will go, and what tools you'll need. Make those tools sometime before the meeting. After each interaction, reflect on what went well and what was difficult or missing. Plan to add that next time.

The key questions with the nitty gritty side are: What makes things easier? What makes things more clear?

These questions are for both you and your customer.

Whenever you can, put your own personal touch on these elements as a way to communicate your brand.

The more you attend to the nitty gritty of business, the more you'll experience smooth sailing in your day-to-day work life and with customer transactions.

☞ Bottom line: The nitty gritty stuff is important. Use imagination and reflection to develop these over time.

Payment Options

There are lots of payment options. You can accept whatever you like; just make it clear to clients, so they are not surprised. In today's world, people are used to using credit and debit cards. If you're not going to accept these, be very upfront, and remind people a lot.

Here are some options:

- Cash
- Check
- Paypal, Square Cash
- Credit/debit cards
- Gift certificates
- Barter/Trades
- Bill pay checks
- Insurance
- Automatic transfers

Do what works for you.

Do what's easy.

For example, if you're a massage therapist and you don't want to take insurance, don't! If you don't like chasing down payments, then collect payments at the time of service.

Start out simply. Then add options as needed, over time. Many self-employed folks start with cash and check only. If people want to use debit cards, then PayPal is often the next step.

If you really need to take credit cards—if this makes your life easier—then you can get a card reader, such as Square or Inner Fence for your phone or iPad. Just be aware that they generally take a 3 to 5% fee.

Invoices and Receipts

Any time you accept a payment, you have to create a record of it for yourself and the purchaser. These used to be known as paper trails...but of course now, they can also be electronic. Personally, I prefer using paper, because I can see many things at once, and I don't have to worry about backing up my records.

Often the terms invoice and receipt get mixed up or used interchangeably, which is a mistake.

An **invoice** is used as a request for payment. It usually details what was purchased.

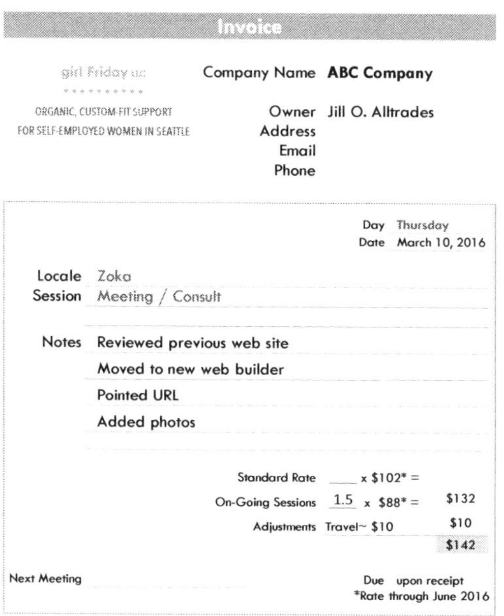

Invoice

girl Friday LLC

ORGANIC, CUSTOM-FIT SUPPORT
FOR SELF-EMPLOYED WOMEN IN SEATTLE

Company Name **ABC Company**
Owner Jill O. Alltrades
Address
Email
Phone

Day Thursday
Date March 10, 2016

Locale Zoka
Session Meeting / Consult

Notes Reviewed previous web site
Moved to new web builder
Pointed URL
Added photos

Standard Rate ___ x $102* =
On-Going Sessions 1.5 x $88* = $132
Adjustments Travel~ $10 $10
$142

Next Meeting

Due upon receipt
*Rate through June 2016

A **receipt** is proof of payment.

Receipt
Girl Friday LLC
[Contact info goes here]

Name Jill O. Alltrades
Amount $142
Paid on March 10, 2016
Method Check
Initials j.m.

:) Jenny

These can be combined into one form. The receipt is what you actually need for tax reporting since it is the evidence that money changed hands. Invoices are most often used when billing clients or when a description is needed.

There are lots of ways to make invoices. You can create them from scratch or use a template from Microsoft Word or PayPal, or use accounting software.

Ideally, your invoices or receipts will include:

- purchaser's name and information
- your company name and information
- description of services or goods
- amount paid
- type of payment
- the date.

Have some fun with these! People often forget that these communicate about you and your business. Take the time to add your logo, favorite fonts, or colors. Perhaps add a personal note, a thank you, or a relevant quote. Select paper that you like—maybe recycled, textured, or just thicker paper. Make your invoices and receipts something that brings you a little joy and shows your clients that you care about them.

Invoices and receipts are also a great place to gently educate your clients about any policies, reminders for the next meeting, or the work that you completed for them.

The primary reason for keeping these records is that they are required as proof for tax reporting. You need to keep these for several years, in case of audit. (Number of years varies by government agency. Here's a statistic I like: less than 1% of people get audited by the IRS.) In addition, keeping records will help you to track what you're bringing in.

On Billing Clients

You'll need to decide on how often you will bill clients and what method you will use. The more you can make a routine and stick to it, the easier it will be.

Pro Tip: The sooner people pay you after a service, the happier they are about the charge. The longer you wait, the more they tend to doubt the charge.

For timing, you can: bill at the time of service or on a regular schedule. A regular schedule could be once a week, twice a month, or monthly. Or, you can select the same date or dates each month, such as the 5th and the 20th.

State when payment is due. Make this policy very clear, so clients are not surprised. If you choose to bill on a schedule, versus at the time of service, you'll need to put time into your schedule for both billing and checking to see if payments have been made. Additionally, you'll want to figure out how to handle reminders and any late payments.

Methods and delivery: you can use paper invoices, which you hand to the clients or send in the mail. Or, you can bill electronically, either through email, PayPal, or a software program.

Be very clear about when payment is due, and if you have a late payment policy, be sure to put that on your form too.

Here's an example of a billing success story: Dana is a private music teacher, and she originally collected payments at each lesson. This was mostly fine, but it meant handling a lot of checks and deposits, all at random times. Also, if a student canceled, she missed out on being paid that day. This meant it was hard to predict her income. We talked it through, and she said it'd be best if she got all her payments at the same time each month. That way, she'd know what her income was, and she wouldn't have to do bookkeeping on a daily basis.

We made a new system and policy—that lessons would be charged for by the month, and that all payments were due by the 5th. She set up a sweet little red mailbox in her studio, with a framed signed next to it, stating the tuition due date—this way, families were regularly reminded of the policy.

It only took a month to get everyone into the new routine. It paid off! She smiled as she explained one day, "It was so easy! Everyone brought their checks, and the students seemed to have fun putting them in the mail box."

•

Once you decide how you want to bill, add it to your *Policies* document (more on this later) and any contracts so that clients know what's expected.

Tracking Lots of Purchases

If you're planning to sell at street fairs, farmers markets, or in stores, you may have to handle a lot of transactions quickly. This means you'll need a way to calculate sales tax (if applicable) accept payments, provide receipts, and most importantly, keep track of all the numbers for inventory and for tax reporting.

Pro Tip: One way to speed up transactions is to include the sales tax in the price, and make it end in .00 for easier adding. In that case, you would have to post, "All prices include WA state sales tax of 9.6%." For example, you might charge $28 for a necklace, meaning the cost is $25.55 and the sales tax is $2.45.

Choose a method that fits your style. There are a lot of options. You might ask around to see what some of your friends or colleagues do. Or go to a sales venue and watch the vendors.

Here are a few favorites among my clients. These first three are well-suited for selling individual items, such as pieces of art, jewelry, clothing, or gift cards, or services.

☞ Carbon Receipts

> Get a carbon receipt book. Record the date, item and price. You might need a calculator for finding totals and sales tax. Use the carbon copies to add all the figures to records later.

☞ Spiral Notebook

> Put columns on each page: *Date, Item, Subtotal, Tax, Total, Payment type*. Record the transaction while the customer is there.

☞ Credit Card Readers

Use readers such as Square, PayPal, or Inner Fence. These work well for credit and debit cards by keeping a record of all transactions and calculating tax for you. If you also accept check or cash, you'll need a separate way to track those.

If you have a commerce site with Shopify, you can get a credit card reader through them and all the transactions be integrated with your Shopify site.

•

If you're selling lots of small items, such as baked goods, candles, or soaps, detailed invoices are often not required, though you may still offer receipts of payment. Use the following.

☞ Bake Sale Approach

Know what you're starting with—the number of items and amount of cash in the box. At the end, calculate products sold and total payments by subtracting from what you started with. At the end of the selling session, record the date, total payments, and total items sold.

Plan for Increases / Raises

Raise your rates regularly.

Rates need to go up for a variety of reasons. One, it's hard to know what to charge in the beginning. We often undercharge, or forget to account for overhead. We need to adjust up to cover these costs. Two, as you get better, you'll be more efficient and knowledgeable. It'll take you less time to do the work. Three, you need to keep up with inflation. Four, many people will expect it anyway!

Always have a date attached to your prices and rates, such as *Fall Prices or Rates good through May 2017*.

This sets the expectation that prices will go up. And it's all about expectations! People don't like being surprised. Usually, it is the element of surprise that stresses people out, not that you're charging more. Give your clients a lot of notice—something between one and three months.

You don't need to rationalize or overly explain these increases. Just state that the prices are changing/increasing. If customers ask why, you can always say "inflation" or "to get up to the market value." They don't need to know if you were undercharging before or that you need to earn enough to buy a new computer. The more comfortable you are, the more comfortable they will be. I've often had clients say something like, "Finally. I thought you weren't charging enough!"

Pro Tip: Review your *Menu of Services* or *Price Lists* one or two times a year. Update as needed.

Discounts

If you are giving a discount, you're giving up part of your profit. In order to make this a win-win situation, be sure that you're getting something in return and that it is something you want.

Discounts can be given for all kinds reasons. Here are some that make sense from a win-win perspective:

- to help sales (when business is slow)
- to get a new customer who is on the fence about hiring you/ purchasing from you (sales)
- as a reward for referrals (customer loyalty)
- clients who will tell others about you (as a form of marketing)
- because it feels good—to friends, family, or a special customer (personal enjoyment).

The last one is tricky...be sure that you can afford this one. If you are hurting for money, this might put you in a lose-win situation. You're losing out, and they are winning. If you do give discounts to friends and family, be sure they understand what your normal prices are, so if they talk about you to other potential customers, they can quote the right prices.

It's a good idea to put the regular price on the receipt or invoice, and then show the discount underneath. Again, if you're giving a gift to someone, it's good for them to see it and realize that they are receiving a gift!

Pro Tip: Do not give discounts because you feel that you have to. This will lead to stress and resentment, and often lower-quality work. This is draining and affects your other work and reputation.

Determine Insurance Needs for Your Business

Insurance needs vary greatly among self-employed folks according to industry requirements and individual preferences. I highly recommend taking some time to determine what you need and want for your business. The point of insurance is to help you both in the future (should the unforeseen happen), and to give you peace of mind right now.

This is one area where I like to rely completely on a specialist. Whenever clients and friends ask for insurance advice, I always say the same thing. Find an insurance agent that you trust, and follow their advice. For this book section, I consulted with our insurance agent and family friend, Tim Quigley, a Certified Insurance Counselor for over 30 years.

Tim says, when it comes to insurance, *always ask!* We talked over the most common topics related to business.

There are Different Types of Insurance Agents

Roughly speaking, there are two types of insurance agents. It's important to know the difference—so that when you're talking to one, you know if they are limited or not with what they can share with you. An agent who works for one company is commonly referred to as a *direct writer*. They only provide the insurance policies their one company offers, and can only speak about the options that they offer. An *independent agent* is one who represents multiple companies. They can speak about each company, compare and contrast different policies, and then help you to select the one that is best suited for your needs.

ProTip: Consider consulting with an independent agent who has demonstrated a higher level of insurance education! Look for one designated as an Accredited Advisor of Insurance (AAI) or Certified Insurance Counselor (CIC). They generally do not charge a fee for their services.

Auto Insurance

Call your auto insurance agent and make sure that your policy covers business use of your vehicle(s). Tim explained that some policies have limits to what they cover, and you don't want to find out the hard way! Consider this worst-case scenario: You get into a car accident. You explain to the insurance representative that you were delivering some new products to a boutique. They say, "Sorry, we don't cover business use." You then have to pay for all the damage and medical bills yourself.

The only way to know for sure is to call and find out.

Home Owners/Renters Insurance for Equipment and Tools

With more people working out of their homes, some homeowner's policies may be willing to amend coverage to include your business. Ask your agent if your homeowner's (or renter's insurance) policy will extend to include your business equipment and any in-home business activities.

ProTip: It's sometimes possible to get extra coverage for items that you take outside of the house—e.g., laptop, guitar, massage table—for a small premium. To get this coverage, it has to be listed specifically on your homeowner's policy. For example, I've added my laptop to our homeowner's policy and pay only $12/year. If I'm at a coffee shop, and it gets knocked off a coffee table or stolen, my insurance will replace it without a deductible. ☺

Commercial Insurance Policy

If you conduct business outside the home—such as in an office, studio, classroom, or treatment room—and want to get insurance coverage in that space, you may need to look into getting a commercial insurance policy. Business insurance is not always expensive and your agent can help you decide what type of coverage is best for you.

When Professional Insurance is Optional

(Some fields require this type of insurance. If this is your case, you likely know what you need.)

Sometimes people working in professional roles (where insurance is not required) wonder if they want or need insurance. It's also possible that clients will sometimes request or require you to be insured. This comes up a lot if when folks are working as a consultant in any field, as a life or business coach, or with marketing work, such as graphic design or copy writing. Deciding whether or not to purchase insurance depends on many factors. A root question to consider is: What is the risk involved if people follow your guidance or utilize your work...and something goes wrong? Do you need coverage for this type of scenario?

Professional Insurance is a specialty type of insurance. Not all agents offer this type of insurance, check with your agent to see if they can offer this type of policy or can recommend someone who does.

ProTip: Another solution is to find and join a professional organization that offers special access to insurance for their members. Usually this is more affordable. For example, my neighbor, Carol, is an education consultant. This year, she joined the APBS (Association for Positive Behavior Support). They work with Forrest T. Jones & Company, to offer insurance to their members. It cost $279 for a year, for a one million dollar policy. (This amount was required by the State).

•

To read a few tips related to medical, dental, and life insurance, please see "How do I find Health Insurance?" on page 355.

ProTip: Sometimes medical and dental expenses can be deducted on your taxes. Check with an accountant to see if this applies to you.

Remember, when it comes to insurance...always ask!

Set Up a Physical Space

Create a space for your business. It can be as small as a shelf or as large as an office. Whether or not you work in the space, you need a place to collect paperwork and to store business-related things.

Having a space is mentally and emotionally important too as it reinforces that you have a business structure to maintain. Knowing where to find things helps you to stay sane. Instead of feeling spread out, you can feel put together.

This is especially key for "pilers"—people who tend to create piles of things—such as myself.

As the week progresses, my nature is to pile projects, receipts and books all over the house. Instead, I've trained myself to put them in my office—on whatever surface I want. (It is a tiny attic office, about 6 x 9 feet.) No matter how cluttered it gets up there, getting stuff into the office allows me to get it out of my visual field so I can "clock out." It also helps me feel secure because I haven't lost anything. If I need something, I know that it's in there somewhere. On Monday, I go up there, sift through things and put stuff away. It's a very pleasant way to warm up to the week.

Make your office a delightful place whether you work in there, or just visit. Find some art, mementos, or favorite furniture. Find things that nourish and encourage you like inspirational quotes, records of achievement, certificates, and testimonials from clients. Even though it can feel cheesy, consider framing your business licenses.

Collect Your Tools and Supplies

What tools and supplies do you need? Make a list, and start working through it. Or, collect these as the need arises. Just know that even the simplest businesses require tools and supplies—often more than you'd think.

To get you brainstorming, here are some categories of things you might need:

- office basics (paper, pens, stapler, etc.)
- mailing/shipping
- billing, invoicing, receipts
- software
- collection tools for bookkeeping (See page 187.)
- books, magazines
- client records, contracts
- thank you cards
- marketing materials

plus

- whatever you need for your service or product making.

As you bring these things into your home or office, find or create a space to put them. Choose a location that is close to where you will use them. Make it easy to put things away. Even if you have a more cluttered style for the rest of your home, I encourage you to be a little neater with your work supplies and space. Self-employment has a lot of stress already...so give yourself a gift, and create an environment where it's easy to find things.

The cost of these things varies so much based on your work. Be sure that your rates or prices are high enough to cover these costs. They are all a part of your overhead. As one accountant said to me, "There are two ways to pay for overhead. It either comes from the client, or it comes out of your kid's lunch money."

Policies

Policies are your friends. We don't make them up to be difficult or more business-y. We have policies to prevent bad situations or give direction when needed. Creating some policies will save you time, stress, and brain space.

For example, it sucks to get paid late, especially if you've had to send a lot of reminders. If you decide to make a late payment policy, it will deter clients from paying you late and give you a little compensation for the extra work and stress. If someone asks you, "Can I send you the check next week?" you don't have to decide. You can simply state the policy, "Sure...if you're okay with the late fee of $25."

The great thing about a policy, is that when you announce one, it sounds like an objective truth. Official. It helps people accept a charge or a rule more easily. It reminds folks that a business transaction is taking place. Personal language makes it sound personal, and perhaps changeable. It sounds like you're making a choice that moment.

Compare:

Well...I'm so sorry about the traffic too. Let's see, I was here waiting for you, so I think I need to charge you for some of this time. I think $45 would be fair. (Too personal and spontaneous.)

I understand about traffic; that's sure a bummer. Well, as you know, the policy for missed appointments is to pay 50% of the meeting fee, which comes to $45. How would you like to handle that? I can send you a PayPal request, or self-addressed stamped envelope. I really am sorry to miss you today! (Steady, confident.)

Of course, you can always waive the fee or policy if you want to. Be sure to point out the rule, and that you are waiving it. It might sound funny, but it allows the client to understand what's expected for next time, and it shows them that you understand and care. It helps build your relationship and loyalty. If you don't bring it up, and just skip charging them, they'll never know that you extended yourself for them.

Whenever you go through a stressful situation, ask yourself, what policies or rules would make this easier in the future. Create a *Policies* document, and write them down. Find ways to communicate policies to clients—in your contract, on your website, or in reminder emails. If you do a client newsletter or group email, you can announce new policies as they are created.

It's helpful to think through some in the beginning, such as:

Late arrivals
Payment due dates
Late payments
Friend discounts
Referral bonuses

Make your policies easy to find; display them as much as possible where they make sense—perhaps on your invoice or in your email signature or reminders. That way, clients have lots of chances to see them…so they can follow them, which makes both of your lives easier.

Travel Time—To Charge or Not to Charge? (Charge!)

A place where new self-employed folks can lose a lot of time and money is traveling to meet clients. Often people are so excited to get the work that they're happy to accommodate, and don't charge for travel. This is a very reasonable feeling. It can be tricky to ask people to pay for travel and hard to know what to charge.

You basically have three choices: a) Do it for free. ...then wait until you're feeling the pain of it, and then ask for a travel fee. b) Bite the bullet and add this now. Or, c) Reduce your travel needs.

Here are some strategies:

- Ask clients to meet you in your neighborhood
- Split the travel time: charge your hourly rate for one direction of travel, but not both
- Have a standard fee for travel
- Have different fees based on regions of the area
- Include the cost of travel in your rates

Put your travel fee, along with all your prices, everywhere—on your website, menus, invoices, and when you give quotes. Learn to say it casually and with ease. Maybe role-play talking about your travel fee with a friend.

Examples:

New client: *I think you're exactly who I've been looking for! I'm ready to start. What are your rates?*

You: *$85 an hour, plus a travel fee of $20 North of the Ship Canal.*

Or, You: *$85 an hour. With a travel fee of $10 if we meet in your studio. Or, no travel fee if we can meet at my local coffee shop _____.*

Sometimes, traveling between clients is a great way to clear your head, warm up mentally for a meeting, or reflect afterward. It's also a nice way to get outside, move a little bit, or listen to music.

Having said that, it still costs money and time, it can be quite stressful in today's traffic, and it puts wear on your car. So find a way to charge for it from the beginning.

Barters

If you choose to barter with someone, make sure that the service or product they are providing is one that you actually want and need. My personal policy is to only barter for services that I would pay cash for, right now.

For example, when I first started, I had two clients who do bodywork—the type that I was already paying for, out of pocket. Whenever one of them wants to barter, I'm ready and willing. As I've gotten new clients who also do bodywork, I haven't bartered with them because I don't need any more services, and therefore wouldn't pay cash for them. Similarly, even though I would love to own more art, it's not in my budget to buy art. So, at this point, I don't barter with my artist clients. (I hope to in the future!)

Here's something that may surprise you. According to the IRS, barters are treated as income. The rule is that you track these costs and you file a 1099-MISC if the bartered services were provided by an independent contractor and worth over $600 (or this year's minimum). See page 141 for more information on 1099-MISC.

A lot of people don't like this rule. For my part, I like reporting barters because it is technically and practically income that I earned. I like to see what I've made, and I want my business to make a good profit, so that if I need to apply for loans, I'm showing a steady income.

With that in mind, I provide invoices and receipts for all barters. And again, this makes me think twice before accepting them!

Here are a few tips for setting up a barter agreement:

- Choose the unit—either time or money
- Do a trial period before agreeing to something longterm
- If possible, create a schedule for the traded services
- Create a deadline or time period for using barter credits
- Decide what happens if one party wants to drop out
- Write up the agreement, or at least verbalize and shake hands

Working for Less As a Way to Get Started

Sometimes it makes sense to work for a reduced rate. Perhaps you're new to your field or new to an area, and it's been hard to drum up business. Or, maybe you're still building your confidence, and it's hard to charge the same as folks who are experienced in your field. Working for less is a great way to get started and/or to build momentum. But be sure to do it only for a short period of time.

If you're going to work for less than the standard rate, first decide on your future rates, and then charge a percentage of that. Communicate both to clients, so they understand that you're giving a discount on your future rate. Provide a reason. You're prototyping a new service or it's a New-to-the-neighborhood special. This helps clients understand why your prices are low; they reflect a special deal, not your level of work.

If you start out with really low rates and don't explain them, clients will have a hard time adjusting up. Customers who are already educated about your type of services or products will wonder why they are so low, and they won't trust you; customers who don't know will get the wrong idea. Plus, you'll fix yourself in a lower pay bracket and will likely start attracting the types of clients who can't actually afford you once you raise your rates.

For example, if you're a massage therapist and you charge $35 for an hour long session, it'll be hard to get clients up to the industry standard of $80. And again, people might wonder why you're so cheap.

One more thought, sometimes it's cleanest to do work for free—again, after you've decided on your future rates. This gets people's attention, and it gets you work and experience. This is essential for both your confidence and building business through word of mouth. Also, it helps people try something they normally wouldn't. And then, maybe they'll continue on. When you do this work for free, be sure you have a price sheet or a website, and be sure that folks have that. Invite them to hire you again.

Contracts / Agreements

Whenever we have interactions with other people, we're relying on agreements or contracts. (These terms can usually be used interchangeably.) Often, they are unwritten and deeply understood. If I pass a neighbor on the sidewalk and smile and say hello, I expect to get a hello, a smile, or at least a nod of acknowledgment. If they do nothing, and totally ignore me, the normal reaction is to think they are being rude. What is wrong with them? We interpret their behavior as rude because as a society, we have a general agreement to greet people in return if they have greeted us.

With business, there are similar agreements. I sell you a service, and you pay the price attached to that service. If I advertise a discount for the month of January, you expect that I will honor that agreement. These are understood and don't need any explicit conversation or paper contracts.

However, there are lots of situations that can be less clear, such as late payments, schedule changes, or bouncing checks. It's common for two people to have very different ideas about what's expected in these situations. That is, to have different ideas about the *contract*, or *agreement*.

When agreements are stated clearly and policies are written, everyone has a chance to understand the contract (actual or implied) and to follow it. Companies often develop explicit policies, and, over time, learn the best ways to remind the customer so that everyone understands what is expected. For example, when I get a confirmation reminder from my chiropractor's office, there's a "courtesy reminder" of the 24-hour cancellation policy. I understand and agree that if I don't show up or call to cancel, I pay a $50 fee. They know that even though I read it once in the initial paperwork, I probably won't remember it. So they put it in every email.

Troubles come when two parties have different ideas about the agreement or contract. When things are written down, you can reference them, and it's easier to either fix your own mistakes or to clearly and gently point out when the other party is mistaken.

With self-employed people, there are lots of fuzzy areas. Frequently things are not spelled out, so misunderstandings can happen, especially since we often work with friends and family, or friends of friends. We don't want to be formal, so we skip steps. Or, maybe we don't know what our policies are yet. Often they are created after a problem has occurred!

So, as a general rule, it helps to be extra explicit and write things down, whenever possible. The closer you are to somebody, the more important this is. Another way of thinking about it is this. The less you think you need a formal step, the more you need it!

Even when things are written, get in the habit of speaking things out, so everyone is reminded what the expectations are, and so it shows that you're aware and that you're following your side of the agreement.

Since I charge hourly, I often make it a point to announce when we move from visiting to working. I say something like, "Well...I'm really excited to see what we can get done today. Let's get started! It's about 11:10 now. Can you go for one hour, until 12:10?"

Or, after the session when I'm filling out the invoice, "Well, we started on work stuff at 3:15, so that'll be 1.5 hours today."

If you are a service provider, it's great to have some sort of *Terms of Agreement*, where you spell out the logistics of working together, what you charge, how you charge, and any policies you have. Schedule time to go over this with clients outside of the appointment, so it is off-the-clock. Have a copy for each of you to sign.

Sometimes it feels a little like playacting, but it is not, and it is very important. It allows both people to be clear about the agreements. It's a way of bringing up issues that the client might not have thought about. And because it is physically outside of you, it feels more real and official. It allows you and the other person to be together looking at it, this third thing. Often, services with a self-employed person can be very friendly and casual. The contract adds some formality, and it reminds them you are a professional. It makes you look legit! It makes you look prepared! This is very reassuring to the client.

Free Help...is Rarely Free

Please be careful of any friend or family member offering to help you for free in your business venture, whether it's a gift or volunteered time. Often people offer to help; they want to, and it gives them pleasure. It might work out fine for a while, but it can easily turn sour in the future.

Consider this aspect of human nature. Most people experience ups and downs in life, times of want, and times of plenty. It's fun to be generous in an up cycle. In a down cycle, it's human nature to review those we've helped and wonder if they can return the favor to us, especially if they have something that we want or need.

Now, let's imagine that someone gave you a gift, and then needs your services some day. They might expect you to work for them for free or for a discount without even realizing it! "I spent 8 hours helping her with her website (three years ago), and now she expects me to pay for a massage?"

I've had lots of clients tell me that a friend or family member was going to set up their website or help them with taxes. What a nice idea, right? The problem is that the gift-giver is doing this work in their free time—so often, they're not giving their best energy, and the project gets pushed off over and over. If they do end up doing work for you, and then afterward you have questions or additional needs, it's common for the gift-giver to develop an attitude—which means that getting answers or making changes takes forever!

To avoid this situation, as often as possible, offer something in return for the help. Even if the the items don't feel equal in value, it will close out the interaction. When you make an agreement, be explicit. Spell it out. Define exactly what they are giving you and what you're giving back— whether it's verbal, in email, or on paper. For example, you might say, "Really, you can help me with my website? That would be amazing. I would love to give you something in return. How about a free massage in return for the landing page, domain name, and helping me write my personal story."

Or, "I would love your help on the website! How much time do you think it will take? I can return the favor with double the hours in babysitting."

Or, "Yes, please! I have five pages I'm trying to build. If you can help me with those, I'll buy you a bottle of top-shelf whiskey."

Expectations can still arise in the future. If they do come up, it's best to air them right away. "I know that you helped me a few years ago with the website. And now, it feels strange to charge you. What do you think?" Or, "You know, you really helped me with the website a few years back. What if I give you two hours now for free?"

Another strategy is to not accept the help. Instead, let the friend know that you're getting the work done, but you'd love their response or review afterward. While it might cost you more money now, you can get the level of service that you want, and it keeps things cleaner with your relationships.

Thinking about Time

Time is a your most flexible and valuable resource, so you'll want to use it mindfully—both to make progress with growing your business and to feel balanced, sane, and happy.

Whether you like things flexible or structured, it's important to be proactive and thoughtful about how you utilize your time, and to have some systems in place. First, we'll look a little at the nature of time itself and some of the challenges of self-employment. Then we'll look at some strategies.

A Few Thoughts About Time

Time is weird. It's bendy; it can feel different based on the activity. When you're doing something you like, the hours race by. When doing a chore, each minute seems to last forever.

Managing time is different from managing energy. Making decisions or actively listening to someone takes a lot more energy than folding laundry. Tasks that take a lot of energy usually need some warm up and cool down time.

If you're used to others managing your time, it will be an adjustment to do it for yourself. It takes time to manage time, and in the beginning, it will take you even more!

Tasks take time to do. Anything that's on your to-do list, no matter how small it seems, will take time to accomplish. I like to say, things take *physical time* or a *quantity of time.* This reminds me to allow that time in my schedule. For example, if I need to call the Department of Revenue with a question, it will take anywhere from two minutes to fifteen or more. If I need to buy printer paper, that's thirty minutes to Fred Meyer and back unless I can tack it onto another chore.

For tasks or meetings that take a lot of concentration, ninety minutes is about the maximum of time your brain can function in this way.

Some Common Challenges for Self-Employed Folks

It is very common to feel like you don't have enough time, and there are good reasons for this.

There's a lot of time overhead when developing anything: new tasks take time to learn, there's deep thinking required to set priorities and make decisions, and you're inventing and designing new tools.

Taking on too much work takes time: saying yes to projects that don't fit, doing all the work yourself (not outsourcing), doing things the hard way because you don't have systems in place.

Time gets chopped into little chunks, making it hard to get things accomplished. This comes from task switching, answering email and calls, and from checking social media.

Some Strategies for Time and Energy

We often think that if we had more time, things would be easier. But the answer isn't more time. It's how you manage your time, and what you allow on your plate.

1 Put time in your schedule for business tasks. You can either create an office day or office hours. It helps to acknowledge some of the chores/tasks of business, and give them an estimated amount of time per week. Many people underestimate the time it takes to do these. If you're not sure, then guess and adjust. Here are a few basics to plan for:

- Email/communications: setting up appointments, following up with people, confirming plans, sending thank you cards

- Bookkeeping: making invoices, collecting and filing receipts, making deposits, sending reminders for payment, checking accounts, paying bills
- Marketing: working on materials, such as websites, flyers, business cards, posting flyers, and/or posting on social media
- Self-Management: setting your next goals, making to-do lists, prioritizing tasks, adjusting your load as needed
- Nitty-Gritty: ordering supplies, tidying your office, doing errands, cleaning the bathroom, fixing technology

2 Put some Flex Days into your schedule. It's common for details and unfinished projects to pile up from time to time. Building in some flex days allows you to catch up when behind. If you're all caught up, you can use them to work on new projects for the business, or take a day off!

3 Write important tasks directly onto your calendar. To ensure that these get done, write them onto your calendar with an amount of time allotted. This will ensure that you have the time and space to finish them.

4 Check your calendar before saying yes. It's so easy to say yes to new clients, barters, networking opportunities, etc. Before you say yes, check to see if you actually have time available, and if you do, how much.

5 Create some structure and limits to stay refreshed. Without planned limits, it'll feel like you're working all the time. Caution: you'll want to because you love your work. The problem is that working around the clock every day can sometimes feel great, but it can lead to burn out. You are the talent for your business, so you have to nurture that talent, which includes giving yourself some rest. Create work hours, such as "9 to 3p.m., Monday through Thursday," and stick to them. Or create a number of hours you want to work each week, for example, thirty. Track those, and when you get there, quit for the week.

6 Plan your OFF time. Write it on the calendar and into your schedule.

7 Use tools (that you like) to manage your time—whether it's an app, a moleskin planner, or a whiteboard. When you capture ideas and plans about time onto a calendar or list, it frees up brain space for the other tasks at hand. In addition, when you can see all your plans at once, it can help to see the patterns and flow of your time and energy, giving you an opportunity to make adjustments.

We'll look at two such tools next—Weekly Flow and Year At-a-Glance plans.

Weekly Flow

There is a natural rhythm to working, and something special about a seven-day week. Tony Schwartz, business author and motivational speaker, talks about the "weekly pulse," referring to how energy builds up at the beginning of the week, holds steady, and then cools down. He advises to work with this pulse by assigning tasks throughout the week to match this energy.

Building on his idea, I like to think about having Weekly Flow—a pattern of activities that flow from one to the other where the transition times can be sort of loose. This allows for some flexibility when needed.

Some people like to plan their time, and others like to be more spontaneous and go where their energy is. **Either way, it helps to create a weekly flow plan, whether you follow it or not.** The act of making it helps you to consider all of the tasks you do and to create time for them, set some limits so you have an end to your workday and work week, and understand how many billable hours you actually have.

The idea is to look at your week as a whole, so you can assign regular activities at the best times possible and to group activities that logically fit together.

Make Your Weekly Flow Plan

There is an example of a complete Weekly Flow Plan on page 294.

1 Use the graphic in this book, or draw your own. There's a blank one on page 295.

2 Put in any activities that are already fixed—from both your personal and work life.

3 Draw in rectangles around your job hours, and mark your OFF day(s).

4 Identify which times are best for doing your high-energy work—where you are creating, writing, and working with clients. For most people this is the middle of the week. Block out this time as your core work time.

5 Assign office hours. These are times allotted for *business doing*: emails and phone calls, nitty gritty stuff, billing, and other various business tasks. You can choose an office day, a half day, or spread the hours through the week.

Pro Tip: These fit really well at the beginning and end of your week. They take less energy and are a nice way to warm up and cool down.

6 Look at what you have, and make adjustments. Check to make sure you have enough time assigned for little breaks and travel between meetings.

7 Post your Weekly Flow Plan somewhere as a gentle reminder. Start reinforcing your plans by saying things like, *Monday is my office day.*

Many clients have found this general pattern to work well with their energy:

Sundays—off
Monday—office tasks, reading, ramping up
Tuesday—work
Wednesday—work
Thursday—work/meetings
Friday—leftover tasks, closing up
Saturday—light writing, reading sometimes

Creating a Weekly Flow helps you have the right energy for the right tasks. It also creates habits, so your brain is ready at these times. It gives you something predictable. Revisit your Weekly Flow Plan from time to time.

Weekly Schedule Example:

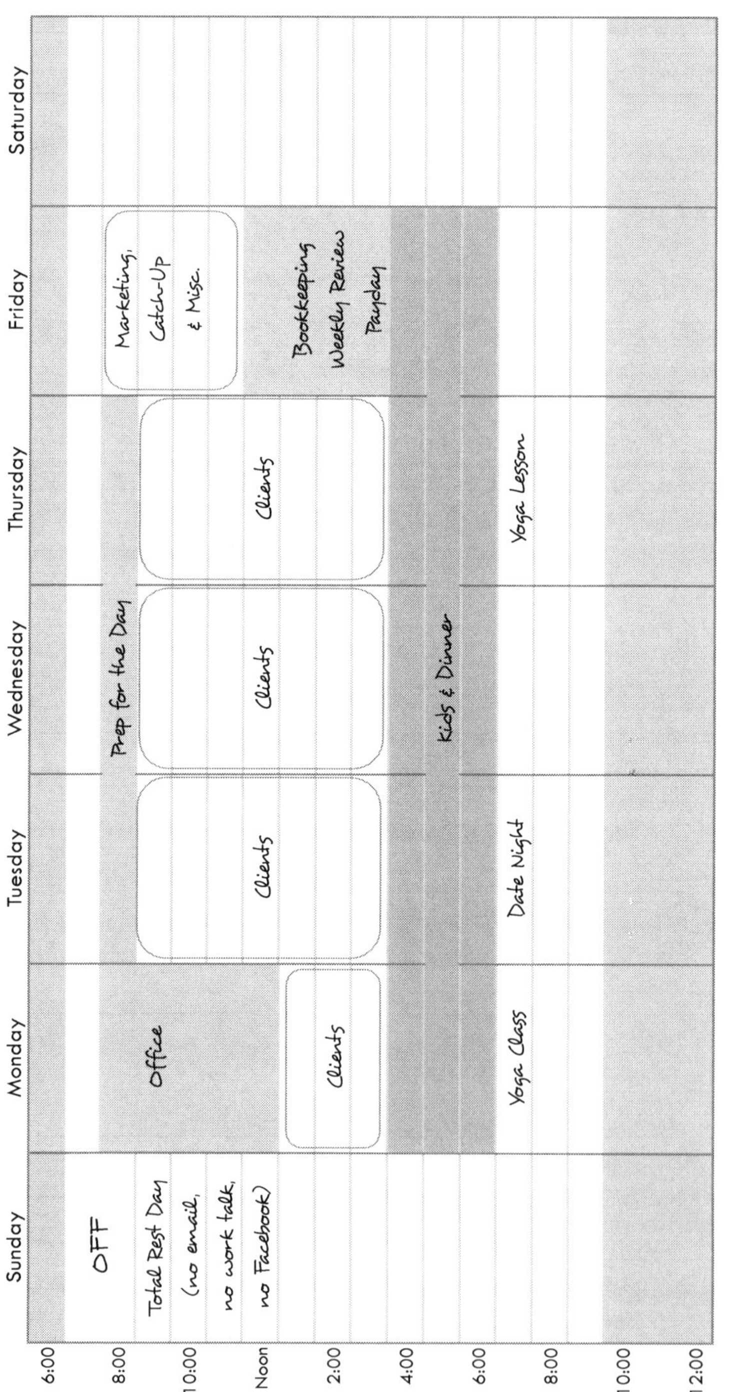

Sunday
Monday
Tuesday
Wednesday
Thursday
Friday
Saturday
6:00
8:00
10:00
Noon
2:00
4:00
6:00
8:00
10:00
12:00
OFF
Total Rest Day (no email, no work talk, no Facebook)
Office
Clients
Yoga Class
Prep for the Day
Clients
Date Night
Clients
Kids & Dinner
Clients
Yoga Lesson
Marketing, Catch-Up & Misc.
Bookkeeping
Weekly Review
Payday

Time blocked for:

Family
Exercise
Marketing
Office - email, creating invoices, organizing, research, reading
Catch-Up - unfinished tasks, typing notes
Weekly Close-out - record income, expenses, reflect, get paid!

Try it for yourself! (There's another blank one on page 378.)

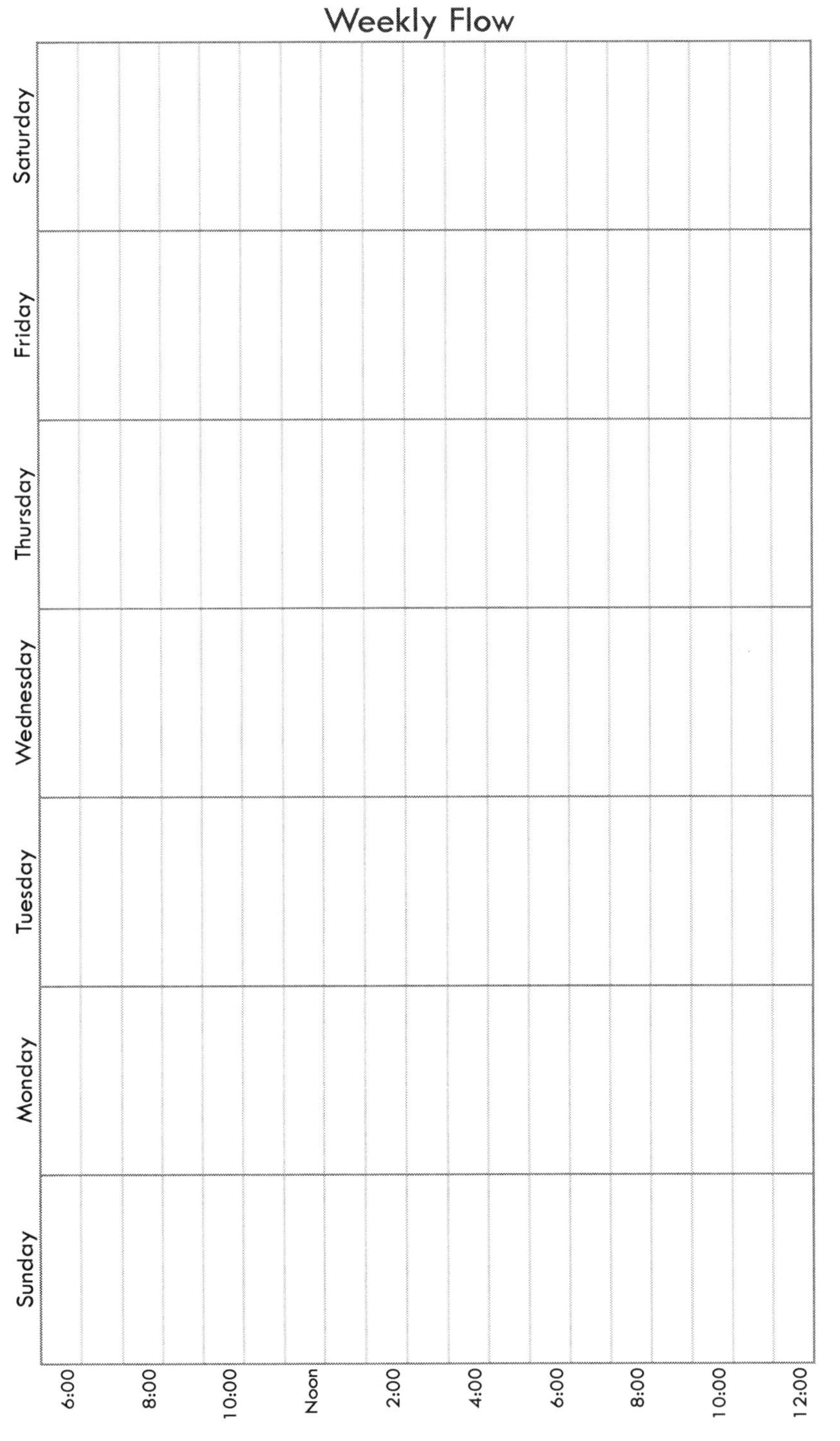

Year At-a-Glance

It is essential to look at your year as a whole at least once or twice per year. Even spending thirty minutes on this activity can literally pay off for you as it helps you charge enough money. In addition, this is one of the best tools for staying sane and happy. It's how you make sure to take vacations and ensures that you have enough time built in for the annual housekeeping of your business and high-level projects.

1. Print out an annual calendar. Or, use the one on page 298.
2. Mark all the time that you want to take off: holidays, regular trips, school, work retreats.
3. Mark the important due dates related to the tax season and anything else for your business.
4. Add in work retreats or trips that you want to take.
5. Now, make some observations:
    - How many weeks are you able to work? (Count the OFF weeks, then subtract from fifty-two.) Use this figure when choosing your rates and prices. See page 171.
    - Which months bring a lot of work and which months are lighter?
    - Does your work typically have a slow season? Can you shift your vacation or any work retreats or trips to this time?
6. Make some changes based on these observations.
7. Write these events onto your primary working calendar. Be sure to include some days dedicated to working on taxes.

There's a sample on the next page. This simple activity will help you to manage your energy, take breaks, and calculate what you need to charge. It also gives a sense of being in control since you chose your schedule. This is helpful for the times that get busy! Consider posting this somewhere in your office or home.

Example of a Year At-a-Glance:

Jan			Jul
		Off	
	Due: WA & Seattle		
Feb			Aug
	Start IRS Taxes		
Mar			Sep
		Writers' Retreat?	
Apr	Due: IRS & County		Oct
	Spring Break		
May			Nov
	Writers' Retreat?		
		Thanksgiving	
June	Extra work		Dec
	(before vacation)		
		Christmas	
		Holiday	

8 weeks off

44 weeks of work

Note: Months are divided into four. (These are not weeks.)

Try it for yourself! (There's another blank one on page 380.)

Year At-a-Glance

Jan			Jul
Feb			Aug
Mar			Sep
Apr			Oct
May			Nov
June			Dec

In Summary—Nitty Gritty

Two of the biggest stresses for you and for clients are being surprised with something unpleasant or not getting something that you need. Often, it's the littlest thing that can trigger these stresses, resulting in losing time, money, and even clients.

In order to get paid, it's helpful to:

- know forms of payment you will accept
- create an invoice and receipt
- choose a billing schedule
- revise your price sheet—labeled with season and year.

Set up your physical space:

- create an office
- collect tools and supplies.

Create some policies to help you and your clients:

- plan for increases
- think about common situations, such as late payments, and referrals
- decide if you charge for travel
- plan discounts you will offer
- decide if you will barter.

Contracts and agreements make things clear:

- create any written contracts relevant to your work
- be aware of verbal agreements
- be careful about taking any free work.

Plan how to best utilize your time—over the week and throughout the year.

Know that you can build these tools, habits, and practices over time.

Self-Management

Things to review, choose, and do. Check when complete, or mark NA.

Getting Stuff Done	Job Description / Take Stock of Your Work
	Create Routines for Checking In
	Adrenaline Changes
	Create Some Deadlines / Milestones
	Outsourcing Willpower
	Forming Habits
	Good Habits for Self-Employed Folks
	Strategies for Dealing with Chores
Getting Support	Know Who's On Your Team (and Who's Not)
	Get Support
Setting Limits	Plan for Time Off:
	One day a week
	Schedule some vacations
	Choose quitting time
	Get Into the Mindset of Saying No
	Ways to Say No
Take Care of Yourself	Define Levels of Self-Care
	Find Ways to Be Inspired
	Plan Your Next Celebration

Introduction to Self-Management

There's a well-proven notion that people don't leave companies; they leave managers. It's no different with self-employment! Often, when people are struggling with their "business," they're really struggling with their manager: in this case, themselves.

There are some good reasons why this is a challenge. First, most people don't realize that this is a part of their new job, so they don't create time for it or get the necessary tools. Second, most people are not taught how to self-manage. Third, few people have any practice at it.

Here's the good news. Self-management is a skill, and like all skills, it can be learned and improved with practice. Also, there are resources and coaches out there. Self-management can even be delegated.

The important thing to know is that you need to do it. You need to get a sense of what is involved in the role, and you need to create some time and the tools to do it.

So, what's involved in self-management? Let's first consider what management is—what it includes, and why it's necessary. To really get the picture, think back to one of your favorite jobs. What made it so great? Chances are, you have some of these responses. *The work was fun to do, and someone cared about me. I had some friends. When I left, I was done for the day. I cared about I was doing. I had a great team.*

If any of these are true, someone was doing a good job as a manager. Their job was to make your work, work. It's easy to take what a manager does for granted—when they do it right. (When they do it poorly, we're pretty clear about what they're not doing.)

A good manager does many of the following. They describe the job—what exactly needs to be done, when and how. Next, they make sure you have the right tools. They make sure that you're using your talents, and that you're delegating what you're not good at. They create deadlines that fit.

They are invested in your growth. They see your potential. Nudge you when needed and reward you when possible. They adjust the load if you have extenuating circumstances and can't be there.

In short, they make sure you can do your work well. They take care of you. So you can take care of the client. We have needs as workers, and they are supposed to meet those needs.

Self-managing means you take the time to do this for yourself. This is where it's helpful to remember there are two yous: the *Talent You* and the *Business You.* (See page 37.) When you're in business/manager role, you take care of your Talent. You get them what they need, and make sure they don't burn out. You adjust the workload as necessary.

If you take the time to manage yourself, you'll stay in the job longer, feel better, perform better, and earn more money. In this section, I present some of the most common strategies and issues that come up for self-employed people. For additional help, you might consult a management book or hire a coach. Meanwhile, employing these strategies should get you pretty far.

☞ Bottom line: It is a skill to self-manage. It is essential to your happiness and the health of your business. Be intentional about developing this skill.

Job Description / Taking Stock of Your Work

Imagine a wild rose bush. It grows in many directions, filling up whatever space it can find. It makes pretty flowers that smell great. However, if it starts to come into the walkway, or gets blight, it needs to be pruned!

The same is true for your new work. The nature of building a business is that you're constantly growing your to-do list in a variety of directions. Every once in a while, stop to take stock of what you're doing, so you can honor your efforts and make adjustments. This is part of growing sustainably! I would suggest doing this once a quarter, at least. For a cue use the changes of season or due dates for quarterly tax payments.

In order to take stock, start by writing down everything you do. Imagine that you're creating a job description for someone else to take over your business. The next step is to make adjustments. Sometimes it's helpful to break this process into two basic categories: *Business You* and *Talent You*.

1. For *Talent You*: List all the things you do related to providing your service or making your product.

2. For *Business You*: List all the things you do related to the five areas of business: legal and taxes, numbers, marketing, operations, and self-management.

3. Make some observations. Such as:
    - How much time are you spending on the various tasks?
    - Is the amount of work correct for one person?
    - What tasks are not getting done that need to do?
    - Which tasks do you like? Which don't you like?

4 Make some changes. Notice what you like and find ways to do more of those things! For the things you don't like:

- Look at Strategies for Chores, page 314.
- Assign different tasks for different times. You don't have to do all these things at once. For example, you might alternate working on business and bookkeeping by month.
- Most importantly, cut back work if you need to. Or, if you need to work more, make a goal around your increased hours.

5 Write up your new job description for the next season. Make an agreement with yourself that you'll stick to this list. Consider posting it somewhere visible so you remember.

The purpose behind this activity is to keep you focused and to do the right amount of work—not too little, but not too much.

Make a Routine of Checking In

Working for yourself is sort of like being an explorer or pioneer. You're out in new terrain a lot. You sort of know where you're going, but you sometimes get lost. You're making progress and working hard! You rely on yourself—even though you sometimes get help from others. To keep up this lifestyle, it's essential to regularly stop, and if you will, make camp, count up supplies, and check your map. Sometimes we get further off course than we think, or we're going through fuel way too fast.

It is important to build some routines for stopping and checking in with yourself, and your vision. The rhythm is up to you. The number one best way to make this happen is to meet with another person, whether it's a business coach, spouse, or colleague. The second best way is to keep a regular appointment with yourself for reflection. Be sure to put it on the calendar and planning for one to two hours at least.

The overarching question: Is what I'm doing effective?

There are many different angles to this. You might use some of these for prompts:

- What's working? What's not working?
- Am I working on the projects that I want to be doing?
- Am I working with the clients I wanted?
- Are my clients happy?
- Is my work aligned with the purpose?
- Is it a pace that works for me?
- Do I have enough time?

Checking in with the big picture naturally dovetails with looking at finances. After all, your progress is reflected in your numbers too. You might make time to look at both together—or keep them separate.

For finances, the overarching question is often: Am I earning the money that I need?

Other questions:

- What am I bringing in each week or month?
- What are my expenses and product supplies (COGS) totaling?
- Am I saving for taxes as I need to?

These check-ins are very much worth the time. Most of my clients have some combination of weekly, monthly, quarterly, and annual check-ins.

Here's what I do:

Weekly I record all of my gross sales. I look to see if there's growth. I reflect on what's going well and what's not. I think about each client and if they are happy.

Monthly I record all of my expenses, and calculate my total take-home pay for the month. I think about new marketing ideas.

Quarterly I create a Profit and Loss Statement. This is for the state (for Apple Care) and for myself. It's just like filling out a Schedule C. I record my total gross sales and all my expenses, in order to see my profit. Doing this exercise gives me a lot to think about. I ask myself if I like my current mix of work activities, and then consider if I need to adjust services or policies.

Annually I reflect on the year as a whole. I consider what I've accomplished, what's changed, what's working, and what needs fixing. I compare the current Schedule C to previous years. I make goals about the year to come—what I hope to earn, how I hope to improve, and what to cut.

These check-ins keep me feeling sane. Otherwise, the business sometimes feels like a huge swirl of details and to-dos. These keep me grounded and refreshed and give clarity to my efforts.

Adrenaline Changes

Your body is likely to go through some chemical changes when you become self-employed. They will affect your mood, energy and motivation, and the changes can be quite confusing. It's important to know what's happening so as not to get alarmed.

[This is my lived experience as a self-employed person. It's also what I've witnessed time and again with my clients who set out on this journey. Frankly, I haven't known anyone who transitioned from a traditional job to self-employment who hasn't experienced these adrenaline changes.]

Consider this: The modern day employee is constantly bombarded with emails, memos, updates, meeting requests, deadlines, and changes in the workplace. These all cause little stresses, essentially creating constant fight or flight responses in the body. In order to take action, your body needs adrenaline. Imagine that every time this happens, a little red button is pushed to release this adrenaline, in turn giving you a quick flux of energy.

This is constant throughout the day.

Seeing the boss > stress > red button > energy.
Someone cuts you off in traffic > stress > red button > anger + energy.

It is tiring for the body to be in this state all the time. It needs recovery. Unfortunately, in our modern world, we rarely get a break. It used to be that time off work at home offered a reprieve, but now with email, cell phones, and a culture of constant communication, we rarely get a break. What's bizarre is that we come to rely on these surges to keep going through the day. Do you ever find yourself pushing the *get mail* button when you're tired or avoiding something? Every time I do this, I picture a rat pushing a red button....

When these triggers are taken away, we can experience an energy low. We can feel very tired and unmotivated. Have you ever had a vacation that was truly relaxing? Where no one asked anything of you? Chances are you felt sleepy, bored, listless, and not like moving.

For better or for worse, self-employment can feel like this in the beginning. You've removed the triggers and are going through adrenaline changes; some might even say withdrawal.

At first, many people are pleasantly surprised by how relaxed they feel. But then, after some time, concerning thoughts start to appear, "Wow, I'm being so lazy! Maybe I can't be my own boss. I guess I just don't have what it takes." Although this is rarely the truth...the feelings are very real. They are in line with what we've been taught in our culture. Unfortunately, these types of thoughts can lead to doubting your venture and quitting before you've actually given things a chance.

Do not give up! Do not despair!

Knowing this will happen is half the battle.

The other half is a combination of learning how to boost your energy in other ways and to create some adrenaline-producing events and routines. After all, some adrenaline is good.

Happily, as your work grows, it will naturally energize you. Deadlines and appointments will force you to get moving. Other strategies include: setting office hours, creating milestones to meet, saying yes to things before you're ready, and creating tools as needed for clients.

After some time, you'll get used to your new normal. Two things are likely true: you will keep yourself moving because of goals you care about, and your body will be in a relaxed state much of the time.

Deadlines / Milestones

Whether or not we like structure, we need it to keep going. When you work for yourself, so many things can be loose and/or flexible, making it easy to let important things slide when they are not urgent. For example, we put off tax preparation, building a website, or meeting a contact for coffee. Use deadlines and milestones to help you to stay motivated and on track

There are lots of ways to make deadlines. Do them however you want. Just be sure to use them regularly to ensure progress.

- Choose a specific date for a task. You can change it later.
- Choose a month and year—e. g., *In September, I will work on the website.*
- Create an event that forces you to get something done.
- Do the math—for time, tasks, and money in order to calculate the deadline. Or, pick deadlines based on your gut instinct.
- Write deadlines on your calendar.
- Make a poster or note.
- Make sequential deadlines: I must finish this, before I do that.

Talent You needs *Business You* to do this.

If a deadline is stressing you out, move it, or figure out why. This is important information too!

Maybe you don't know how long something will take. Just guess! And adjust. Or, schedule some time to figure it out.

Deadlines remind you to do the task. They help you to reserve time. They help you to say no to other things. They help you to prioritize.

ProTip: After setting a deadline, block out work time in your calendar. If you find there's not enough, then move the deadline.

Outsourcing Willpower

The research is clear: willpower is limited. When you're in charge, you're doing a million things and everything can take a little bit of willpower—email this client, get started on a project, fix the printer, etc.—because you have to make yourself do these things. It can be easy to run out of willpower.

Give yourself some help. Find ways to outsource your willpower. That is, create dates, appointments or events with other people...so that it forces you to get something done.

Have you ever noticed how you magically get the house all cleaned before a party? Or, if you sign up for a 5K, you somehow find time in your schedule to train...that you didn't have before?

Use this awareness to add some juice and focus to your work efforts.

In business, you might:

- Say yes to a new offering or product. Then make it/develop it in time for that person.
- Plan a workshop, and advertise it. Then, you'll be forced to create it.
- Tell a friend that you want to celebrate a finished project on a certain day. Then, figure out how you'll get it done before then.
- Make an appointment to do something hard—alongside someone else.
- Make an appointment in your calendar in the future. Sometimes just seeing that it's scheduled makes it feel less like a choice.
- Ask someone to check with you about something.

Forming Habits

There are lots of little details when doing business, and they are important to get right, whether they're for good customer service, ease of working, or legal or tax requirements. However, this need to manage details can lead to feeling overwhelmed and spread too thin. *Today I have to buy a ream of paper, track mileage, make some invoices, call the state, find my keys, and post on Facebook!...in addition to actually doing my work.*

Tracking all these details often requires long lists and a lot of task switching. It can be a drain on your energy. Even worse, it takes up brain space, making it harder to do your job. This is where habits come into play.

Forming habits is an important part of staying sane and keeping up on everything. The beautiful thing about habits is that once they're formed, they don't take any willpower. By definition, they are automatic. They don't take any thought or energy, which are two important commodities you need to grow your business.

But what habits do I need, and where do I start?

There are a handful of good habits that apply to most self-employed folks. (See page 313.) The rest you'll figure out over time. A good place to start is to look at anything that's giving you some stress. Work through these steps:

1. What is something that you're always losing, forgetting, or missing?
   Example: I'm always losing my car keys.
2. What is causing this?
   Example: I set them down in different places, and then they get covered up.
3. What's a tool or strategy that can help? What are solutions you've seen?
   Example: Key hooks....

4 Will this strategy work for you? If not, why? And what would be better?
Example: Hooks feel like too much work. I just want to throw them somewhere. Maybe a bowl would be better.

5 Set it up and start immediately.
Example: Find a bowl right now. I can find a prettier one later.

6 Commit totally to this goal.
Example: Even if the dog gets loose out the front door, I will put the keys in the bowl first.

The process of training yourself takes time and can be a challenge. It's tempting to let this slide because it feels like *small stuff*. Stay strong! The small stuff adds up to the big stuff. You'll be so glad that you did.

A few tips and ideas:

- Habits usually take three to six weeks to form. Give yourself time.
- It can be useful to pair activities—a new habit with an old one. Or, give yourself a cue. For example, I now take out recycling when brewing coffee.
- Only work on one or two at a time.
- If there are lots of habits you want to form, write each one on an index card. Keep just one out at a time to remind you to work on it. Once it's established, put the card away, and pull out a new one.
- Some can be tied to the calendar. For example, write "Billing" on every Friday.
- If they don't work right away, it's okay. Take a moment to evaluate. What's making it hard? Is there anything I can shift? Then start again.
- Find a visual reminder.
- Celebrate habits that have taken hold.

☞ Turn the page to see eight habits that really pay off.

Eight Great Habits for Almost All Self-Employed Folks

Always:

- Use business checking for all business purchases.
- Deposit all payments into business checking.
- With every deposit, immediately transfer 30% to business savings (40% if you collect sales tax).
- With paper receipts, write your business name on the top immediately after the cashier hands it to you.
- When you get home, after you set your keys down, find any paper receipts (from business expenses or material supplies) and put them wherever they are collected.
- Every time you get into the car for business, log into your mileage app or reach for your tracking notebook.
- During the first week of every month, fill out the Monthly Income Tracking chart for the previous month to see what you earned. Find the chart that matches your business in *Appendix 5: Tools*.
- Deposit checks either the day you receive them or on the same day of every week.

Strategies for Dealing With Chores

Every job, including a dream job, includes some chores. By this, I mean things that must be done...that maybe you don't like to do. It's very tempting to keep putting chores off, but the danger is that they will weigh on your mind. Here are a few strategies.

☞ Have a Chore Day. Maybe this is once a week or once a month. Make a list of all the little tasks you need to do, and do them all at once on that day. Be sure not to plan anything else on that day, so you can really get in the groove. Perhaps plan a fun event that night as a reward.

☞ Write each chore on an index card. Each day, select one and work on it. You could pull them out randomly from the stack, or you can select the easiest one each time.

☞ Make a list of all your chores. Then write each one on your calendar, just as you would write in a dentist appointment. Select a day and a specific time. Allot the amount of time you need to do this task. For example, you might write in: *Add Expenses to Excel Sheet* from 3:00 to 5:00 p.m. on Friday, June 10th.

☞ Try this helpful trick inspired by David Allen, author of *Getting Things Done.* Write your list of chores out. Next, for each one, write down the first actual action step. For example, you might write *Add expenses to spreadsheet* first. Next, you would add the first action step, *Print bank statement from last month.*

☞ Make a problem/solution list. Make three columns: chore, problem, solution. Write down each chore. In the Problem column, record what makes this chore difficult, e.g., *boring, don't know how to do it, feels hard*. Later, figure out a solution for each one. Some solutions might be to pair with something fun, get some help, or find missing pieces of information.

If certain tasks persist in being major bummers, find a way to outsource them if possible.

What are some of your work chores?

It's Good to Know Who's Really on Your Team (And Who's Not)

Lots of people love to give advice. This may or may not mean they are on your team.

People on your team hope the best for you, believe what you tell them, and they believe in you. They show interest, ask questions, and listen. They share information that seems relevant. They don't tell you what to do. They ask what kind of feedback you want. They ask if you want help before offering it. They understand that this process takes time.

Then there are people who *seem* helpful, but aren't really. They give you advice. "You know what you should do? You should…". They offer ideas before asking what yours are. They interrupt your thought to give you theirs. They tell you about things to watch out for, under the guise of being helpful, such as business ventures that have failed or scary statistics. They give lots of feedback you didn't ask for. "You know, your website could use some more pictures." They tell you what worked for a relative or friend. They act as if there's one right way.

And then, there are people who are obviously not being helpful. They say things that highlight the negative all the time. They ask questions that sounds biased already. "Can you earn enough doing that? Aren't there already a million photographers in the area?" They talk like any dream job is just a pipe dream. "Yeah, we all wish we could do that, but we have to grow up. "

Recognize who's who in your mind. For the Negative Nellies, the best thing to do is to *not* discuss business stuff with them. The more you say, the more they have to react to, and it will generally leave you with a sour feeling. Often these folks mean well but don't know how to be supportive. The best general method is: don't talk business with them, ever. Don't bring it up.

Pro Tip: If Negative Nellies ask about business just share a quick, positive summary, and change the subject. "Oh yeah, business is great. We're hoping to get out of town in February. How about you? "

On the flip side, it's also helpful to recognize the different kinds of supporters. Good listeners let you process. People with information, such as specific relevant facts and resources, can help you save time. Idea people can help you solve problems. (Just be sure they understand all your needs and constraints first.) Ambassadors are amazing and help build your reputation by talking to everyone about you.

Learn to utilize these folks. When you have a specific need for support, go to the person who can best help. This saves you time and honors their gifts.

Get Support

The best solo performers have support teams. Consider a cyclist on the Tour de France. They've got a van carrying their food and equipment. A race car driver pulls into the pit for his car to be serviced by the crew. Actresses have a beauty team to choose their clothes and hairstyles.

Self-employed people are often independent by nature. A common mistake is to start out on this journey alone and expect it to work.

It is not a sign of weakness to need help. It's a sign of being smart.

You need a team. This team can work any way that you want— it can be an informal, unrelated set of folks, or an organized group that is named.

Whoever they are, look for people who:

- Believe in what you're doing
- Get excited about your accomplishments
- Listen when you need it
- Understand what you're doing and why—so their ideas match your needs
- Answer questions
- Support your health and happiness

Some supportive professionals you might consider:

- Business coach
- Accountant and/or bookkeeper
- Marketing Consultant
- Designer
- Technology specialist
- Therapist

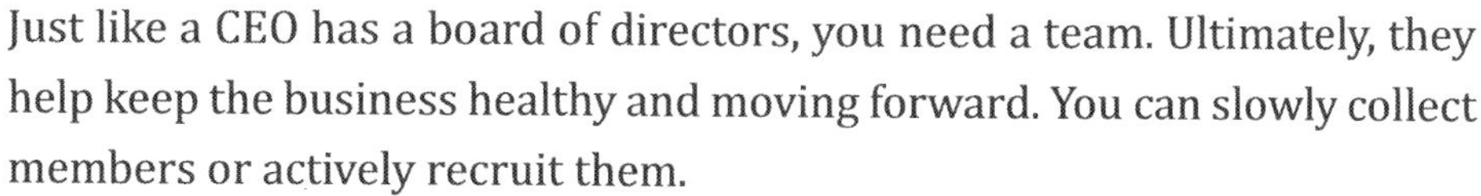

Just like a CEO has a board of directors, you need a team. Ultimately, they help keep the business healthy and moving forward. You can slowly collect members or actively recruit them.

Who's on your team?

Who would you like to add to your team?

Time Off is Essential

Repeat after me. "Time off is essential. Time off is essential. Time off is essential."

Consider how muscles are built. When you exercise, you create tiny, microscopic tears. During rest, the muscle rebuilds itself with bulkier tissue, making itself stronger for next time. Work and rest are both ingredients to stronger muscles, and, therefore, better performance.

The same is true for your new business. It will require both work and rest for you to stay strong, be effective, and to grow.

This is very counterintuitive and counter to our work culture. Although the business literature is starting to come around, few managers promote time off. It's also counter to our training, so even if you value rest, it can be hard to make it happen.

In addition, there are all kinds of temptations to work a lot. You are doing a job you love. You want to make more money and build your reputation. There is a strong instinct to work more and more when things get tough, especially if you care.

So how do you make rest happen? You have to plan it, write it on your calendar, and stick to it!

Here are some general recommendations:

☞ Make one day a week off sacred.

☞ Schedule vacations on your calendar—at least two per year, to start.

☞ Decide on your quitting time each day, and then quit at that time.

A couple things to note—

When you take time off, don't read or talk about work. Put it all in the back of your mind! This is your time to relax or work on the other parts of your life.

Be aware of the transition. At the beginning of your time off, your brain will want to keep working on your work. Just give it time to let go. If possible, distract it. This will become more natural with practice.

If you make rest a regular habit, you'll have better energy for clients or your creations. You'll be sharper, happier, and more insightful. (The creative process actually requires time when you're not thinking about the problem or project.)

Pro Tip: A rule of thumb from my observations is to imagine that every hour of intense work requires one-two hours of rest.

Learn to Get Comfortable Saying No

It is normal to say yes to almost everything that comes your way in the beginning...even if what you're saying yes to includes: jobs that aren't in line with what you do, clients you have reservations about, taking payments late, overbooking projects, and taking meetings during vacations.

There are some strong drivers. You're thinking might be:

> *I need this work. I don't know if more is coming my way.*
>
> *Maybe she'll be fine to work with, and I'm being too critical.*
>
> *Getting paid later is better than not getting paid.*
>
> *Maybe this project will lead to more work.*
>
> *I don't need a vacation....*

Additionally, it just feels good to say yes to people. If you're a woman, it's likely you were raised to always say yes to make people happy. It also proves to yourself and loved ones that you're serious about what you're doing.

Here's the rub. Whenever you're saying yes to one thing, you're actually, *always*, saying *no* to something else. And vice versa.

Consider this. Saying *yes* to a problem client is saying *no* to time spent in another manner, perhaps advertising for better fit clients, writing your blog, or organizing your work space.

When you say *no* to a potential problem client, you're saying *yes* to more peace of mind, happier working days, and room in your schedule.

Put more simply, when we say *yes* to things that aren't quite right, we're saying *no* to ourselves.

Of course, there are lots of times to say *yes*—to great fit clients, projects that pay well, raises, vacations, etc.

So, why are we talking about saying *no* so much? Because, you will be offered many, many opportunities. Some are good for you, and others are not. In the beginning, you might not be sure which is which. It's common to find yourself spread wide and thin, like a hose set on the mist setting. This can weaken you, causing stress and fatigue, and weaken your product or service. It impacts your ability to grow and move forward on goals. As you learn to say *no*, you become more potent and powerful—like a hose on the jet setting.

Getting in the Mindset of Saying No

Believe that saying *no* is good for you. Rationalize it however you need. Relate saying no to your own values. For example, if helping others is very important to you, you can say to yourself, "I can help people better, if I say 'no' sometimes." Or, if it's income, say "If I say 'no,' I will give higher-quality service, and I can spend extra time on advertising. "

Figure out what you are saying *yes* to! If you have a plan for yourself that includes knowing who your ideal clients are, taking time off, and experiencing less stress, it's easier saying no to compromise situations because you know what you're choosing.

Know that it gets easier with practice! Know that it is normal to have to say no.

Think of it like pruning a fruit tree. Trimming some branches makes the tree stronger, healthier, and it will bear more fruit.

Ways to Say No

- Delay the answer. Often, in the moment, we can get confused or want to please. Make it a habit to say, "Let me think on that. I'll get back to you."

  Pro Tip: Keep your "calendar" at home. This way you always have to check before giving an answer.

- Offer an alternative. It feels a lot easier to say no when we offer a different resource. Create a list of providers and businesses that offer similar products or services. "Your project is beyond my normal scope of work. You might try ____."

- Share what you do—very specifically—as a way of explaining why you want to pass on the opportunity. "My focus is helping women in North Seattle who don't have employees. Sorry, I'm not the right fit for you."

- Say you're "at capacity" or have a "full schedule." This can be true, even if you need more client work, because your other time is spent on advertising, bookkeeping, and building your future business. Your plan is to fill your schedule with ideal clients, business development, and even rest times.

- It's okay to be clear about the *no* and vague about reasons. "I need to pass on this project, but thank you for the opportunity."

Self-Care

You are the talent of your company. It's important to take care of yourself so that you can do excellent work, feel great, avoid burnout, and be a happy human being. This is good for you and good for business. You can stick with your venture longer, you'll make better decisions, and you'll attract and keep clients because people like being around others who are happy!

Professional athletes have coaches who make sure they are staying hydrated, stretching, eating right, and getting massages. You'll have to do this for yourself. It helps to have a plan, and to put things on the calendar.

Self-care also fills your reserves. Sometimes, last minute deadlines or emergencies come up where we have to draw on these. Make sure your tank is full! Stay ahead of the game by making self-care a constant practice.

List all the things you do to take care of yourself:

For example: massage, going to Ladywell's, drinks with friends, exercise, talk therapy, hobby time, sleeping in, TV in bed, community acupuncture

Now, identify these different levels of self-care. Bronze is the minimum you require, Silver is moderate, and Gold is maximum self-care. These might change according to the season.

Bronze Plan

List two or three.

Silver Plan

Include the bronze plan and add two more.

Gold Plan

Include the silver plan and add two more.

Which plan can you afford right now?

Pro Tip: Type this up, and hang it up somewhere visible, such as the fridge or in your office.

Pro Tip: Put these appointments and actions into your weekly flow schedule.

Stay Inspired!

Being inspired means that we believe in what we're doing, and we feel motivated or enlivened to take action. We need this energy to keep going through the tough times.

Connecting with others, whether in books, virtually, or in person can help us to stay inspired. Others show us that we're not alone and that our dreams are real. They stretch us beyond our limits and prove that ventures like ours can work!

Make a practice of getting inspiration. Here are a few ideas:

☞ If you know anyone who's self-employed, get their story! It's amazing what people will share if you offer them lunch and listen well. Try this—"Hello _______, I know you've been self-employed for a while. Any chance I can buy you lunch in exchange for your story? I would love to know more about how you got into your work, and how you like self-employment. "

☞ Reading books can be great if the people they're about are similar to us. Personally, I loved *$100 Start Up* by Chris Guillebeau. *Shop Class as Soul Craft*, by Matthew Crawford is another one. There are tons more. (You can write these books off as a business expense!)

☞ There are business-networking groups—both in person and online. These groups offer great referral networks, as well as the chance to have colleagues and friends.

☞ Find a friend who has a project that's important to them and have a regular lunch. Share what's going well, and what's tough. Maybe do a show 'n tell.

I believe that a habit of connecting with others pays off both figuratively and literally. Collecting more stories about similar people helps to normalize your journey, it's energizing, often offers strategies to use in your work.

Celebrations Are Important and Fun!

Celebrations are fun and serve so many purposes. They:

- reward you for hard work
- provide a moment to catch your breath
- give an opportunity to share with family and friends
- create a chance to close the loop on a long effort
- mark a change
- are motivating.

Find ways to celebrate accomplishments big and small.

One of the addictive qualities of video games is the visual reward that you get after intense efforts. These designers understand that the rewards keep you going! Utilize this strategy for yourself to keep you in the self-employment game.

You can set up celebrations ahead of time. These can be events with others or specific rewards for yourself. Putting them on the calendar and involving others can sometimes create a helpful accountability.

You can also choose a reward after the fact. One thing to be aware of is that we're sometimes too tired to celebrate!

Create a list of options...so you can choose from it when you get there. Or get in touch with a friend and say, "Hey, I just finished this big project. Want to celebrate with me somehow? "

Some celebration ideas are champagne, dinner out, spa treatment, happy hour, small party, purchase of some kind, an engraving, a weekend getaway, or a deposit toward a travel fund.

In Summary—Self-Management

One of the keys to developing your business is sticking with it over time. That's what self-management is all about. You create ways of working that are sustainable and pleasant.

You treat yourself well by developing habits that make work easier. You reflect to refine your practices, learn to say no, and celebrate accomplishments, just to name a few.

At first, many of these practices may feel strange and even indulgent. Stick with them! Over time, they will become more natural and will pay off.

It is a skill to self-manage. It is essential to your happiness and the health of your business. Be intentional about developing this skill, or figure out ways to delegate it.

Regularly celebrate milestones and achievements!

It's important for your clients that you learn to rock this aspect of business. The only way to serve them is to stay in your job.

Onward

Staying in the Game

•

Safe Travels

Staying in the Game

Introduction

By now, your life is likely different from before. You've got new benefits and freedoms. You also have some new challenges.

After the honeymoon period, it's common to have doubts about your choice of self-employment, especially if you're not earning what you need yet.

It can also feel lonely sometimes. People won't always understand your choices and may have a hard time relating to your new lifestyle. Additionally, if you ever need to vent or talk out any problems, friends and family might not be able to help any more. Many clients report to me that their loved ones encourage them to go back to an employed position at the first mention of difficulty.

Most of these issues resolve over time, but in the middle of the journey, they can put extra strain on you. At this point, it's all about staying in the game!

Remember the grapevines? And how most species need three to six years in the ground before producing usable grapes? All of that time, the gardener still needs to water and care for the plants to eventually produce the fruit.

This chapter presents the most common issues and hurdles that come up for self-employed people as well as some strategies and frames of mind that help.

Remembering Why

Sometimes the efforts and unknowns of self-employment can be a drag. It's important in these times to remember why you're choosing this path and what you're getting out of it.

Consider journaling with these questions or talking them over with a friend.

1 What are the reasons you started this journey?
2 What do you like about your new lifestyle?
3 How many days are you happy and satisfied?
4 What new things are you able to do now?

You might be making less money, but you're probably gaining other rewards. Often we get accustomed to the good new things in our lives and start to take them for granted.

For example, many clients report the following:

- less stress
- better sleep
- more time with family
- more time with home
- easier errands in the daytime
- access to early-bird or midday discounts.

Pick five things you love about self-employment from the list above, or add your own answers. Write them down, and post them somewhere.

OR

Perhaps you chose self-employment to accomplish a big objective—like working only during the kids' school day. Write down what this does for you, and post that.

We Tend to Forget the Hard Parts from Before

Pretty quickly...we tend to forget the hard parts of our old work life, such as traffic jams, long meetings, tough supervisors, coworkers that get under our skin, working lunch hours, and having less control.

Having autonomy and doing things in our own rhythms is such a wonderful and natural feeling that we very easily slip into this new state, and old stresses fade quickly. This is normal. The brain quickly acclimatizes to new realities. In addition, we probably don't want to remember the unpleasant parts of our old jobs and lifestyles. The memories get buried, especially if there are no cues to bring them up.

What results is a selective amnesia—which has some risks. When money is tight or times get tough, it can be easy to fantasize about working for someone else and idealize what this did for us. It can be tempting to throw in the towel and go back to your old lifestyle, as if it will solve all of the problems.

For some people, becoming an employee again is the right choice. The self-employment path isn't for everyone. However, before you take that step, it's important to call up the entire reality of being an employee. Be sure that you consider both the good and bad parts of that old work life, not just the good ones.

If you decide to keep going, it's helpful to remember from time to time all of those old stresses, because their absence is one of the perks to your new life. This automatically happens for me when I hear a friend complaining about something related to work. I listen and think, *Oh yeah, I don't have to deal with that anymore!* In fact, I am almost surprised with what people tolerate in their jobs. I listen and empathize with my friend, and on the inside I think about how good I have it now.

Perks and Trade-Offs

It's common to experience a lack of money and time when you begin to work for yourself. You might have to cut back on favorite purchases or activities for the transition period.

However, it's important that you still get some perks. It's helpful to identify the things that really make you happy as well as the things that you're willing to give up in order to get them.

I invite you to think through the perks and trade-offs by answering the questions below. (For what it's worth, it really does help to actually write out your answers.) I would like to further suggest that you consider both personal and professional items when filling out these lists.

What are three things that you always want to have?
My example: a mac computer, good face lotion, premium denim

1

2

3

What are some things you're willing to give up?
My examples: new shoes and clothes, attending concerts, and going out to eat

1

2

3

Living on a Lower Budget

It's usually possible to maintain your quality of life even if your budget is reduced. You can do this through a combination of little efforts and new awareness.

Here are a few thoughts and ideas to get you started. There are, of course, many great books and websites if you want to explore the topic further.

First, you might actually need less money than you did before. Working has its own costs, such as commuting, work clothes, dry cleaning, meals out, stress-related purchases, convenience foods, and *I-work-hard-I-deserve-this* impulse buys.

Second, when you have more time, more breathing space, and more happiness, it's easier to be intentional with money and to not buy more than you need. Naturally, many people spend less money without even trying or noticing.

Third, there are lots of little ways to cut spending. Some common tricks are: when eating out, split meals, have one fewer drink, or eat before going out. Cut back on coffee and pastries on the way to work. Take time to find clothes on sale. Shop using a list. Buy larger containers instead of pre-packaged convenience foods. Cook from scratch.

You can also find ways to pay less for the same thing. Learn when Happy Hours are. Use cash discounts. Do more comparison shopping. A penny saved really is a penny earned.

Pro Tip: Use cash as much as possible! (Instead of a debit or credit card). When we start with a handful of cash and then see it disappear, we feel its loss in a more visceral way. This leads us to being aware of our limits and thinking more carefully when we spend. This simple habit cuts down unnecessary spending quite a lot.

Reducing what you need to spend is like giving yourself a raise.

Considering a Side Job

If your income is growing too slowly, a second job might be a good way to fill the gap.

In addition to the helpful extra income, there are other purposes for a second job. It can give you a sense of security, provide networking opportunities, give you a break from your business, teach you a skill that you need, provide you a chance to be around other people, and provide a sense of structure to your week. Depending on the position, you might be able to get a discount for something you need or want for your business.

Just be careful that your second job doesn't slow your progress or become a detour. Some warnings to watch out for are jobs that cost you money, give you a lot of stress, don't pay that much, or tire you out.

When finding a side job, be sure that it fits in with your overall plan and that it supports you and your efforts. Some people decide that they actually prefer to keep a part-time job alongside their business.

If your desire is for your side job to be temporary, be sure to define the time period or earnings goal so you remember to leave when it's time. Otherwise, it can be very easy to stay longer than you intend—either from the comfort, or from loosening your spending so that you feel the need to stay longer for the money.

Perseverance

The first year or two takes some perseverance. Along with doing your new job, you're building the business side too, which demands new knowledge and new skills. On top of that, it can take a lot of courage to keep putting yourself out there. Often, you've taken a pay cut, which means less money to spend on the fun stuff and requires other sacrifices.

This period doesn't last forever! Eventually, you will have things like a website, print materials, routines, and policies. The business side will take less energy. You will have ambassadors to promote you, a business reputation, and sustainable self-employment. If you know this up front, it might make it easier to get through it.

Alongside all these challenges, you are likely to have some great energy boosters as well. Hopefully, you are enjoying your work! Other people's lives are improving because of you! Maybe your commute is shorter. Hopefully, you love the people you work with. Other life tasks might be easier because you can do them at convenient hours. Grocery shopping, for example, takes half as long in the middle of a weekday as it does in the evening. The newness and the achievements will carry you for a while.

Then, at some point, you may arrive at this feeling: *I just want to do my work! I don't want to worry about the website any more, and I'm tired of doing free work or rounding down on my bill.* It's an exhausted, tired feeling. And it can feel like defeat. *When will this end? I didn't go into self-employment just to deal with marketing and minutiae!*

Believe it or not, this a good thing. Many of us start to let down near the finish line, so this is likely a sign that you're near the end of building your business foundation. This feeling of exhaustion often leads to two great outcomes. First, it allows you to relax some of your standards and just let things be as they are. This creates a more sustainable work environment, which leaves more time for other aspects of your life. (This is especially helpful for anyone with perfectionist standards.)

Second, it means it's time to give yourself a "raise" by doing some of the following: refusing to do free work, charging for all your time, and maybe even raising your rates. These actions are often hard in the beginning but are a lot easier after hitting this point.

Finding Co-Travelers

It's great to be unique, but it's tiring to feel alone. You need to vent, celebrate, and process with people who understand. Validation comes when people really understand what you're going through because they've been there, or they're on a similar journey. Find some co-travelers to give you company and support.

Whether they are in your field or doing different work, co-travelers can be other self-employed folks or anyone pursuing a unique path that they really care about.

How do you find them? Formally, you can join networking associations such as BNI (Business Networking International), or community groups such as the F Bomb Breakfast Club, your chamber of commerce, or look for a meet-up group. There are also great co-working spaces, such as The Riveter or The Inc. Usually, even paying for the most basic membership allows you access to events where you can meet other members.

Informally, you might run into some other folks when working in a coffee shop or purchasing supplies. If you connect with someone, you might suggest having work dates, or swapping stories over lunch.

Find some people who get it, and stay connected.

Get Used to People Not Understanding You

Most people are not self-employed. They commute, answer to a boss, and work fifty weeks a year. Therefore, they may not understand your self-employed lifestyle. They might make comments and ask questions that show this misunderstanding. Sometimes they are funny, and sometimes they are irritating. Here are some things I hear a lot:

"I could never work from home! I need to be around people."

My reality: I spend over half of my work hours with people! In fact, I'm working with people so much that I now need to schedule alone time on the weekends.

"How does your husband like retirement?"

Our reality: My husband Alex is far from retired. He's self-employed and works a lot—building his businesses, writing, doing construction, cooking, and taking care of the kids.

"I could never work for myself. I don't know the first thing about business."

My reality: I didn't either—but I learned, and none of it is that complicated.

In my experience, sometimes people listen to your answers, and sometimes they don't. At first, I felt sort of sad that so many people didn't understand, or even try to. But then I got used to it as my *new normal*, and I remembered that I'm unique and doing something special, so it's normal for others not to understand. How could they?

With that awareness, I now get less irritated, and I either answer with more patience or change the subject.

Picture the Future That You Want

The point of any job is to support you as a person—both to provide for your basic needs *and* to offer you the lifestyle that you want to live.

It's important to remember what you're working for, that is, the lifestyle that you're trying to build, whether it's to have more time for your kids or travel, to do unique work, help people, or maintain a sustainable work schedule so that you stay healthy and well.

This is like setting the North Star on your map. It guides you, lights your path, and gives context and orientation for all that you do. In order to keep your hope alive, develop a clear picture of this lifestyle and how your business is a part of it.

Imagine that it's three years from now. Your business has grown steadily. You have the workload and the income that you want. What does your life look like?

To develop this picture, journal or think through these questions:

- What does your work week look like? What activities does it include?
- How many hours are you working?
- Who are the people that you're working with?
- After paying your bills, what money is left over? How do you want to use it? Hobbies, travel, savings, art, furniture, or...?
- How do you want your days to feel week in and week out? What is your year like—as far as seasons, work times, and off times?

Once or twice a month, try calling up these images—perhaps when you're driving around, falling asleep, or standing in the grocery line. The more you imagine the life you want, the more real it will become.

You Might Need Some New Hobbies

If you've built a business out of something that you love to do, it is now your work. This means you need some new hobbies.

Why? To be a happy human who is good at your job, you need to get a break from work! It's important to think about other topics, to play, to have fun, and to learn new things. Hobbies provide all of that in a no-pressure setting; you're engaging in activities because you want to, not because you have to. No matter how much you love your work, you need to be able to switch gears from time to time.

Be aware that if your new work used to be your hobby, you'll have to re-train your brain; it's in the habit of thinking about work during your off hours.

For example, before working as a self-employment consultant, I used to read about behavioral science and best business practices in my free time. This was fun for me—and was both entertaining and relaxing. But now it's so related to my job that reading these types of books naturally makes me think about work. That's okay sometimes, but my brain still needs a break. I had to train myself to stop reaching for these books on Saturdays, and to not chat about these topics too much on the weekends. Once I identified some new hobbies, it was a lot easier!

So, give yourself some time to identify new possible hobbies, to explore them, and to learn how to "turn off work" in your off time.

What are some areas of interest that you'd like to explore?

In Summary—Staying in The Game

Sometimes being self-employed can feel lonely and challenging. Therefore, it's important to have strategies to stay in the game.

To keep your challenges in context, remember why you've chosen this path as well as the challenges of being employed that you've likely forgotten.

Figure out what perks you still need in your life, and what you're willing to give up.

Find ways to live on a lower budget, and perhaps consider getting some side work—as long as it supports your primary work.

Persevere. Time is a major ingredient.

Find some company! Connect with others who are self employed. Also, get used to people not understanding you sometimes.

Remember, this is all about lifestyle.

Lastly, you might need some new hobbies.

Safe Travels

I wanted to leave you with a few of my favorite quotes and concepts—the ones I reach for whenever I hit any bumps in the road. (These authors are all mentioned in Appendix 2.)

When the business side or marketing starts to feel too complex, I get focused again by Chris Guillebeau's words:

> "Make something worth talking about and then talk about it."

•

Whenever I doubt what I'm doing, I remember Steven Pressfield's concept of Resistance—the complex and "repelling force" that pops up and attacks whenever one is doing anything creative, for growth or for the soul. In one section called "Resistance Plays for Keeps," he writes:

> "[Resistance's] target is the epicenter of our being: our genius, our soul, the unique and priceless gift we were put on earth to give and that no one else has but us."

I take this to mean that Resistance is proof when I'm getting close to my most important work. It's confirmation that I'm headed in the right direction.

•

When I'm tempted to work too hard, or too long at something, I think of the 4th Agreement, written by Don Miguel Ruiz:

> "Always do your best, no more, no less."

•

Whenever I ask, Who am I to do this work, or take this on? The answer comes back, "Who are you not to?" ...just one small snippet from a beautiful, famous quote by Marianne Williamson. (Full quote in Appendix 2.)

•

Here's one of my own pet theories and a few related thoughts. There's no role model for being you. To be our own authentic self, we have to make it up, figure it out, and go out into unknown territory, because we can't just follow someone. This takes courage on many levels. And doing courage is different than reading about it. It's hard, and there's no shortcut.

Even so, it's totally worth it! It feels amazing to be on my own pathway. There's a sense of integrity within myself, and of being alive. I see this in my clients too: aliveness, radiance, participation in life.

Wishing you safe and happy travels in your journey. :)

Appendices

Appendix 1: **Common Roadblocks to Starting, FAQs and Myths**

Appendix 2: **Recommended Reading**

Appendix 3: **Tax Season Checklist**

Appendix 4: **How To Close Everything**

Appendix 5: **Tools**

Appendix 6: **Glossary of Terms**

Appendix 1: Common Roadblocks to Starting, FAQs, Myths

I don't like business.

What does that mean exactly? Many of us have connotations about that word *business* that are very specific and negative, such as: being profit-focused, doing anything for a buck, caring only about money, greed, etc. But are these associations true? Are they helping us now?

Let's redefine and reclaim that word. At its core, doing business is simply an exchange of value between two people—usually this includes providing a service or a product for money.

Also, let's remember that you're not trying to build a stand-alone business...you're becoming self-employed to make a job for yourself that you really like. You are required to own a business to be self-employed, but that doesn't mean you need to be a *business person*.

Sometimes, I'll use the word "business" in place of the phrase "your self-employment work" because it is easier to write and read, and the word business gets at the aspects of your work that are different than your service or product.

Finally, you can still be self-employed, even if you don't like "business".

I don't like numbers.

This is a big one for a lot of people. What does that word numbers mean to you? For many, it pulls up dark memories of math or statistics classes, or accounting jargon they've heard but don't actually know—monsters in the closet.

Great news! The numbers that are a part of your business will be meaningful to you. How many clients do you have? How many hours did you bill for this week? How many products did you sell? Can you pay all your bills? Is there money leftover? Could you pick up the check at the restaurant? Can you buy the new boots you want for winter?

The actual math involved is quite simple. And, there are a lot of apps and software programs out there to do it anyway.

More good news—you can outsource a lot of number stuff! You can hire an accountant or find someone to help with your bookkeeping. Sometimes, if you have a number-savvy life partner, you can get them to take on this role.

It seems too complicated.

I hear you. Even though I have tried to boil this process down to its simplest form, I acknowledge that it looks complicated. It's most complicated before you've started—when you're still on the outside looking in.

Getting started will help. Let's say there are ten things you don't know. Do one or two. Do what you understand. Then, you only have eight things left. Do one or two more. Those things can be moved out of your field of vision for a bit, so now you're looking at six things. It starts to get clearer.

For the stuff that is really hard, or, as one client says, "makes me feel stupid," slow way down. Watch a video, get a friend to explain it to you, or hire a consultant who is friendly and patient. Take a class. Be nice to yourself. You'll get through it.

I think I need a business plan.

Probably not. This is the number one roadblock that I hear. Business plans serve two major functions. They help you think through the aspects of having a business, and they are often required for a bank loan or investors.

The problem is that often the moment you press *print* on the plan and get started, you're veering from the projections. The plan becomes moot.

If you need to get funding, then by all means, do a business plan. I suggest looking at Guy Kawasaki's approach. Either search online for his plan, or find the book, *The Art of the Start*.

Otherwise, instead of a business plan, work on a transition plan. Figure out how you can earn enough money while building your business. Work through this book, and learn by doing.

I like to do things all the way. (I don't like doing this at a low level of quality.)

Chances are, you are a high-achiever. You're used to doing things well. Probably, your habit is to craft and revise multiple times before sharing your product or service. So, if you're used to working at a certain level of quality, it can be intimidating to add tasks that you're new at or nerve wracking to do things at a lower level of quality.

For example, maybe you've never set up a website before, and now you need one. You have an expectation that yours will be perfect. (Or why do it?) So, you expect that you'll read several books, maybe take a class, and that you'll figure it out. The idea of outsourcing isn't appealing because it costs money and the web designer might not do as good of a job. But there's a problem in this. It takes lots of time to learn and do new things, time you don't have. You might find that weeks go by, and it's still not done.

In this case, it helps to lower your standard and recognize that part of being a high-quality business is having all the pieces in place, even if they're not top-notch. So do the best you can, or be okay with hiring out. Over time, you can keep polishing your work to get it up to the quality level.

I don't have any money saved. OR I don't have enough time/energy on the side of my current work.

You can still get things started. Think about your business idea like a one-credit college class. If you can find one to two hours a week to spend on it, you can make a lot of progress in a few months! Define a set number of hours to spend on this venture, and when you're ready for a few clients, start putting the word out.

Use this income to pay for your start–up costs, then start saving any extra money. This gives you a way to try your dream and will help you discover if you have a viable idea. Then, if possible, find ways to reduce your work hours with your job, in order to have more time for your business.

One of my first clients had this very issue. She was working full-time as a massage therapist. She started doing a few massages a month on her "off" days in her living room. Friends were comfortable in that setting; after all, once you're on the table with eyes closed, it doesn't matter where you are. She saved all that cash. Eventually, she was able to sublet a massage room one day a week. Later, she went up to two days a week and started cutting back on her main job. Only a year later, she was able to quit her job at the clinic and she now makes the same amount of income working three and a half days a week.

I don't have the perfect name yet.

Some people are lucky enough to find the perfect name quickly. For others, (like myself) it's a six-month process. Do what you need to find your perfect name. Just don't let it slow down your process. Pick a placeholder in the beginning. (Remember, you can register one name, and then change it later!)

Keep in mind things that seem perfect now, weren't always in the beginning. Over time, they became perfect.

One idea is to give yourself a time limit—whether it's a set number of hours or a deadline. For example, you can say: *After ten hours of research, list making, etc. I will pick the top contender.* Or, *September 30th is the deadline for knowing the name.*

Another idea is to pick your top three. Try each one on for size for a week. Start talking to people, using the current name. *I'm thinking about this....* Maybe, make a pretend business card. Ask potential clients what they think.

What if I can't earn enough money?

There's only one way to find out. Do the work. Monitor your earnings. Give yourself prove-it-by dates.

Example: I have six months to build earnings to $2000 a month. Then one more year to get to $4000 a month.

Be creative—what about a part-time job to supplement? Ways to cut your spending? Could you rent a room out?

What if I'm not that good at it?

The simple answer: Try it and see.

When we're in a learner state, we look to the greats for knowledge and guidance. And then, we compare ourselves to them. By this standard, we always fall quite short. Comparing ourselves to greats isn't a realistic gauge of how we're actually doing.

Instead, try working with others outside of your field. It's amazing—once you start working with the public, you realize you know more than you think! Doing your work will both teach you, and give you more confidence. So get started.

Often, when we have ideas, they are perfect in our imagination. They can also change immediately. Once we start acting on them, the reality pales in comparison. This is common. Everything pales to the imagination.

When this happens, you have to trick your brain. Tell yourself it will be perfect in the future. Tell yourself you can change things. Get excited about the idea that you're bringing new things into existence. Your first business card! Your first website landing page! Your city license on the wall!

Or find one area to do things all the way, without compromise. Maybe you'll have the best business cards, stationary, or website. Enjoy how awesome that thing is.

Try to see yourself from others' points of view. They're noticing the overall accomplishment. *Wow, she is so amazing! She started up a consulting business on the side of her job!*

What if it fails? What will I think? Or say to others?

Even if your venture fails, it's possible for you to still be a winner. You will know that you tried. This will likely give you a deep sense of satisfaction, and you can move on. Or, you can try again in the future— with more experience! No matter what, you'll have more self-knowledge, business knowledge, and additional skills. It's also possible that you can now bargain for a higher pay rate when applying for jobs.

Sometimes talking to others can bring up the feelings of failure. Turn that around. Try this: When talking to others, create a short version of the story that is true and positive.

Example: *I gave myself a year to try it out. I decided that I missed the structure of a job.*
Or: *I liked the work, I just decided that I didn't like the marketing aspect.*
Or: *There was less demand than I expected. I'm going to do something else for a while, and might go back to it.*

A friend or family member had a business that failed. I don't want to follow in their footsteps.

You are not your friend or family member. You know this, logically...but emotionally, you might think that you'll behave similarly to them. Times change. Opportunities change. You likely have different skills, knowledge areas, types of friends, etc. from this person.

Having said all that, this emotion is a deep one and is likely to affect you. It's worth talking it through with a trusted friend or therapist.

One helpful tool is to make a list of how you're similar to your friend or family member, and how you're different. What contributed to their business not working? How can you counteract those things? Make a plan that deals specifically with these issues.

Maybe quiz them and learn from their experiences.

Family and friends think I'm crazy. And I don't know what to say to them.

Doing anything new or different looks crazy to other people. It's normal for them to doubt you, or to not understand. The best thing to do is give it time. Once you've built some things like a website, an online store, and a list of clients you've served, they'll start to understand. Adopt a "show, don't tell" policy.

In the beginning, keep your stories about your business brief and confident. Focus on what's working. For example, "It's going well. I've got my website up, and have two new clients." Or, "I'm working to double my sales by December."

If someone close is truly worried about you, then take some time to hear what they have to say and to share your plans. Arrange a time to sit down in a relaxed way. Acknowledge their concern and ask them exactly what they are worried about. Show them you understand, and thank them. This will help them to feel heard, and should go pretty far to calm them down. You don't need the answers to their questions. Mostly, people just want to be heard.

Helping them calm down will help you.

If they don't calm down, you can think: *Time will tell!* In that case, just keep doing your thing.

How do I find Health Insurance?

This is beyond the scope of this book. Here are a few ideas to get you started on your own research.

Pro Tip: Make appointments on your calendar to do this research. Otherwise, it can be too easy to keep it on the back burner!

To get health insurance in Washington State, you have two basic options:

1 Purchase a policy directly from an insurance company, such as Premera Blue Cross or Group Health Cooperative.

OR

2 Use the Washington Health Plan Finder, www.wahealthplanfinder.org. It will ask you questions about yourself and family (if applicable), and then give you policy options, based on your income.

If your income is low enough, you might be enrolled in Apple Health Care, meaning some or all of the cost will be subsidized. In this case, you'll need to send in proof of your income to the Washington Health Care Authority, the Medical Eligibility Department in the form of a Profit and Loss Statement (P and L). A Schedule C is an example of a P and L, see page 177.

I already have Medical Insurance. Will this cover me while I'm working?

Your personal medical insurance policy may not apply to on-the-job injuries. Call your insurance company and ask. If they do not, you might consider getting some coverage through the state. Call the State Department of Labor & Industries and investigate the possibility of opening an account for yourself. The number is: 800.547.8367. Generally speaking, L&I includes both significant medical insurance as well as coverage for loss of wages and other benefits for those injured on the job.

How about Dental Insurance?

Sometimes your health-insurance provider will offer dental insurance as well. This is probably the easiest and most cost-effective way to get coverage.

If you need to find a stand-alone policy, here are two tips—

- If you already have a dentist, call their office and talk to the person who handles billing. Ask which policies they take and about their experiences with the various companies.

- If you don't already have a dentist, try asking friends and family members about their dentists and dental policies.

Something to know ahead of time is that, often, major dental work (such as crowns) will not be covered right away. You may have to wait six to twelve months.

Life Insurance Policies

There are many, many kinds of life insurance with different benefits and rules. Working with an agent you trust is an excellent way to decide if this is coverage you want and what type of policy best fits your needs.

Be sure to ask about a Term policy. This is an excellent way to obtain low-cost life insurance. With this type of policy, you select the number of years that wish the policy to remain in effect e.g., 10 years, 15 years, etc. You make payments that entire time. When the term ends, you may be able to convert this policy to a permanent or universal life policy.

Pro Tip: Be sure that the rates for the term policy cannot change during the policy term and that you have the option to convert the policy to a permanent plan, if you want. Also be sure there is no penalty if you choose to cancel the policy before the end of the selected term.

What if I want to hire an employee?

Hiring employees adds some layers of complexities. It takes time to find the right person, train them, and to manage them. Even more importantly, as an employer, you will have additional legal responsibilities to meet. A few examples are: to set up an L&I account with the state and to make payments for your employee(s), to withhold federal taxes, get Employer Identification Number (EIN), and to follow legal hiring policies to name a few.

I generally tell clients to research this thoroughly first by meeting with a lawyer, getting help with Greater SCORE of Seattle (www.seattle.score.org), or by calling the state Business Licensing Service at 800.451.7985.

Do I need to hire a lawyer?

I cannot answer that question exactly. Every business is different. There are many tasks that we are legally allowed to do, without a lawyer. These include: forming a single-member LLC, creating contracts, registering copyrights and trademarks.

Having said that, some folks prefer to hire a lawyer to aid in the above situations—since a lawyer can speak to all of the legal requirements of business, different tax laws, choices of business entities, how contracts work, etc.—giving some peace of mind and aiding in decision-making. Lawyers can also do some of that work for you, saving you time. Having good advice early on can also save you major headaches in the future.

Here are some situations where a lawyer is required or highly advised:

- ☞ If making $100K or more. A lawyer can look at changing to a different business entity, such as an S-corporation, which may save you money.
- ☞ Setting up any legal partnerships.
- ☞ Protecting intellectual property. Especially for patents.
- ☞ When considering hiring employees.

Why should I do this again?/ Am I crazy?

You are doing this because you have an idea or a dream. Maybe it's to have more free time, a different lifestyle, for a change of pace, or to help people.

I believe this is important. It is worth exploring, and it will lead somewhere.

What's the worst that can happen? Maybe your self-employment venture will flail and flop. So be it. You will have learned something. Maybe you don't love that service or product. Or, maybe you do, but you need more resources for the next go-round. Maybe this will lead to a different job. Maybe you can use your new knowledge in your field. Maybe you'll have more confidence to ask for a raise or negotiate a higher salary in the next job.

Maybe it'll grow slowly and steadily. Or, maybe it'll take off. There are all kinds of results. At the least, you'll be trying out your dream.

Appendix 2: Some Favorite Books to Recommend

If You Can Only Read Three Books

The Art of the Start
Do the Work
Be Excellent at Anything

(Complete title and author information follows.)

17 of My Favorite Books

General Business + Marketing

The Art of the Start: The Time-Tested, Battle-Hardened Guide for Anyone Starting Anything *by Guy Kawasaki*

The $100 Start-Up: Reinvent the Way You Make a Living, Do What You Love, and Create a New Future *by Chris Guillebeau*

The Boss of You: Everything A Woman Needs to Know to Start, Run, and Maintain Her Own Business *by Emira Mears and Lauren Bacon*

Brand Yourself: How to Create an Identity for a Brilliant Career *by David Andrusia*

Legal and Taxes + Numbers

Accounting Made Simple: Accounting Explained in 100 Pages or Less *by Mike Piper*

Independent Contractor, Sole Proprietor, and LLC Taxes Explained in 100 Pages or Less *by Mike Piper*

Your Money or Your Life: Transforming Your Relationship with Money and Achieving Financial Independence *by Joe Dominguez and Vicki Robin*

Nitty Gritty

Getting Things Done: The Art of Stress-Free Productivity *by David Allen*

Organizing from the Inside Out: The Foolproof System For Organizing Your Home, Your Office and Your Life *by Julie Morgenstern*

Self-Management

The 7 Habits of Highly Effective People: Powerful Lessons in Personal Change *by Stephen R. Covey*

Be Excellent at Anything: The Four Keys To Transforming the Way We Work and Live *by Tony Schwartz*

Do the Work: Overcome Resistance and Get Out of Your Own Way *by Steven Pressfield*

First, Break All The Rules: What they World's Greatest Managers Do Differently *by Marcus Buckingham & Curt Coffman*

Now, Discover Your Strengths: *by Marcus Buckingham and Donald Clifton*

Inspiration

The Four Agreements: A Practical Guide to Personal Freedom (A Toltec Wisdom Book) *by Don Miguel Ruiz, Janet Mills*

The Diamond Cutter: The Buddha on Managing Your Business and Your Life *by Geshe Michael Roach, Lama Christie McNally*

Peace Is Every Step: The Path of Mindfulness in Everyday Life *by Thich Nhat Hanh, Edoardo Ballerini*

Quote from Marianne Williamson

(Mentioned in Safe Travels)

"Our deepest fear is not that we are inadequate. Our deepest fear is that we are powerful beyond measure. It is our light, not our darkness that most frightens us. We ask ourselves, 'Who am I to be brilliant, gorgeous, talented, fabulous?' Actually, who are you not to be? You are a child of God. Your playing small does not serve the world. There is nothing enlightened about shrinking so that other people won't feel insecure around you. We are all meant to shine, as children do. We were born to make manifest the glory of God that is within us. It's not just in some of us; it's in everyone. And as we let our own light shine, we unconsciously give other people permission to do the same. As we are liberated from our own fear, our presence automatically liberates others."

—Marianne Williamson, *A Return to Love: Reflections on the Principles of "A Course in Miracles"*

Appendix 3:
Tax Season Checklist

Dec. 31	Renew Business License with Seattle
Jan. 31	Make Report to Seattle (Send in city B&O tax If you earned over $100K)
	Make Report to DOR
	Send in any required tax to DOR: sales tax collected, use tax, B&O tax
Apr. 15	Include Business Income with IRS filing
	Pay Income and Self-Employment Taxes
Apr. 30	Report to King County (Pay any taxes, if applicable)

	If Applicable—
______	*LLC Renewal - on the anniversary month*
______	*Order 1099-MISC forms*
Jan. 31	*Submit 1099-MISC forms to Payees*
Jan. 31	*Submit 1099-MISC forms to IRS*
______	Additional Tasks for Your Business— (Add to your list: renew professional insurance, renew permits, other requirements.)
______	
______	
______	
______	

1. Renew City of Seattle Business Tax Certificate—by December 31st

The standard fee is $110. It's $55 if you earn under $20K.

1 Go to filelocal-wa.gov*. Sign in. (Create an account, if necessary.)

2 On your home page / dashboard, look for "Renew a License".

3 Follow instructions.

4 Pay and print your receipt.

*Or, go to Seattle.gov, search for "renew business license", follow links to FileLocal.

Call the city if you need help: 206.684.8484

2. Make a report to the City of Seattle—by January 31st

The city collects its own B&O tax. If you earn less than $100K, then you will NOT owe any tax. You still must make a report.

You'll need to report Gross Sales in each category:

Services	Wholesale	Royalties
Retail	Manufacturing	

1 Go to FileLocal-wa.gov, sign in. (You may have to create an account.)

2 Select "File a New Tax Form".

3 For the "filing period" select December of the last year.

4 Follow instructions on each screen. If you do any work in the Services category, you'll have to fill out a pop-up worksheet. It's kind of confusing. If you get stuck, call the city! 206.684.8484. (Or, check out my walkthrough on seattlebusinessapothecary.com.)

5 If necessary, pay B&O tax.

6 Print your receipt.

3. Make a report to the Department of Revenue (DOR) of Washington State—by January 31st

If you are an annual filer, this is your only report to make each year. Some of you may be on a quarterly or monthly schedule.

You may call the DOR to get help with filling out your form. 800.647.7706. If necessary, send sales tax collected, pay use tax, and pay B&O tax.

You'll need—

Gross Sales in each category:	Services	Wholesale
	Retail	Manufacturing
	Royalties	

Sales Tax Paid at the Source—if Applicable
If you made products or resell items, you'll also need the subtotal of purchases where you paid sales tax already. This is for a deduction called, Tax Paid At the Source.

Totals for Use Tax
Total up all purchases made for which use tax is owed. This includes items bought out of state or online, where you were not charged WA state sales tax.

Heads Up! The state is changing their portal soon.

1 Go to dor.wa.gov.

2 Login to your account*.

3 Find "File A Return".

4 Look for "Returns to be Filed"—select link below.

5 Follow instructions.

6 Confirm and pay.

7 Print receipt.

*If this is your first time logging in, you may need to set up your account. For this, you will need your UBI number and a PAC code. The state usually sends your PAC code in the mail. You may also call them to get the code at 800.647.7706.

If necessary, you will send in any sales tax collected, and pay any B&O tax and use tax.

4. Report business income (or loss) to the IRS—by April 15th

This report gets added to the standard tax form, the 1040. (Once you have a Schedule C, you must use the full 1040. Once you have business income, you may NOT use the 1040-EZ or 1040-A.) You may file online, hire an accountant, or use paper forms, for which the business will require filling out the Schedule C, SE and possibly some additional forms.

You'll need:

Gross Sales
COGS and Inventory—(if applicable)
Expenses by category—including mileage and square footage of dedicated office space

From those figures, you, the accountant, or the online program will calculate:

Business Income or Loss
Self-employment tax owed
Self-employment tax deduction

If necessary, you will pay income tax and self-employment tax on business income.

5. Report value of "personal property" to King County—by April 30th.

Personal property refers to tools, equipment, furniture, and supplies owned by the business. If the value is over $7500, you may need to pay tax.

You must make a report every year, even if you don't owe any tax.

Go to: www.kingcounty.gov/depts/assessor/Personal-Property/eListing.aspx. To see instructions.

Call the King County Assessor's office at (206) 296-5126 if you need any help.

6. If applicable: Renew LLC with the Business Licensing Service—due the anniversary month of formation

The current cost is $60. When you renew your LLC, you're making an annual report. For a single member LLC, this essentially includes confirming your name and address.

1 Go to https://ccfs.sos.wa.gov/#/
2 Sign in
3 Find "Business Maintenance Filings" on the left
4 Select "Annual Report"
5 Search for your business
6 Follow instructions
7 Pay fee and submit

7. If applicable: Order and submit 1099-MISC forms—due January 31st

These are free. You need to order directly from the IRS or access via specialized software. They are carbon forms.

1 Go to www.irs.gov.

2 Search *online ordering*.

3 Select *Online Ordering for Information Returns and Employer Returns*.

4 Scroll down to find Form *1099-MISC*.

5 Put in the desired quantity for the correct year. (Usually, there are two columns.)

6 Follow the instructions to complete your order.

7 Meanwhile, double check that you have collected a W-9 form from each payee. See page 141.

When they arrive—

1 Fill out the 1099-MISC as instructed.

2 Fill out the included 1096 form; it's like a cover page for all of your forms.

3 Submit copy to payee by the due date in instructions.

4 Submit copy to the IRS by the due date in instructions.

5 Keep copies for your records.

Bravo! Celebrate your completion of the tax season!

Appendix 4: How to Close Everything

It's easy enough to close up shop. There are two phases—

1 Let all the government bodies know that your business is closed.

2 Participate in your final tax season, by completing your reports and making any tax payments.

Here's what to do for each agency:

- For the IRS, there is no account to close. Simply file your final Schedule C.

- To end your LLC (if you have one):

  Secretary of State
  File a Certificate of Dissolution
  It's a paper form. Go to: sos.wa.gov/corps/ClosingaLimitedLiabilityCompany.aspx
  OR
  Search: "close LLC washington state" to find current link.

- To close your state business license and your state tax account:

  Business Licensing Service & the Department of Revenue
  File a form online, or print and send in the mail.
  Go to: bls.dor.wa.gov/close.aspx
  You must include trade names. This closes both your state business license AND your account with the DOR.
  Make reports and submit any state tax through your next reporting cycle—you'll either be on a monthly, quarterly, or annual schedule.

- To close your account with King County:

  King County Assessor
  File an Advance Tax Request form—within 30 days of closing
  Request from the Personal Property Section
  Email: personal.property@kingcounty.gov
  Or call: 206.296.5126
  Or, go to: www.kingcounty.gov/depts/assessor/Forms.aspx
  Look for Advance Tax Request Form

  You'll be asked to report what you did with all of your business equipment—what was sold, kept, disposed of, etc. After that, the county will determine if you owe any final taxes, and will let you know that amount. Any taxes are due until the following April.

- To close your city business license tax certificate:

  City of Seattle
  Use an online form or send an email
  Go to: www.seattle.gov/licenses/cancel-a-business-license
  (Simply not renewing, doesn't count. You need to let the city know that you're closing your business...or they might send you some unpleasant letters.)

Appendix 5:
Tools and Worksheets

Contents~

About the Journey

- ☞ You are stepping into a new way of working. You need some new mental frames and strategies to deal with the challenges.

- ☞ Think of building your business as if you're going to graduate school. Make a Transition Plan that includes a way to earn enough money to pay all your bills, so you have time to develop your business.

- ☞ Realize, there are now two versions of you: *Business You* and *Talent You*.

- ☞ Learn the requirements of business. This empowers you and brings peace of mind. Give yourself time; it's a learning process.

- ☞ Think sequentially. Work on projects in order, not all at once.

- ☞ Do things your way! You'll enjoy your work more and it'll be more sustainable.

- ☞ Don't do this alone. Do what you like, and get help for the rest.

- ☞ Other people won't understand. Be ready for them, and don't take it personally.

- ☞ Plan to build as you go. It's called *iterative design*. You can make changes in response to customers and experiences.

- ☞ Pick dates to get something started. Put these on the calendar and talk about them.

- ☞ Be inspired by people who've gone before you! Be an inspiration to others. What will be the story we tell about you?

Important Dates A:

If You File Annually With the State (DOR)

Note: All of the IRS dates shift when they fall on a weekend.

Jan 15	IRS - Estimated Quarterly Tax Payment	$
Jan 31	City - Make Report to Seattle	*Pay B&O tax, if you earned over $100K*
Jan 31	State - DOR Annual Report	*If required: pay B+O taxes, send sales tax*
Jan 31	IRS - 1099-MISCs to Independent Contractors	
Jan 31	IRS - 1099-MISCs due to IRS	
Apr 15	IRS - Annual Tax Filing	*Pay Income and Self-Employment Tax*
Apr 15	IRS - Estimated Quarterly Tax Payment	$
Apr 30	County - King County Assessor Report	*Pay taxes if required*
Jun 15	IRS - Estimated Quarterly Tax Payment	$
Sep 15	IRS - Estimated Quarterly Tax Payment	$
Dec 31	City - Renew Seattle Business License	*$110*

☞ *Add Anniversary of LLC, and any specialty license or permit renewals*

Important Dates B:
If You File Quarterly With the State (DOR)

Note: All of the IRS dates shift when they fall on a weekend.

Jan 15	IRS - Estimated Quarterly Tax Payment	$
Jan 31	City - Make Report to Seattle	*Pay B&O tax, if you earned over $100K*
Jan 31	State - DOR Tax Report for Qtr 4	*Pay taxes if required*
Jan 31	IRS - 1099-MISCs to Independent Contractors	
Jan 31	IRS - 1099-MISCs due to IRS	
Apr 15	IRS - Annual Tax Filing	*Pay Income and Self-Employment Tax*
Apr 15	IRS - Estimated Quarterly Tax Payment	$
Apr 30	County - King County Assessor Report	*Pay taxes if required*
Apr 30	State - DOR Tax Report for Qtr 1	*Pay taxes if required*
Jun 15	IRS - Estimated Quarterly Tax Payment	$
Jul 30	State - DOR Tax Report for Qtr 2	*Pay taxes if required*
Sep 15	IRS - Estimated Quarterly Tax Payment	$
Oct 31	State - DOR Tax Report for Qtr 3	*Pay taxes if required*
Dec 31	City - Renew Seattle Business License	*$110*

☞ *Add Anniversary of LLC, and any specialty license or permit renewals*

Business Expenses by Category

This is what you can deduct when filing federal taxes with the IRS

Category	Amount	Examples
Advertising	$	*website, business cards, flyers, design fees*
Car and Truck	$	*mileage or actual costs, parking, ferry, tolls*
Commissions and Fees	$	*official ones, e.g. broker fees*
Contract Labor	$	*independent contractors (**not** profeesionals)*
Depreciation / Section 179	$	*items, tools that cost over $100*
Insurance	$	*includes professional, general liability*
Interest	$	*credit card for biz expenses, business loans*
Legal and Professional	$	*lawyers, accountants, supervising therapists*
Office expense	$	*paper, ink, folders, notebooks, postage*
Rent or Lease	$	*for office, equipment*
Repairs and Maintenance	$	*computers, tools, equipment*
Supplies	$	*stuff you need for your service or products, books, magazines, professional dues*
Taxes and licenses	$	*business licenses, B+O tax*
Travel	$	*airfare, lodging, meals during travel*
Meals (Half of $______)	$	*meals + entertainment in town*
Utilities	$	*cell phone, Dropbox, wi-fi, % home utilities*
Wages	$	*to employees*
Other - Bank Fees	$	*fees from banks, credit cards, PayPal, Stripe, etc.*
Other - Prof. Development	$	*classes, meetings wi/consultants, conferences*

Note: Three standard categories are removed from this list: Depletion, Employee Benefit Programs, and Pension and Profit Sharing

Monthly Income Tracking A: Service Providers (No Sales Tax)

	Total Sales*	Expenses	Profit	IRS Taxes† Profit x 30%	Paycheck Profit x 70%
Jan		-	=		☺
Feb		-	=		☺
Mar		-	=		☺
Apr		-	=		☺
May		-	=		☺
Jun		-	=		☺
Jul		-	=		☺
Aug		-	=		☺
Sep		-	=		☺
Oct		-	=		☺
Nov		-	=		☺
Dec		-	=		☺

*Does NOT include sales tax
†Estimated

Monthly Income Tracking B: Service Providers (With Sales Tax)

	Total Sales*	Expenses	Profit	IRS Taxes† Profit x 30%	Paycheck Profit x 70%	Sales Tax Collected
Jan		-	=		☺	
Feb		-	=		☺	
Mar		-	=		☺	
Apr		-	=		☺	
May		-	=		☺	
Jun		-	=		☺	
Jul		-	=		☺	
Aug		-	=		☺	
Sep		-	=		☺	
Oct		-	=		☺	
Nov		-	=		☺	
Dec		-	=		☺	

*Does NOT include sales tax
†Estimated

Monthly Income Tracking C: Product Makers

	Total Sales*	Expenses	Product Supplies	Profit	IRS Taxes† Profit x 30%	Paycheck Profit x 70%	Sales Tax Collected
Jan		–	–	=		☺	
Feb		–	–	=		☺	
Mar		–	–	=		☺	
Apr		–	–	=		☺	
May		–	–	=		☺	
Jun		–	–	=		☺	
Jul		–	–	=		☺	
Aug		–	–	=		☺	
Sep		–	–	=		☺	
Oct		–	–	=		☺	
Nov		–	–	=		☺	
Dec		–	–	=		☺	

*Does NOT include sales tax
†Estimated

Weekly Flow

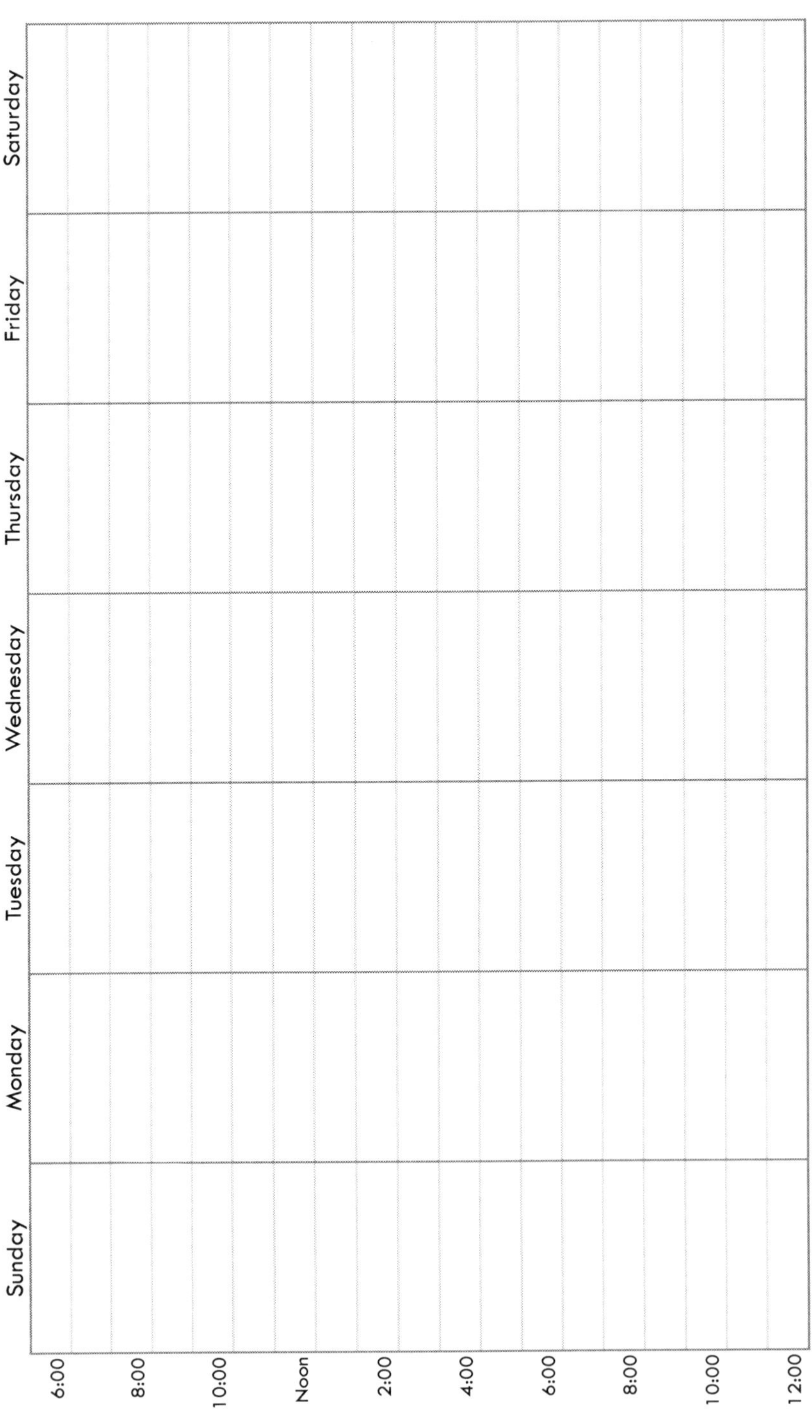
Saturday
Friday
Thursday
Wednesday
Tuesday
Monday
Sunday
6:00
8:00
10:00
Noon
2:00
4:00
6:00
8:00
10:00
12:00

Year At-a-Glance

Jan			Jul
Feb			Aug
Mar			Sep
Apr			Oct
May			Nov
June			Dec

Marketing Snapshot

Foundation	You • • • •	Customer • • • •
Story		
Brand	• •	• •
Brand Elements	font(s): colors: imagery:	keywords: special touches:
Advertising	Where are customers?	1 2 3 4 5
Tools	• • •	• • •

Appendix 6: Glossary of Terms

Accounting The story you tell about your numbers: tax reporting, and analysis, e.g., growth percentages, predictions, ratios like cost per unit.

Advertising Actions you take so people know about your business—such as online blurbs, flyers, commercials, and spots in a magazine. It is one element of marketing.

B&O Tax Business and Occupation tax. The state collects some, and so does the city. Rates vary according to each business activity and by industry. If you make less than $100K, you don't owe any for the city of Seattle. If under about $46K (depending on the industry) you don't owe any to the state.

Bookkeeping How you track the numbers in your business: recording expenses, creating invoices, billing customers, making deposits, tracking time and mileage, etc.

Branding The story you tell about your business. It creates a mood or feeling.

Business and Occupation Tax See B&O tax.

COGS (Cost of goods sold) The cost of items you buy that get sold to customers. These are not business expenses. For example, if you make graphic T-shirts, it'd be the cost of T-Shirts and artist fees for the designs.

Cost of Goods Sold See COGS.

DBA Stands for *Doing Business As*. Also known as a trade name. This is a name you choose for your business that is different than your legal name. For example, my business' legal name is Girl Friday LLC. I could choose a DBA of: Jenny MacLeod, Girl Friday.

Disregarded Entity This is a label that the IRS uses to refer to single-member LLCs. It means that they don't care about your legal status as an LLC because you will file as a sole proprietor. Your status is disregarded, because it doesn't fit their categories. This designation is given to you by default. (You may elect to file as a different type of entity, such as partnership or corporation by using those forms.)

Doing Business As See DBA.

EIN Employer Identification Number. This is a tax ID number assigned by the IRS. It has a different format than SSNs; the EIN format is 00-000000. It is required if you have employees. If you do not have employees, the IRS instructs that you use your SSN for all business purposes. Often, you'll be asked for an EIN because it is sometimes equated as a business tax ID number. This is a common mistake. Having said that, some self-employed folks prefer using an EIN to keep their social security number private.

Employer Identification Number See EIN.

Entity As in *business entity*. When you set up a business, you are creating a new organization. There are different business entities, each with their own structures, rules, and benefits. They are typically considered separate from their founders, and are taxed separately. (Sole proprietor is the exception.) Most self-employed folks choose a sole proprietorship or an LLC. Some choose an S-corp.

Expenses The costs of doing business. Examples include your computer, printer, advertising, and gas. Deducted on Section II of the Schedule C. These are different than the merchandise or supplies that go into merchandise (COGS).

FEIN Another term for EIN. (See above.) Stands for Federal Employer Identification Number.

Gross Receipts The total of all your sales, that is, the total amount that was paid to you by customers or clients, *including* sales tax. (This is different than profit or income.)

Gross Sales The total of all your sales, that is, the total amount that was paid to you by customers or clients. This NEVER includes sales tax. This is different than profit.

Hobby Business When someone creates a business structure in order to write off expenses, often to support a hobby. These businesses generally do not make much profit. The IRS has a rule if your business takes a loss in three out of five years, it will put you in the Hobby Business category. Once in this category, you may not deduct your expenses in the same way, and you have to use a different form than Schedule C.

Legal Name The name of your business on all of the licenses and tax forms. You can use a different name for doing business. (It is like the name on your birth certificate—it's legal, but you can have other names.) If you are a sole proprietor, your legal business name is the same as your personal legal name.

Limited Liability Company (LLC) A type of business structure that protects the owners (members) from liability. In Washington State, it must be set up through the secretary of state. It may be owned by one or more members.

LLC See Limited Liability Company.

Marketing The system of managing, creating and implementing all of the actions and policies related to getting new customers. May include advertising efforts, such as online ads, emails, newsletters, and print materials, as well as attention in the media, special promotions, or great customer service.

Managers of an LLC People who run the business and/or operations of a limited liability company. They work for the members (owners) of the LLC.

Members of an LLC All of the owners of a limited liability company. If there is only one owner, it's called a Single Member LLC.

Net Loss When your expenses are more than your business income. For example, you earned $8000, but your business expenses came to $10,000. Your *net loss* is $2000.

Net Profit When your business income is more than your expenses. For example, you earned $24,000. Your expenses came to $6,000. Your *net profit* is $18,000.

Operations Anything that is related to making your product or providing your service. All of the tools and supplies used, how they're organized, and procedures defined.

Registered Agent Someone who is authorized to accept mail and conduct legal business on behalf of the business. It is used on the LLC application. This is you or anyone you name as an agent.

Sales Tax Tax collected on certain items and services, at the point of the sale. In Washington, there's a state sales tax and a city sales tax. Both are collected by the state. Check dor.wa.gov for current rates.

Social Proof A term used in marketing. It is providing evidence that other people have liked a service or a product, e.g., testimonials, reviews, or number of likes.

Tax Registration Number A generic term for a number assigned to you when you are required to collect taxes. In Washington State, this is the same number as the UBI—unified business identifier. Even if you do not need to collect taxes, every business is given one by the state.

Taxpayer Identification Number (TIN) A term used by the IRS. This is an umbrella term referring to the number you're assigned for tracking your federal taxes. For individuals, it's your SSN, *social security number.* For businesses, it's the EIN, *employer identification number*. Non-residents use an ITIN, *individual taxpayer identification number*. **Please note:** if you have a single-member LLC, you are required to use your SSN.

TIN (Taxpayer Identification Number) A term used by the IRS. This is an umbrella term referring to the number you're assigned for tracking your federal taxes. For individuals, it's your SSN, social security number. For businesses, it's the EIN, employer identification number. Non-residents use an ITIN, individual taxpayer identification number. Please note: if you have a single-member LLC, you are required to use your SSN.

Trade Name The name use for doing business. That is, whatever name is on print materials, business cards, flyers, or on your website. It can be the same or different than your legal name. You must register trade names. Also referred to as a DBA, doing business as. Example with LLC: a legal name is Root Down Massage Therapy LLC. A trade name might be: Root Down Massage and Aesthetic. Please note: a trade name may NOT contain LLC (or any version). Only the legal name has that ending. Example with a sole proprietorship. The legal name would be Jane Doe. The trade name might be Jane's Cupcakes.

UBI Stands for Unified Business Identifier. It is a number assigned to your business by Washington state. It is used specifically as your tax account number with the state and any cities where you pay business tax. And, in general to identify your business—for things like setting up a bank account, applying for licenses, and as providing proof of owning a business.

Unified Business Identifier See UBI.

Use Tax One of three types of Washington state tax. It is...basically sales tax for things bought out of state. For example, if you buy a computer for your business in Portland, you would owe 9.6% use tax on it here in Washington. You pay use tax whenever you file your WA state excise form.

Book Credits

It really took a village to write this book! I hold the deepest and sincerest gratitude for all of these amazing folks.

Publishing

Alex MacLeod

Editors & Expert Reviewers

Developmental: Valerie Pacino
Copy: Anne LeWarne
Proof: Alex MacLeod
Legal: Justin R. Jensen, Esq.
Accounting & Tax: Valerie Moseley, CPA
Insurance: Tim Quigley, Certified Insurance Counselor

Design

Cover: Jina Constantin, Brandscape LLC
Endpapers: Jina Constantin, Brandscape LLC
Book Design: Jenny MacLeod, Alex MacLeod

Beta Readers

Amy Tipton, Jodi Wade, Jessica Pelkey, Roxie Jane Hunt, Valerie Pacino

Illustrations, Charts, and Tools

Charts, Tools, Illustration Concepts: Jenny MacLeod
Illustrations: Liza Brown

Contributions

Alex MacLeod, Claire Gardipee, Carling West, Erika Dorje, Liza Brown, JaLynn Montes, Jeff Williams, Sadie Frederick, Tavia Kachel

Special thanks ~

To authors Guy Kawasaki and Steven Pressfield, whose books helped me to *get going* and *do the work.*

To the writers in my life: Gretchen Bear, Jeff Williams and Karen MacLeod, for being great role models with writing and at finishing projects...and for offering just the right encouragement at the right moments.

To Anne Viggiano, my business muse. To Carol Frodge who helped me discover this work. To Tavia, for the coaching session that got me started on this book project.

To Jodi Wade for cheerleading me through the middle, Valerie Pacino for being my pacer to the home stretch, and to Liza Brown, for her energy and help in the final mile.

To Erika for lots of listening, ideas, and always pointing to the truth; for sharing both the highs and the lows along the way. To both Jessica Pelkey and Jessica Chen for all the times we played with theories about people and human nature, and for sharing restful and rejuvenating moments. To Siri for going with me on errands (cheerfully), letting me complain, and being so ready to laugh.

To Alex for providing all of the right kinds of support: space, belief, humor, and book design. And, for being a most interesting man.

xoxo

Jenny

Clients and Friends Mentioned

Alan Alabastro .... alabastro.photoshelter.com
Alex MacLeod ....morerealthings.com
AmyLeah Paul and
Catherine Alberg..................etsy.com/shop/twocrowslaughing
Anne Viggiano .... avcolordesign.com
Carlie Williams .... facebook.com/carliewilliamslmp
Carol Frodge .... cnfrodge.com
Charles Mickelson .... seattleqwiktour.com
Claire Gardipee .... postscriptapparel.com
Dana Parker .... thepianoparlor.com
Emily Peterson .... quietthymewellness.com
Gabe Strand .... strandwoodworks.com
Gretchen Bear.. firsttimelandlord.com
Heidi Bracher .... rootdownhealingarts.com
Jeff Williams 320sycamorestudios.com
Karen MacLeod ....kemacleod.com
Jeff Williams .... lizamodernartmedia.com
Nikki Jacoby ....nikkijacoby.com
Robyn Thompon .... contextyoga.com, livingproofoods.com
Roxie Jane Hunt ....howtohairgirl.com
Sadie Frederick..sadieaccounts.com
Sally-Anne Sadler .... shootingstartgardens.wordpress.com
Sandy Nelson ....sandynelsondesign.com
Shawn Nichols ....shawnhnichols.com
Tavia Rhodes ....taviarhodesmusic.com

About the Author

Jenny MacLeod lives a country-paced life in the city, specifically in a half-finished house in Green Lake. Interests include Iyengar yoga, jigsaw puzzles, classic cocktails, reading, and collecting old technology. She has two teenagers who give her a lot of joy, and is married to Alex, a poly-hobbyist.

Jenny moved to Seattle in 1995 and put down roots immediately. She loves the vibe here—a mix of urban lifestyle and nature all in one place.

She started her unique business as a self-employment consultant/Girl Friday in 2013 by following her nose and figuring it out along the way. Since then, she has helped hundreds of clients and readers make the self-employment lifestyle work for them.

Jenny loves spending time with people who are figuring out how to live life in their own unique way. Being a new-fashioned Girl Friday is her dream job.

Photo Credit: JaLynn Montes, 2017

I Would Love to Hear from You!

If you have any further questions, comments, or
suggestions for improvements,
please get in touch.

If this book helped you in any way, I would love to know. If you have the time to tell me your story, I'd be honored to read it.

Email me at:

jennygirlfriday@gmail.com

You're my Hero.
I want to be your Sidekick!

Get help with the chores of business. Save time, money and stress.
So you can get back to being awesome at your real work!

Tax + license deadline reminders, links to how-to articles,
inspiration, helpful resources and more ... delivered right to
your email box. Sign up is FREE.
Asking for an annual donation of $5 - $120.

Tailored for Seattle, still helpful in other cities. :)

Join today at:

jennygirlfriday.com

Made in the USA
Lexington, KY
12 December 2019